Whisk of the Red Broom

STALIN & UKRAINE, 1928–1933

M. Andrew Holowchak

Series in World History

Copyright © 2025 Vernon Press, an imprint of Vernon Art and Science Inc, on behalf of the author.

All rights reserved. No part of this publication may be reproduced, stored in a retrieval system, or transmitted in any form or by any means, electronic, mechanical, photocopying, recording, or otherwise, without the prior permission of Vernon Art and Science Inc.

www.vernonpress.com

In the Americas:
Vernon Press
1000 N West Street, Suite 1200
Wilmington, Delaware, 19801
United States

In the rest of the world:
Vernon Press
C/Sancti Espiritu 17,
Malaga, 29006
Spain

Series in World History

Library of Congress Control Number: 2024931691

ISBN: 979-8-8819-0179-0

Also available: 978-1-64889-860-0 [Hardback]; 979-8-8819-0020-5 [PDF, E-Book]

Cover design by Vernon Press. Image by Freepik.

Product and company names mentioned in this work are the trademarks of their respective owners. While every care has been taken in preparing this work, neither the authors nor Vernon Art and Science Inc. may be held responsible for any loss or damage caused or alleged to be caused directly or indirectly by the information contained in it.

Every effort has been made to trace all copyright holders, but if any have been inadvertently overlooked the publisher will be pleased to include any necessary credits in any subsequent reprint or edition.

To my longest and closest friend, Charles, ever in charge.

Table of Contents

	List of Figures	vii
	Preface	xiii
	Introduction	xxi
Chapter 1	Man of Steel	1
Chapter 2	The Death of Lenin	19
Chapter 3	Stalinism & Ukraine	27
Chapter 4	Collectivizing Ukrainian Farms	47
Chapter 5	Compulsatory Collectivization	61
Chapter 6	The "Need" of Dekulakization	75
Chapter 7	The Process of Dekulakization	89
Chapter 8	Ukrainians' Resistance to Dekurkalization	107
Chapter 9	Respite & Resumption	121
Chapter 10	The Problem of Nationalization	131
Chapter 11	The Great Ukrainian Famine of 1932–1933	151
Chapter 12	*Holodomor*, Causes & Consequences	169
Chapter 13	Stony Soviet Silence	181
Chapter 14	Stalin's Marxist Utopia	199
	Afterword	211
	Figure Credits	225
	Index	229

List of Figures

Map 1.	Ukraine's Ecological Zones, 1937, courtesy Ukrainian Research Institute, Harvard	ix
Map 2.	Wheat-Growing Areas of Ukraine, 1937, courtesy Ukrainian Research Institute, Harvard	x
Map 3.	Collective Farms in Ukraine, 1932, courtesy Ukrainian Research Institute, Harvard	xi
Map 4.	Deaths in Ukraine, 1933, Due to Famine, courtesy Ukrainian Research Institute, Harvard	xii
Fig. 1-1.	Joseph Stalin, 1920	9
Fig. 1-2.	Lenin Speaking in May 1920 in Sverdlov Square, Moscow, with Leon Trotsky and Lev Kamenev	14
Fig. 2-1.	Lenin, Confined to Wheelchair, March 1923	22
Fig. 3-1.	Leon Trotsky, c. 1936, Reading *The Militant*	28
Fig. 3-2.	Stalin with Lev Kamenev, Alexei Rykov, and Grigori Zinoviev in 1925	30
Fig. 4-1.	Woman Goading Emaciated Horses on a Collective-Farm, Author Unknown	48
Fig. 4-2.	Vladimir Krikhatsky, *The First Tractor*	55
Fig. 4-3.	Serednyaks, Bednyaks, and Kulaks, 1926	58
Fig. 5-1.	Ivan Vladimiro, *Prodrazvyorstka*, 1922	62
Fig. 5-2.	Peasant-Farmers Headed for Work	66
Fig. 6-1.	1930s' Poster, "Get Kulaks off Collectives"	79
Fig. 6-2.	Buksyors Showing their Spoils	83
Fig. 7-1.	"Liquidate the Kulaks" Parade	93
Fig. 7-2.	Solovky Special Camp	100
Fig. 8-1.	Exiled Female Kulaks Deforesting, 1930	117
Fig. 9-1.	Haymakers, Volodymyr Orlovskyi, 1878	127
Fig. 10-1.	Bourgeoisie, Priest, and Kulak Pulling Alexander Kolchak, Viktor Deni, 1919	135
Fig. 10-2.	Mykola Skrypnyk	141
Fig. 10-3.	Ukrainian Kobzars Mykhailo Kravchenko and Petro Dravchenko, Old Postcard, 1902	143
Fig. 10-4.	Ivan Vladimirov, Confiscation of Church Property in Petrograd, 1922	148
Fig. 11-1.	Children Starving from the Famine in 1922	154
Fig. 11-2.	Cartful of Ukrainian Corpses, 1922	156
Fig. 11-3.	Activists on Watchtower	159

Fig. 11-4. Starving Ukrainian Woman with Son, c. 1932	160
Fig. 11-5. Populational Decline in Ukraine, 1929–1933	164
Fig. 11-6. Stamp Commemorating Pavlik Morozov, 1948	167
Fig. 12-1. Red Brooms (Buksyors) "Appropriating" Foodstuffs from Oleksiyivka, Kharkiv, 1932	171
Fig. 12-2. Mass of Graves near Kharkiv, 1933	172
Fig. 12-3. Dr. Lev Kopelov, 1980s	176
Fig. 13-1. Soviet Guard by Granary, c. 1932	186
Fig. 13-2. Nadezhda Alliluyava, Stalin's Second Wife	188
Fig. 13-3. Cartoon Drawing of Starving Peasant Asking a Russian Soldier for Bread, 1933	192
Fig. 13-4. Ukrainian Peasants Fleeing from their Village in Search of Food, 1933	193
Fig. 14-1. Joseph Stalin at the Tehran Conference, 1943	201
Fig. 14-2. Soviet Anti-Religion Poster of Unknown Date	204
Fig. A-1. Sergey Kirov	212
Fig. A-2. Nikolai Bukharin, 1926	216
Fig. A-3. Stalin with Yezhin	220
Fig. A-4. Stalin without Yezhin	220

Map 1. Ukraine's Ecological Zones, 1937, courtesy Ukrainian Research Institute, Harvard

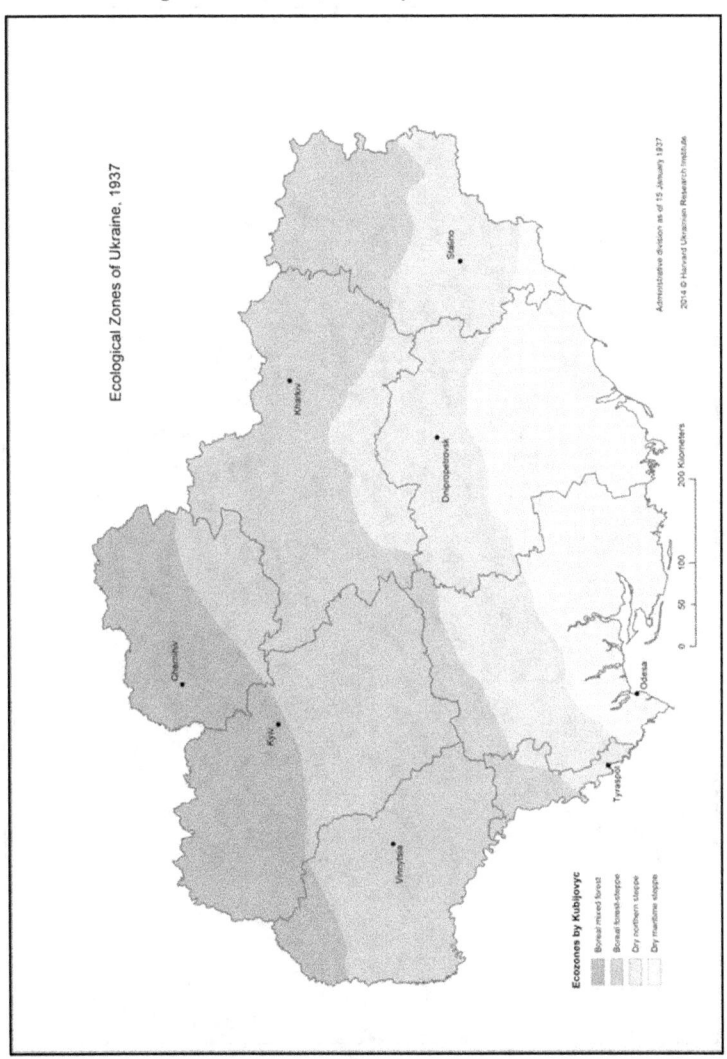

Source: Ukrainian Research Institute, Harvard University.
© 2023 The President and Fellows of Harvard College

Map 2. Wheat-Growing Areas of Ukraine, 1937, courtesy Ukrainian Research Institute, Harvard

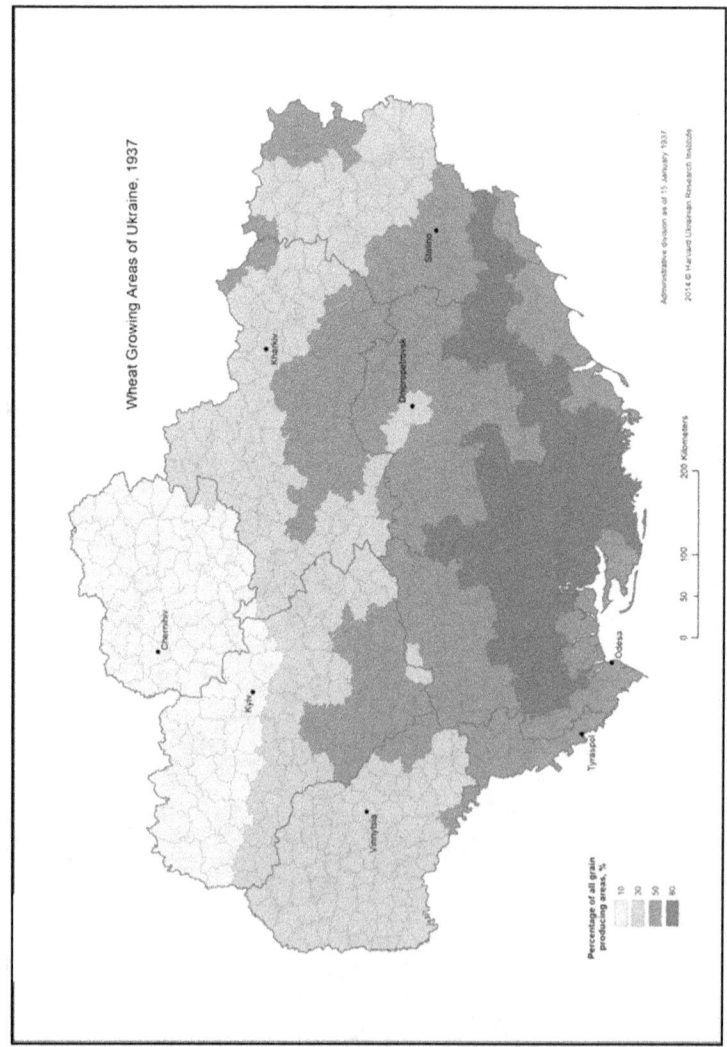

Source: Ukrainian Research Institute, Harvard University.
© 2023 The President and Fellows of Harvard College

Map 3. Collective Farms in Ukraine, 1932, courtesy Ukrainian Research Institute, Harvard

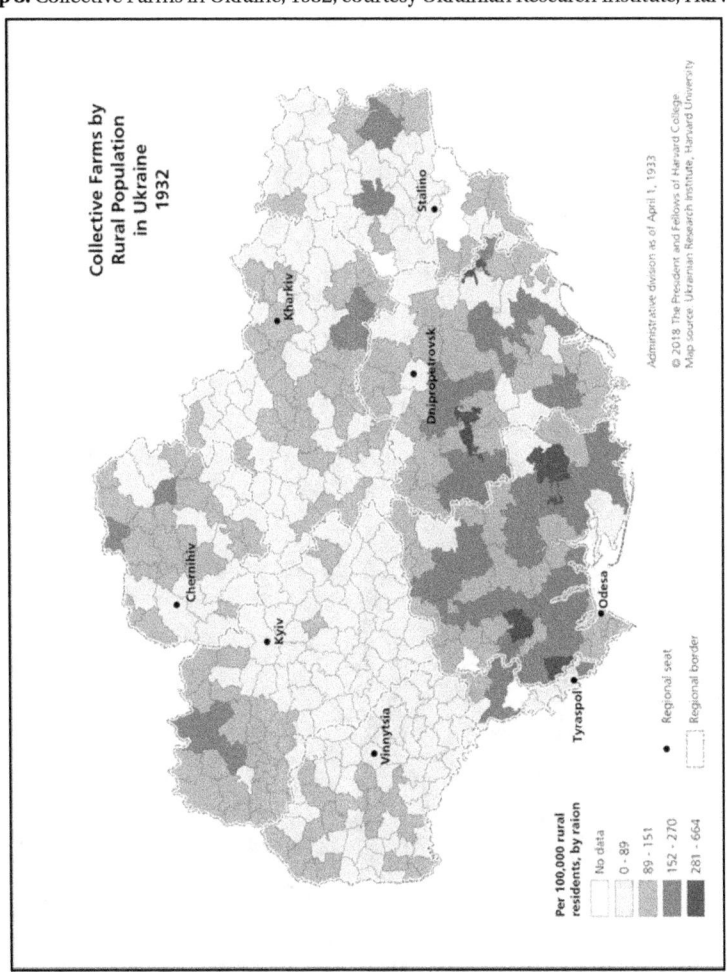

Source: Ukrainian Research Institute, Harvard University.
© 2023 The President and Fellows of Harvard College

Map 4. Deaths in Ukraine, 1933, Due to Famine, courtesy Ukrainian Research Institute, Harvard

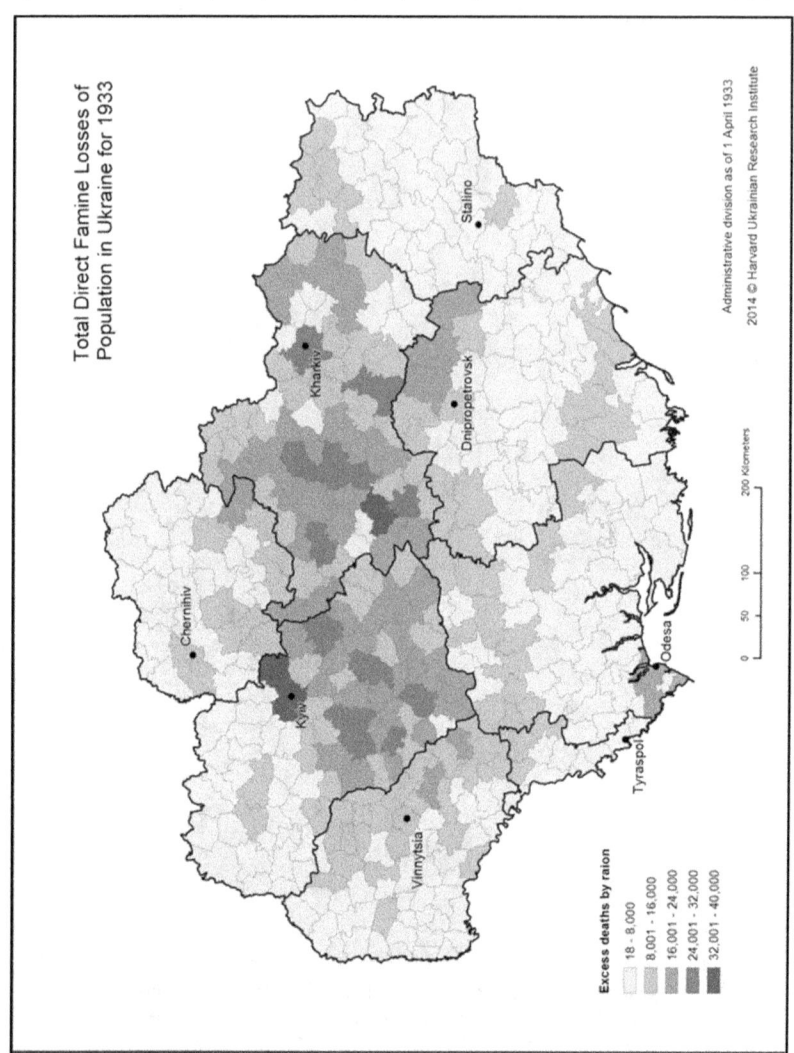

Source: Ukrainian Research Institute, Harvard University.
© 2023 The President and Fellows of Harvard College

Preface

Ukrainian Ivan Bahryany relates a singularly frightful event, ineffaceably imprinted in his mind as a boy of 10 in the year 1920. A band of Russian soldiers came to his home, spoke threateningly to his uncle and grandfather—the latter, a man of 92 years and with one arm—and then thrust their bayonets repeatedly into the two men, after which they "shot at the bloody bodies on the ground [with] their pistols and roared with laughter." All of that was under the old linden tree, under which were the icons of his grandfather's beloved St. Zozym and St. Savativ and near his grandfather's beloved apiary. On that same day, all the old peasant-farmers of the village were murdered along with the village's priest by members of the Soviet Cheka.[1] Bahrayany's grandfather was singled out because he, owning almost 100 acres of land, was a well-to-do farmer and openly against the socialization of Ukraine. His uncle was singled out because he was a Ukrainian soldier in Ukraine's struggle for independence in 1917 and 1918. Bahryany and the rest of his family would later be arrested and sent, without trial, to the prison camp, Solovky.[2]

What happened to Bahryany and his family was occurring throughout Ukraine after the fall of the tsars. Ukrainians were arrested, exiled, and murdered, and millions were forced to try to suffer through, in some measure, two famines in successive decades—the second, State-sanctioned. What was happening in Ukraine was happening also, but to a much lesser extent, in other parts of Soviet Russia.

According to official Soviet records, adds Bahryany, Soviet Ukraine had a population of 32 million people in 1927, and yet, in 1939, there were only 28 million Ukrainians. The natural increase in the span of 12 years, without some cataclysm, ought to have been some seven million, but there was a decrease of four million. In a union of Soviet republics in which, according to the Russian Party's line, industry in Soviet cities had been flourishing and peasant-farmers

---

[1] Established in December 1917, the Cheka was the commission for protection against counter-revolution—the Bolshevik Secret Police, or formally, the Extraordinary Commission for Combating Counterrevolution and Sabotage by Officials. It would become the State Police Directorate (GPU) in 1922. In 1917, the Peoples' Commissar for Internal Affairs (NKVD) was formed to conduct policing and oversee prisons. The GPU became part of the NKVD in 1930, though it was common for people to refer to it as Cheka or GPU.

[2] Ivan Bahryany, "I Accuse," in *The Black Deeds of the Kremlin: A White Book*, ed. S.O. Pidhainy, Vol. 2 (Detroit: The Basilian Press, 1955), 4–5.

in the countryside had been, with a little encouragement, gleefully forming thriving collective farms, a marked decrease in the population of Ukrainians ought not to have happened.[3]

While punitive measures were not exclusive to Ukraine, Ukrainians were especially targeted, once Bolsheviks assumed control of Russia and its republics, because Ukraine was rich in natural resources. Its large and fertile steppe could, when cultivated, provide grain for much of the Soviet Empire. Moreover, it was a natural buffer to any hostilities of Western nations toward Russia, and there was always antagonism, given the Bolsheviks' insistence on fomenting a global revolution to overthrow Western capitalism. Like other Russian rulers before him, Stalin generally considered Ukraine to be part of Russia and Ukrainians to be Russians—albeit, Little (uncultured) Russians. The Ukrainian language, for Stalin, was merely a vulgarization of the Russian tongue. Thus, Stalin was ever agitated by many Ukrainians' mulish insistence that they were culturally distinct from Russians. They had, Ukrainian intelligentsia insisted, their own religion, their own traditions, and their own language, and that culture was rooted in the rural villages of peasant-farmers, scattered throughout Ukraine.

Ukraine's peasant-farmers would ever pose a problem for Stalin—especially from the year 1928 to the year 1933, when Bolshevik activists, "brigadiers," on account of directives by Stalin, pressed aggressively to collectivize the Ukrainian countryside and the lands, arable or not, of all the USSR's member republics. Stalin uniquely maintained, *pace* fellow Bolshevik Leon Trotsky, that Russia and its republics were not such backwaters that they could not be socialized without the contagion of socialism in heavily industrialized Western nations like Germany. Heavy capitalist Western nations, for Stalin, were far from embracing Marxism, and thus, after the death of Lenin in 1924 and Stalin's sly boots assumption of the lead of the Party—one could viably argue that he was already directing matters of the Party in 1922 as Secretary-General with Lenin's debilitation after a stroke—Stalin pushed to socialize Russia and its post-war republics independently of the West. He quickly socialized many Soviet cities—in some instances, he created cities where there was nearby, abundancy of natural resources—and pressed for great improvements in heavy industries in those cities. The lofty aim was gigantism: to do what the Western capitalist nations were doing but to do it better and bigger to prove the superiority of socialism. Stalin wished, through socialism, to industrialize to bring economically Russia into the twentieth century and to guard against the possibility of a war with the West. Western nations, as I have already noted, were

---

[3] The numbers are roughly correct. Ivan Bahryany, "I Accuse," in *The Black Deeds of the Kremlin: A White Book*, ed. S.O. Pidhainy, Vol. 2 (Detroit: The Basilian Press, 1955), 3.

ever suspicious about the USSR, given the "inevitability" of Marxist socialism as a global phenomenon—*viz.*, the unavoidable demise of capitalism.

With Stalin's push to industrialize the USSR, there was a considerable migration of peasants from the countryside to the growing Soviet cities, though some two-thirds of the population was still rural. To feed the laborers in the cities, the peasant-farms needed to up agricultural production. With the socialization of cities leading to large increases of the production of goods like military vehicles and weapons as well as tractors, plows, and all sorts of materials for building, Stalin wished to "urbanize" the rural farms throughout the USSR—Ukraine especially. In short, Stalin aimed to impose the model of a large, "efficient" factory in the country. He aimed for peasant-farmers to give willfully their possessions—land, buildings, animals, tools, and so on—to the State, and the State would then turn the numerous individual farms into large and efficient collective farms, State-owned and State-run. That, at least, was the plan.

Stalin, from the beginning, recognized two difficulties: the independant spirit of peasant-farmers and cultural differences among peasant-farmers in different regions or different republics. Collectivization, he was often to say, could only work if peasant-farmers willfully collectivized and if activists of the Party were respectful of cultural differences in different republics when aiming to rally peasants to collectivize.

The first difficulty was gargantuan. Peasant-farmers, after the break with the feudalism under the tsars, were accustomed to farm as they saw fit to farm and did not take kindly to Bolshevik urbanites, who were sent to oversee collective farms and who had, most often, little knowledge of farming, telling them what crops to grow and how to grow them to maximize yield. Moreover, they were unwilling to give all that they had over the years worked so hard to acquire—grubbed acreage, plows, and other tools, animals, barns, and perhaps even their tractor—to the State, which in return promised them in return nothing substantial. Again, peasant-farmers were averse to sell their grain at State-fixed prices, substantially lower than market prices. They rightly recognized from the start that Stalin aimed to fatten the State at their expense, while to Stalin, peasant-farmers, especially the successful ones, were but liberal capitalists and were albatrosses to Soviet socialism.

The second difficulty was not as weighty as the first, but it needed to be addressed. Different republics of the USSR and even different regions of a republic were in some measure culturally distinct, and any attempt to impose a one-size-fits-all model of agricultural production, indifferent to cultural differences, might meet with staunch opposition. Stalinist Marxism, for instance, was secular and religiosity-intolerant. It would thus have to face the difficulties that God-fearing peasants presented, such as time away from agricultural concerns to attend religious ceremonies and festivals throughout the year. The nodus of removing God from peasants' itinerary would prove Bunyanesque.

Stalin, however, was wont not to address possible nodi until they were actual nodi. He merely assumed that once a collective was running, its efficiency of yield soon would make all, or most at least, eager to join the collective. There was never the consideration that socialism, which seemed to be taking root in urban areas, might be ill-suited for rural areas. Stalin merely followed the gospel of Marx. Capitalism, which followed neatly and inevasibly after the collapse of feudalism, would itself implode and socialism would inevasibly take its place. That is how things had to be, because that is what Marx said. There could be no concord between capitalism and socialism—*viz.*, no halfway Marxism, no proletariats in the cities and classes of capitalist peasants in the countryside.

Resistance to socialism, rife in rural areas, was sensibly enough strongest from the wealthiest peasant-farmers, whom Stalin derisively called kulaks (Ukr., kurkuls). The wealthy peasant-farmers formed the backbone of every village and their well-being sustained their village. They, for instance, governed the village, offered loans, shared tools, and gave advice to farmers, poorer and less knowledgeable. In short, villages thrived when their best farmers thrived. No farmer, say, with 100 acres of land, with many domesticated animals, and with steel plows or perhaps even with a tractor was willing to give everything to the State, at the discretion of one official or a few urban officials from the Party.

Because they formed the backbone of each village, Stalin came to grasp that collectivizing agriculture could not occur without sanction of the wealthiest farmers, who firmly opposed collectivization. And so, Stalin quickly turned to aggressive measures of dealing with kulaks, on the assumption that once the wealthiest peasants' resistance was overcome, all peasant-farmers would readily collectivize. Stalin imposed heavy, crippling taxes on the wealthier peasant-farmers and soon brought in Soviet collectors of grain to search farms for hidden grain that might be sold at market prices, instead of to the State. Meeting still with stiff resistance from peasant-farmers, collectors turned to doubly aggressive, even violent measures. Peasant-farmers with hidden grain were exiled, even shot.

Imposing a Marxist grid on the peasant-farmers, Stalin divided them into classes: wealthy farmers, poor farmers, and farmers neither wealthy nor poor. He then tried to incentivize, through material gain or merely eschewal of disfavor of the Party, the non-wealthy peasant-farmers, chiefly the poorest through poor-peasant committees, to turn against wealthy peasant-farmers by becoming activists of the Party, e.g., informants or collectors of grain.

The policy of classifying peasants and turning peasant against peasant was only partly successful. For one, the division into classes was more contrived than it was clean, so it was difficult to discern who was to turn against whom. Moreover, there was perhaps jealousy of, but seldom enmity toward, the wealthy farmers by the less wealthy, for the relationship between the two was more symbiotic than frictional. Finally, a poor peasant who gained materially from turning against wealthier farmers might find himself to be considered in time wealthy, and thus, an enemy of the Party—a kulak. Therefore, many peasant-farmers turned to sabotage: destroying grain, killing farms' animals, or refusing to work their fields in resistance to the aggressive, often sanguinary, Stalinist measures.

The scenario in Ukraine was decupled, and that is the focus of this undertaking. In Ukraine, Stalin faced the problem of resistance to collectivization as well as the problem of many Ukrainians' wish for independence. His shock-brigadiers, the most unscrupulous of his collectors, hit Ukrainians hardest of all, and that led eventually to the Great Famine of 1932–1933, what is commonly called by Ukrainians *Holodomor* (death by starvation). Millions of Ukrainians died from want of food—the scenario was so dire that parents sometimes ate their own children—as well as from the harsh conditions of exile to the Russian gulags of the nether-regions in the frigid Northeast, where Ukrainians, along with other enemies of the Party, were forced to labor in squalid conditions and without sufficient food or drink. Along with the push to liquidate the Ukrainian kulaks "as a class," the Ukrainian intelligentsia—philosophers, poets, novelists, scientists, professors, politicians, bishops and priests, and former high-ranking officers in the Ukrainian Army, or anyone who might justifiably be accused of nonconformist thinking—were gathered up, interrogated, tortured, and sent to prison camps such as Kolyma, Solovky, and Franz Joseph's Land, or simply shot. In effect, any Ukrainian thought capable of non-conformist or independent thought was suspected of inciting nationalist sentiments among Ukrainians.

Stalin consistently denied, we shall see, that there was any such widespread famine in Ukraine or elsewhere in 1932–1933. It was a Trotskian ruse, he said, thought up by enemies of the Party. Those who died from want of food were the indolent, the ignorant, or the intransigent: the counter-revolutionists, who deserved to die.

Yet today, it is well-known that Stalin knew of the famine. Moreover, the famine was all the while, in some measure, I shall argue, planned, not an accidental consequence of strategies concerning the aggressive collection of grain. It could not have been otherwise. The belligerent Bolshevik steps in seizing the grain of member states of what was then called the Russian Socialist Federative Socialist Republic (RFSFR) in 1921 had resulted in a large famine and the deaths of millions in the "federative." Stalin could not have not known that aggressive, crash-collective policies beginning as early as 1928, would lead to widespread famine. He likely thought that the deaths of numerous Ukrainians in the early 1930s might serve as lessons to other Ukrainians not to resist collectivization and to push no longer for independence or nationalization.

This book is a critical analysis of Stalin's Ukrainian policy with a focus on the span from 1928 to 1933, from the year that begins Stalin's Five-Year Plan, a reversal of Lenin's New Economic Policy, to what is generally considered to be the end of the Great Ukrainian Famine. It comprises 14 chapters. Chapters 1 through 3 cover the development of Stalin's Marxism, prior to and just after the death of Lenin, and the immediate problem that Ukraine posed for socializing the USSR. In chapters 4 and 5, I discuss Stalin's plan for collectivizing Soviet farms and his movement toward ever aggressive, heavy-handed means of achieving complete collectivization. Chapters 6 through 9 are a critical analysis of Stalin's strategy for dealing with what he perceived to be the main obstacle to success at collectivizing: the pesky wealthy farmers or capitalist kulaks. Stalin settled on "dekulakization," which aimed at riddance of kulaks as a class, and the means included intra-peasant antagonism, aggressive measures of "appropriating" grain and other foodstuffs, and dispossession of kulaks' property as well as exile or even extermination of kulaks. Peasant-farmer mightily resisted collectivization. I pepper those chapters with numerous illustrations of Stalin's tactics and Ukrainians' means of resistance. The focus throughout is on Ukraine. In the next chapter, I look at and analyze the thorny problem of Ukrainian nationalism and why Stalin thought that eradication of nationalism and dekulakization in Ukraine were mutually entailing. Chapters 11 through 13 deal with the Great Ukrainian Famine of 1932–1933—a natural result of Stalin's aggressive, often sanguinary measures of collecting Ukrainian grain and eventually all foodstuffs that could be found on a farm. Millions of Ukrainians died from want of food, which was readily and relatively cheaply available in Russia, while Stalin and other high officials merely turned a blind eye to the calamity. I end in chapter 14 with some discussion of Stalin's vision of the socialist utopia through a critical look at his theoretical writings on Stalinism. I follow with an afterword.

While there is today widespread acceptance that Stalin was a brutal, unfeeling tyrant whose hostility to Ukraine was strong because Ukrainian peasant-farmers were reluctant to collectivize and because many Ukrainians, in some measure, considered themselves to be culturally distinct from Russians, there has been much too little written on Stalin's Ukrainian policies prior to and during the Great Ukrainian Famine of 1932–1933. Stalin hated Ukrainians not because they were ethnically distinct—Stalin was never vitally pushing Russification of the Soviet republics because he considered Russia culturally superior to other republics—but because of Ukrainians' united unwillingness to accept socialism, which entailed cultural uniformity of some sort for maximal economic efficiency. Failure of Ukraine, the largest and most resource-rich Soviet republic and the one dearest to Russia, to accept Stalinist Marxism would disincentivize other Soviet republics to follow the Stalinist model. That was the greatest obstacle that Stalin faced early in his tenure as dictator of the USSR. That is why Stalin hated Ukrainians.

Of the books written on Stalin and Ukraine with a focus on the years prior to and through the Ukrainian Famine, not enough attention has been given to Stalin's speeches and writings that have a bearing on those policies. This book draws plentifully from Stalin's speeches and writings to show the vacillating mind of an increasingly paranoiac, self-indulgent autocrat. Much more than other early Bolsheviks—e.g., Vladimir Lenin, Nikolai Bukharin, Grigori Zinoviev, and Lev Kamenev—Stalin was driven by titanolatry, or love of power, as well as by the ideals of Marxism, personalized to suit his tastes. In time, acquisition of and maintaining power became more important than the triumph of socialism. Unwilling to lose what he so cunningly acquired, he trusted no one.

Once firmly at the head of the Bolshevik Party—he was never titular head—Stalin was wont to remove all officials of the Party who might conceivably pose a problem for his dictatorship—especially in the final years of the 1930s, the focus of the epilog. Though he was more than anyone else unofficially running the Party by the time of Lenin's death in 1924, Stalin, some years after Lenin's death, became the Party, and he habitually acted inconsistent with principles that he, early on, deemed axial for the rooting and spread of socialism. Wishing to hold on to and increase his power, rivals were forced to submit to his will, or face potentially fatal consequences. Stalin knew only one method, force, and when force failed to produce results, he tended to apply greater force. Failures along the way—and failures were much oftener than successes—were always on account of saboteurs: the ever-present "kulaks," "counter-revolutionists," "anti-Leninists," or "enemies of the Party." The verdicts of the Party, which were in time Stalin's verdicts, were infallible. We shall see this application of force-failure-blame, and then, when the time was kairotic, application of greater force at play in his attempts to collectivize Ukrainian farms and to discourage Ukrainian nationalism.

One of the unique features of this book is that the historiography is unabashedly "analytical." My decades of experience both as an analytic philosopher and as a historian of psychoanalysis give this book, I hope, a critical, analytic dimension that other books that treat Stalin and Ukraine do not have. For instance, in Chapter 1, I proffer an account of Stalin's early chaotic years to help us understand his lust for power and control, his relative disdain for quiet, and his unconcern for the wellbeing of anyone except himself.

Before ending, I add four procedural points. I am wont to capitalize "Party" and "State" throughout this book, because Stalinist Marxism would become, certainly by the time of the Great Ukrainian Famine of 1932, the great Soviet religion, with Stalin as the godhead. Next, all references, with assumption of Stalin at the head of the Bolshevik Party, to "socialism," "Stalinist Marxism," "Stalinist Leninism," and "Stalinism" should be taken identically, to indicate Stalin's take on socialism, rooted in Marx and Engels, and the Marxism that was adopted by Lenin. Third, all Russian and Ukrainian terms have been Romanized. Finally, I make large use throughout of an invaluable source of first-hand testimonies in a two-volume collection of testimonies by Ukrainians who had suffered through Stalin's challenges concerning collectivizing Ukrainian peasant-farms and especially the *Holodomor:* S.O. Pidhainy's *The Black Deeds of the Kremlin: A White Book.*[4]

---

[4] For a critical analysis of the books and Pidhainy's motivation for collecting the testimonies, see Bohdan Klid, "*The Black Deeds of the Kremlin*: Sixty Years Later," *Genocide Studies International*, Vol. 8, No. 2, 2014: 224–235. Klid makes the persuasive argument that despite the "political objectives" of the editor, the collection does a service invaluable to the English-speaking audience, largely in profound ignorance of the goings on just prior to and during *Holodomor*.

Introduction

Vladimir Putin, on July 12, 2021, writes "On the Historical Unity of Russians and Ukrainians." As the title suggests, the argument therein is genealogical. Russians and Ukrainians, says Putin, are one: They have their roots in ninth-century Kyiv-Rus', they have one language (Old Russian), they are economically tied, and they embrace the Orthodox faith. Moreover, *Okraina* is Russian for "borderland," which is itself suggestive of Ukraine being merely a Russian frontier. Thus, the notion of a Ukrainian people independent of Russia is nonsensical.

Yet since the independence of Ukraine and its formal declaration of nationhood in 1991, there has been constructed an artificial cultural and political "wall" between Russia and Ukraine. Putin adds: "We respect the Ukrainian language and traditions. We respect Ukrainians' desire to see their country free, safe and prosperous." Nonetheless, "true sovereignty of Ukraine is possible only in partnership with Russia," because "our spiritual, human and civilizational ties formed for centuries and have their origins in the same sources, they have been hardened by common trials, achievements and victories. Our kinship has been transmitted from generation to generation. It is in the hearts and the memory of people living in modern Russia and Ukraine, in the blood ties that unite millions of our families. Together we have always been and will be many times stronger and more successful. For we are one people." Russia, he adds, has never been anti-Ukraine. And so, he sums, "what Ukraine will be—it is up to its citizens to decide."[1]

Putin's comments are both political and ethnic—the last derivative of the first. Yet there are certain oddities in Putin's statements. First, that he has never been anti-Ukrainian does not imply that he was ever pro-Ukrainian. His choice of words here is noteworthy, and suggestive. That intimates that he is not against Ukrainians having their own sense of culture so long as they do not take themselves as a separate nation, or so long as they do not look to the West for political succor. Moreover, he acknowledges the right of Ukrainians to decide their political fate, and that right is generated by some recognition that they are, in some meaningful sense, a separate people. Nevertheless, partnership with Russia, he says, is a needed condition of Ukrainian sovereignty. Put

---

[1] Vladimir Putin, "On the Historical Unity of Russians and Ukrainians," http://en.kremlin.ru/events/president/transcripts/6784, accessed 30 Sept. 2023.

plainly, Ukrainians are free to decide their political future as long as their decision entails a partnership with Russia.

On February 24, 2022, just over six months later and in what will doubtless go down as one of the most historically singular addresses of the twenty-first century, Vladimir Putin declares that he is about "to protect people who, for eight years now, have been facing humiliation and genocide perpetrated by the Kiev regime." The aim is to the "demilitarization and denazification of Ukraine" and to bring to justice those persons who have committed sanguinary crimes. The operation does not include the occupation of Ukraine nor the imposition of "anything on anyone by force." He adds: "Let me remind you that the people living in territories which are part of today's Ukraine were not asked how they want to build their lives when the USSR was created or after World War II."

"Freedom guides our policy, the freedom to choose independently our future and the future of our children. We believe that all the peoples living in today's Ukraine, anyone who wants to do this, must be able to enjoy this right to make a free choice."[2] Thus, there began Russia's war to "liberate" Ukrainians from the oppressive Kyiv regime—to free them from the neo-Nazis of Kyiv.

Soviet autocrats, beginning with Lenin, have long paid mouth honor to the notion that satellite republics during the tenure of the USSR, beginning in 1922 and ending in 1991, were "willful" members of the USSR and, thus, have had at any time the right to secede. V.I. Lenin, for instance, says in "Manifesto to the Ukrainian People" in 1917, "We, the Council of People's Commissars, recognize the people's Ukrainian Republic and its right completely to secede from Russia or to make a treaty with the Russian Republic concerning federal or other similar relations between them."[3] Stalin, as we shall see throughout this book, often voiced his concern that integration in the union of Soviet republics must be willful, and that strongly suggests that member republics could secede at any time.[4] Such sentiments are expressed with undue optimism: Ukrainians must merely recognize that membership in the USSR would produce

---

[2] Vladimir Putin, "Transcript of Vladimir Putin's Speech announcing 'Special military operation' in Ukraine," trans. Mary Ilyushina, https://www.smh.com.au/world/europe/full-transcript-of-vladimir-putin-s-speech-announcing-a-special-military-operation20 220224-p59zhq.html, accessed 2 Oct. 2023.
[3] V.I. Lenin, "Manifesto to the Ukrainian People with an Ultimatum to the Ukrainian Rada," 3 Dec. 1917, in *Marxists Internet Archive*, https://www.marxists.org/archive/lenin/works/1917/dec/03.html, accessed 3 Feb. 2023.
[4] J.V. Stalin, "Question of the Union of the Independent National Republics" (18 Nov. 1922), in *Marxists Internet Archive*, https://www.marxists.org/reference/archive/stalin/works/1922/11/18.htm, accessed 15 Dec. 2022.

innumerable boons to Ukrainians and failure to adjoin would be baneful because the benefits of socialism, as Marx noted, were obvious.

Nevertheless, Russia's sanguinary "Special Military Operation" (SMO), begun early in 2022, makes a wolf in sheep's clothing of Putin. It makes it impossible to take his statements literally. The aim is Russian irredentism. There are territories of Ukraine that are predominantly Russian in ethnicity (e.g., Donbas and Crimea). That, however, does not mean that they have always been so. Crimea in 1795 comprised nearly 88 percent Tatars, just over four percent Russians, and just over one percent Ukrainians. Yet by the 2021 census, those figures have changed to 76 percent Russians, 13 percent Tatars, and eight percent Ukrainians. Over the decades, Russians were moving into Crimea; Tatars were subtly removed.[5]

Still, the SMO aimed for the heart of Ukraine, Kyiv, and that shows plainly that the plan was more than Russian irredentism: Putin was striking at Ukrainians' right to self-determination. He aimed to make the whole of Ukraine a part of Russia and very likely to return Russia to its glory days as the leading state of the Union of Soviet Republics. Thus, "what Ukraine will be" is not "up to its citizens to decide," but for Putin to decide.

What is Ukraine, and what does it mean to be Ukrainian?

Ukraine, though it has only become a country in 1991, has a long, complex history, and there is no consensus among historians apropos of precisely what does and does not belong in that historical narrative. Key to disentangling the ravelment comes with the term Ukraine, which means "borderland." Any attempt to understand what it means to be ethnically Ukrainian by appealing to the history of the peoples who have occupied the territory that is now modern-day Ukraine will meet with two sizeable albatrosses. First, so many different peoples from different parts of Europe and Asia have over the centuries occupied modern-day Ukraine at different times. Second, scholars who attempt a history of Ukraine very often politic their history: e.g., Soviet socialists write from a Marxian dialectical perspective, disciples of the great Ukrainian historian Mikhailo Hryuhevsky trace Ukrainian identity back at least to the period of the Kyiv-Rus' Empire, beginning in the late ninth century. That is why many Ukrainian historians—e.g., Paul Magocsi and Serhii Plokhy[6]—opt for a "territorial" approach that allows for multicultural explanation and helps

---

[5] Editors, "Russian Census 2021," https://view.officeapps.live.com/op/view.aspx?src=https%3A%2F%2Frosstat.gov.ru%2Fstorage%2Fmediabank%2FTom5_tab1_VPN-2020.xlsx&wdOrigin=BROWSELIN, accessed 2 Oct. 2023.

[6] Paul Robert Magocsi, *Ukraine: An Illustrated History* (Toronto: University of Toronto Press, 2007) and Serhii Plokhy, *The Gates of Europe* (New York: Basic Books, 2021), xxiii.

us to understand the term Ukraine. A territorial approach has its own problems. Imagine, for instance, a territorial approach to the history of the United States. Also, one might say that it, as a pragmatic solution, sidesteps the issue of what it means to be Ukrainian. Yet it is, in my estimation, the most feasible approach. Though nearly 80 percent of today's Ukraine comprises "ethnic Ukrainians," what it means to be ethnically Ukrainian is perhaps still up for grabs, unless one merely appeals to data from censuses. Those who identify as Ukrainians are composed of Jews, Poles, Russians, Belarussians, Romanians, Hungarians, Moldavians, and Crimean Tatars, and the religions practiced by Ukrainians are many.[7]

Both Russians and Ukrainians today claim ancestry from the Kyiv-Rus' Empire. While the former stake their ancestral claims in a manner that includes Ukrainians as "Little Russians," the latter stake their ancestral claims as a people ethnically distinct from Russians. Why is that genealogical link so important for legitimacy?

One answer is foundational. Throughout history, nation-states have typically sought to justify their claim to a parcel of land or to glorify their history by adopting a foundational myth, evident in stories, for instance, in the founding of Sparta and Rome. Writes Ukrainian historian Paul Magocsi:

> Russian historians could draw on a conceptual framework developed in the fourteenth century by medieval churchmen. At that time, when the Muscovite state was in its early stage of development, monastic scribes recopied earlier historical chronicles, which they then "improved" and expanded in order to show the descent of their own secular rulers, the Muscovite princes, from the rulers of Kievan Rus', who belonged to a dynasty that could be traced back to the ninth-century semi-legendary ruler of Novgorod, Riuryk. The Muscovite princes were ostensibly the direct descendants of the Riuryk dynasty, which after the early seventeenth century was continued by the Romanovs.[8]

A problem with that tack is that ethnographic research, which includes linguistic analysis, has shown that there are considerable ethnic differences between Russians and Ukrainians. To account for the differences, Russian historian Mikhail Pogodin posited, perhaps somewhat tendentiously, that the

---

[7] While most Ukrainians are religiously Orthodox Christians (72 percent), there are large numbers also of Catholics (nine percent) and atheists/agnostics (10 percent) as well as very small percentages of those who practice Islam, Buddhism, Hinduism, and Judaism. Andrew Evans, *Ukraine* (Chalfont St. Peter, UK: Globe Pequot Press, 2013), 32–46.

[8] Paul Robert Magocsi, *A History of Ukraine*, (Toronto: University of Toronto Press, 1996) 16.

Muscovites who occupied the lands around Kyiv-Rus' were displaced by the Mongolian invasion in the thirteenth century. With Muscovites abandonment of Ukraine, Poles and Lithuanians moved into the vacated lands, hence the progenitors of modern-day Ukrainians, who are not linked with Kyiv-Rus'. Ukrainian history, so goes the Russophilic account, begins roughly in the fourteenth century, not in the ninth century.[9]

Another, more feasible, answer to the question of legitimacy is economic/political, and it concerns the value of Ukraine's land. Ukraine is rich in resources such as coal, manganese, iron ore, natural gas, and oil in Eastern and Southern Ukraine. Moreover, there are many significant ports on the Black Sea (e.g., Odesa, Sevastopol, and Yalta), and thus, control of Ukraine would allow Russia to have a greater economic and military presence on the Black Sea. Furthermore, the black soil of Ukraine's vast steppe of its fertile plains and the climate of the country are ideal for the growth of nutrient-rich cereals such as wheat, oats, and rye. Those plains are complemented by a system of rivers (e.g., Styr, Horyn, Southern Buh, Dnister, Donets, and Dnipro Rivers) that facilitate travel and communication throughout the country. Last, Ukraine, as a borderland, is a buffer to the NATO countries of Turkey, Romania, Hungary, Slovakia, and Poland. Consequently, by claiming that Russians are of the lineage of those of the Kyiv-Rus' Empire, they can claim, as Putin is wont to do, that the land of Ukraine belongs to Russia.[10]

The tension between Russia and Ukraine after the breakup of the USSR has been large and constant. There were questions to ponder about liberalization and centralization that had marked implications for the new country's foreign relations and economic stability. Should Ukraine move à la much of the West toward a free-market economy and work toward partnership with European nations and the United States, and if so, should the move be quick or tardigrade? Should Ukraine continue with tight control by the state of its politics and economy and work toward rapprochement with Russia, divest of its satellite republics? Should Ukraine aim for some middle position concerning staying the course or Westernizing? Answers to those questions were doubly problematic given regional, ethnic, and even religious differences throughout Ukraine: e.g., the heavy industry of and number of ethnic Russians in Eastern and Southern Ukraine (e.g., Crimea) and the prevalence of Christianity in Western Ukraine. Ukrainians, so long accustomed to the State's control over all aspects of daily life, did not know how to Westernize and attempts toward it were thwarted by political blunders; citizens' ignorance of

---

[9] Paul Robert Magocsi, *A History of Ukraine*, 16.
[10] A problem for this tack is that less than half of modern Ukraine was territorially part of Kyiv-Rus'.

liberalism, privatization, and decentralized markets; widespread crime, including murders; and governmental corruption. Westerners, interested in helping Ukraine jump-start its economy, were thus constantly disincentivized—sometimes by assassination.[11]

Because of massive economic difficulties after the independence of Ukraine in 1991, its citizens displayed ambivalence about Westernization. Yet key events after independence—e.g., the Orange Revolution of 2004–2005 that occurred because of corruption in the election of Ukraine's president;[12] the backsliding of President Viktor Yanukovych (tenure, 2010–2014) on the issue of the path for a free Ukraine to take[13] and the subsequent Revolution of Dignity, which began on November 21, 2013, and ended with a new government in 2014; Russia's annexation of Crimea in 2014 and war in the Donbas between Russian separatists and the government of Ukraine; and Putin's 2022 Special Military Operation—have pushed many, if not most, citizens of Ukraine to Russophobia.

In sum, Putin's assault on Ukraine in 2022 is an extension of the continued tensions between Ukraine and Russia since the dissolution of the USSR and Russian remorse about losing a republic, rich in natural resources and suitable as a buffer to NATO countries to its west.

What is most noteworthy—and the reason for the inclusion of this introduction—is that Putin's strong-arm tactics vis-à-vis Ukraine have their precedent in Joseph Stalin's strong-arm tactics vis-à-vis the Ukrainians in the Ukrainian Soviet Socialist Republic of his day. Stalin was the first to use violence both without and within the Bolshevik Party as an acceptable means of achieving socialist or Stalinist ends. Stalin's long reign as autocrat of the USSR (1922–1952) has made Realpolitik or Machiavellianism the Soviet/Russian *modus operandi* and has much led, as one scholar notes, to Russians over the decades defining themselves "not in terms of their cultural area, as do the

---

[11] See Janucz Bugajski, "Ethnic Relations and Regional Problems independent Ukraine" and Ariel Cohen, "Ukrainian and Russian Organized Crime: A Threat to Emerging Civil Society," in *Ukraine: The Search for National Identity*, eds. Sharon L. Wolchik and Volodymry Zviglyanich (Lanham, MD: Rowman Littlefield, 2000), 165–81 and 285–302, respectively.

[12] Serhii Plokhy, *The Gates of Europe*, 333–34.

[13] His tenure saw much backsliding from democratization of Ukraine (e.g., restrictions to freedom of the press, cronyism, and jailing of oppositional opinions). Sergii Leschchenko, "Yanukovych: The Luxury Residence and the Money Trail that Leads to London," in *Open Democracy*, 8 June 2012, https://www.opendemocracy.net/en/odr/yanukovych-luxury-residence-and-money-trail-that-leads-to-london/, accessed 29 Nov. 2023.

Ukrainians, but in terms of the power of the state."[14] And so, no territorial or ethnic approach to the history of Russia can help us to understand modern Russia. For that, we must come to terms with Joseph Stalin and his legacy of terror, and no story embodies that sanguinary legacy better than Stalin's Ukrainian policy from the years 1928 to 1933: the story of this book.

---

[14] Paul A. Goble, "Establishing Independence in an Interdependent World," in *Ukraine: The Search for a National Identity*, ed. Sharon L. Wolchik and Volodymyr Zviglyanich (Lanham, MD: Rowman & Littlefield, 2000), 109.

Chapter 1

Man of Steel

"It is not heroes that make history, but history that makes heroes."

~Joseph Stalin

The focus of this book is Joseph Stalin's policy concerning Ukraine from the years 1928, when he was the unquestioned leader of the Bolshevik Party after the death of Vladimir Lenin in 1924, to 1933, which is generally regarded to be the final year of the Great Ukrainian Famine that began to surge in 1932. Ukraine had ever been the most coveted of Soviet republics because of the fecundity of its land, its numerous other natural resources, its proximity to Europe, and its southern border, on the Black Sea. Over the centuries, Russia considered it historically as "Little Russia" (*Malaya Rossiya*)— that is, as part of Russia, not as an independent state, or even as a territory with a viable claim to be considered an independent state. That claim is likely based not so much on a shared history, but instead on the measure of Russia's value of the Ukrainian land and its natural resources.

Stalin, who was himself not Russian, but Georgian, could, of course, sympathize with Ukrainians for their desire for independence from Soviet Russia, but his inflexible commitment to Leninist Marxism and the revolution of the proletariat made it difficult for him to prioritize cultural concerns when socialism held the promise of true democracy through obliteration both of classes and of private ownership of goods. In short, Soviet republics that strove for independence threatened the viability and success of the socialization of the Soviet Union of Republics. As a committed Marxist, Stalin tolerated cultural autonomy only when intolerance threatened his socialist experiment. For him, it was convenient for Soviet republics to Russify, not because Russia had a culture and history richer or better than any of its republics, but because the central authority of the USSR was in Moscow and ease of communication to implement socialist reforms demanded a large degree of cultural uniformity—a common language being the foremost desideratum.

To understand Stalin's policy concerning Ukraine from the years 1928 to 1933, we must first have something to say about Russia and Ukraine prior to Stalin's assumption of leadership. That is the first part of this chapter. Then, I turn to a brief biography of Stalin as much as the events of his life shaped his Leninist Marxism.

"The struggle for grain is the struggle for socialism"

Ukraine & Pre-Stalinist Soviet Russia

Prior to the start of World War I, the Ukrainian peasantry was becoming increasingly troubled by Russia's imperialism at the hands of the tsar. Serfdom was officially abolished in 1861 by Alexander II, but conditions for peasants changed little. Early in the twentieth century, conditions were ripe for revolution.

Yet the revolution in Russia began, for all intents and purposes, on January 22, 1905—on "Bloody Sunday," on which some 1,000 protestors, led by Orthodox priest Georgy Gapon, were injured or killed in St. Petersburg. The rioting resulted in Tsar Nicholas II's recognition of the need for some civil liberties on behalf of the citizenry.[1]

On July 31, 1914—not long after the provenance of World War I, in which 34 nations would participate—Germany declared war on Russia. The war would exhaust Russia, whose soldiers were poorly equipped, like no other nation. In early March 1917, there were labor strikes and, subsequently, several public anti-war protests in Petrograd (formerly St. Petersburg, changed largely due to anti-German sentiments from WW I). On March 15, Tsar Nicholas II abdicated, and the Provisional Government was established with Alexander Kerensky as minister of war and a major player in the provisional government.[2]

Despite the abdication of the tsar and extraordinary intra-national strife, Russia continued to participate in the war. Late in October 1917 and amid the tohubohu, Bolshevik revolutionists—few in number[3] and preaching to the masses of a government by "provisional" representatives of the masses—seized nearly bloodlessly Petrograd, which, then being the capital, was recognition of their control of Russia. In the confusion, Vladimir Lenin, who had been exiled to Switzerland, returned to Petrograd to lead the Bolsheviks. Lenin announced immediate withdrawal from World War I, which formally took place on December 15, 1917. The Bolsheviks signed the Treaty of Brest-Litovsk on March

---

[1] Richard Pipes, *The Russian Revolution* (New York: Vintage Books, 1990), 191–94 and chaps. 7 and 8, and Abraham Ascher, *The Revolution of 1905: Russia in Disarray* (Stanford University Press, 1988), chaps 1–3.

[2] Richard Pipes, *The Russian Revolution, chaps. 7 and 8,* and Abraham Ascher, *The Revolution of 1905, chaps 1–3.*

[3] There were only some 24,000 Bolsheviks early in 1917, but the number swelled to 350,000 due to discipline, tight and capable centralization, and propaganda that appealed to the masses. Orest Subtelny, *Ukraine: A History* (Toronto: University of Toronto Press, 1991), 348.

3, 1918, and lost Ukraine, Poland, and the Baltic states. The treaty gave Ukrainians hope for a nation. The Central Powers pledged to offer Ukraine military succor, while Ukraine pledged to offer foodstuffs to the Central Army.[4]

Bolshevik control over Russia would not go uncontested. With the overthrow of the tsar, there broke out a civil war chiefly between the Russian Reds (Leninist Bolsheviks and sympathizers) and the Russian Whites (a hodgepodge of conservatives, monarchists, pro-capitalists and anti-Bolsheviks), supported by the Volunteer Army of the Kuban steppe. So great was the confusion concerning who was fighting whom and for what reasons that the Allied Army, having offered some succor to the Whites, withdrew that support.[5] The Russian Civil War would be a protracted event whose end is a matter of scholarly disagreement today, though 1922 is commonly asserted.[6]

The Russian Civil War was propitious for Ukraine. By 1918, the Austro-Hungarian Empire fell. There was never a more kairotic moment for Ukrainians to act toward sovereignty. Ukrainians took the first steps toward it—there was a formal declaration of independence on January 26, 1918, and the formation of the Central Rada[7]—but Ukrainians failed to take the remainder of the needed steps, viz., to act on that declaration. Though the time was right, Ukrainians were merely unready for that opportunity. While the Germans fulfilled their end of the agreement in the Treaty of Brest-Litovsk, Ukrainians failed on their end. And so, on April 28, Germans marched into Kyiv and disbanded the Ukrainian Central Rada. The problem for Ukrainians is summed by Orest Subtelny, "The Central Rada was forced to begin state-building before the process of nation-building had been completed."[8] Its governing body, the Central Rada, lacked a disciplined army and proper administrative authority. While the Rada busied itself with squabbling over technical issues of statehood, the opportunity for nationhood was lost. And so, when the Treaty of Versailles was signed in 1919 to stipulate the terms of peace between Germany and the Allied Armies (28 June 1919), there were borders for several new states: Poland, Austria, Yugoslavia, and Czechoslovakia, but not Ukraine.

---

[4] Abraham Ascher, *The Revolution of 1905*, chap. 6 and chaps. 10–13.
[5] Richard Pipes, *The Russian Revolution*, chaps 10 and 11.
[6] See, e.g., Evan Mawdsley, The Russian Civil War (New York: Pegasus, 2007), and David Bullock, *The Russian Civil War, 1918–22* (Oxford: Osprey Publishing, 2008).
[7] Lasting only from 1917 to 1918, the Central Rada became Ukraine's provisional government. It worked toward independence and a parliamentary democracy with proclamation of four "universals," but it was seen as bourgeois and counter-revolutionary by the Bolsheviks. See Orest Subtelny, Ukraine: A History (Toronto: University of Toronto Press, 1991), chap. 19, and Arkadii Zhukovsky, "Central Rada," in Internet Encyclopedia of Ukraine, http://www.encyclopediaoftheukraine.com/display.asp?linkpath=pages%5CC%5CE%5CCentralRada.htm, accessed 17 Jan. 2023.
[8] Orest Subtelny, *Ukraine*, 353–54.

Bolshevik Russia, under the leadership of Vladimir Lenin from June 1918 to early 1921, was subject to "War Communism." War Communism was an economic policy intended to stabilize the fluctuant Russian economy, at least to benefit the Bolsheviks in their fight for hegemony during the period of post-war revolution, by having all economic affairs directed by the Bolshevik government—that is, forced, centralized socialism, inasmuch as Bolsheviks, under the capable leadership of Lenin, could enforce that policy. Private businesses were expropriated, industry became nationalized, and the Bolsheviks assumed a large measure of control of surplus grain and other foodstuffs.

War Communism eventuated in bedlam. Industrial production was meager. There were numerous protests and labor strikes, because of the chaos. Again, there was a large decrease in the production of grain and other crops. Without markets to determine prices for farmed goods, there was little initiative for peasant-farmers to produce beyond immediate needs, for all surplus production would be seized without remuneration. Inflation spiraled out of control, and so, money was valueless.[9]

During the time of War Communism, there was an armed conflict between Bolshevik Russia and Ukraine. The Bolsheviks under Lenin had no intention of seeing Ukraine, rich in arable lands and other natural resources, become an independent nation. The chief issue for Lenin was Ukrainian grain, much needed in the struggling Soviet cities, and Ukrainians were unwilling to part with their grain to aid the Bolsheviks, who, fighting merely to stay alive, cared nowise for Ukrainian nationhood. Lenin stated emphatically, "The struggle for grain is the struggle for socialism."[10]

Yet the government at the time did not have money to pay for Ukrainian grain, so it simply "expropriated" grain by sending into villages troops of soldiers who took whatever grain, and other foodstuffs, that they could find.[11] Armed troops, called Poor-Peasant Committees (*komnezamy*),[12] were formed and tasked with preventing the transport of bread into Ukraine. A March 1919 issue of *Pravda* states, "After hard and bloody battles, the Red Army has opened the road to bread, because it has taken Ukraine." Said Ukrainian Alexander Shlikhter, People's Commissar of Food of what was then called the Russian Soviet

---

[9] Robert Himmer. "The Transition from War Communism to the New Economic Policy: An Analysis of Stalin's Views," in *The Russian Review*, Vol. 53, No. 4, 1994: 515–29.

[10] Lev Kopelev, *The Education of a True Believer* (New York: HarperCollins, 1980), 12.

[11] N. Popov, *Outline History of the Communist Party of the Soviet Union*, Vol. 2 (London: Martin Lawrence Limited, 1934), 36.

[12] For more, see James E. Mace, "The Komitety Nezamozhnykh Selyan and the Structure of Soviet Rule in the Ukrainian Countryside, 1920–1933," in *Soviet Studies*, Vol. 35, No. 4, 1983: 487–503.

Federative Socialist Republic (RSFSR) on March 22, 1919: "You all remember when Ukraine was becoming Soviet, every day's forward movement of the Red Army brought us and you relief: Ukraine, full of wealth and bread is ours! ... We have four central military departments of supply. All our hopes are on them! We have a mass of dispatched workers [from Russia to Ukraine], who will know how to take over Ukrainian villages. We always remember that the eyes of the proletariat of Russia are all turned toward Ukraine."[13]

War Communism was not only a period of fighting between Soviet Russia and Ukraine, but there was also the prohibition of all manifestations of a Ukrainian culture independent of Russia. Ukrainian newspapers were banned. Ukrainian schools were closed. Anyone speaking Ukrainian was suspected to be a counter-revolutionist and arrested, and sometimes shot.[14]

Ukrainians, however, were not compliant. Between April 1, 1919, and June 19, 1919, there were 328 Ukrainian uprisings.[15]

Soviet Russia's relations with other republics, due to economic devastation, were also severely strained, and things were not well in Russia, as noted by numerous uprisings in Russia—especially the Kronstadt Rebellion of Soviet sailors in 1921.[16]

Such aggressive measures to impose socialism in Russia and Soviet republics were catastrophic. The harvest of grain in 1921, with peasant-farmers aiming for subsistence, was 63 percent of what it had been in 1913. Soviet industries produced merely one-seventh of their output prior to World War I. Consequently, Russia and all its republics suffered from suffocating inflation.[17]

The moribundity of the Soviet economy was acutely felt in Soviet cities. With most peasant-farmers producing only for self-sufficiency, food was scarce, and many urbanites were starving. Famine broke out in 1921. There were no landlords to upkeep the houses, as they had been socialized. Lack of fuel hampered public utilities—water plants, sewage plants, power plants, and gasworks—so many buildings were without heat in the winter. With little food, insufficient clothing, and frigid houses, typhoid fever raged. Urbanites

---

[13] Petro Dolyna, "Famine as a Political Weapon," in *The Black Deeds of the Kremlin: A White Book*, ed. S.O. Pidhainy, Vol. 2 (Detroit: The Basilian Press, 1955), 10–11.
[14] Petro Dolyna, "Famine as a Political Weapon," 11.
[15] Petro Dolyna, "Famine as a Political Weapon," 12.
[16] For more, see William Henry Chamberlin, "The Crisis of War Communism: Kronstadt and NEP," in The Russian Revolution, *Volume II: 1918–1921: From the Civil War to the Consolidation of Power (Princeton, NJ: Princeton University Press, 1935), 430–450.*
[17] Petro Dolyna, "Famine as a Political Weapon," 13.

swarmed for refuge in the rural villages. There were numerous uprisings in Russia and other republics.[18]

Vladimir Ilyich Lenin (1870–1924), who had assumed control of the Bolsheviks, introduced in March 1921 his New Economic Policy (NEP) in some effort to stabilize the moribund Russian Soviet Federative Socialist Republic. NEP was a matter of relaxing the strictures of socialization by returning domestic commerce and agriculture to private ownership in the short term, while the meatiest economic concerns, like foreign trade, banking, and heavy industry, would remain the government's capacity. Peasant-farmers, for instance, now merely owed a tax to the government, and once paid, they were free to do with their produce what they wished to do with it, and so agricultural production, incentivized, improved markedly. Small businesses, no longer under the eye of the State, also regained strength. Money took the place of ration-cards. Thus, NEP was paradoxically a concession that some measure of capitalism was needed to jumpstart communism. Yet Lenin likely thought that it was not a dastardly concession, for Marx had taught that capitalism would implode in due time because of its internal inconsistencies. NEP—disliked by Stalin and by the Soviet heroes of the civil war who likely wondered, with the large concessions to capitalism, if their efforts in the revolution were in vain—was to last till 1928, four years beyond the death of Lenin.[19]

With the adoption of NEP, Moscow's attitude toward Ukraine changed, too. There was tolerance of Ukraine's cultural differences—Soviet Comstockery had gone—and it was treated by Moscow as one of several equal republics of the union of Soviet republics—when it became in 1922 the Union of Soviet Socialist Republics (USSR). Ukraine would then become the Ukrainian Soviet Socialist Republic (UkSSR), which was tightly bound to Moscow but, on paper, had the right to secede from the USSR, if it wished.

As early as 1923, Ukrainians began to occupy significant political positions in the Soviet republic. The Ukrainian language was no longer banned. Ukrainian schools were reopened. Poets and painters were allowed to express their patriotism. Ukrainian newspapers and printing presses again appeared. There were Ukrainian entertainment venues, such as radio and plays. Ukrainian patriots, exiled, were allowed to return to their homes. Even the celebrated Red Army, to encourage Ukrainian integration into the Soviet system, was in part Ukrainized, for there began, in it, education of a Ukrainian officers' class.[20]

---

[18] Petro Dolyna, "Famine as a Political Weapon," 13–14.
[19] Petro Dolyna, "Famine as a Political Weapon," 14–15.
[20] Petro Dolyna, "Famine as a Political Weapon," 16–18.

Such Soviet concessions to Ukraine were grudging and chiefly aimed at the obdurate peasant-farmers, where Ukrainian culture flourished. Ukrainization (Rus., *korenizatsiya*[21]) was allowed, in effect, because it could not readily be disallowed at the time, and short-term concessions might have long-term implications for the slow and invisible integration of Ukraine into the Soviet Union.

Allowance for the Ukrainization of Ukraine led to a push for Ukrainian independence by certain members of the Ukrainian intelligentsia, who recognized that Moscow was in a giving mood, and giving much, might be in position to give all. Other Ukrainians, embracing what Moscow had given, feared reprisals for asking for too much. Ukrainian political activist Mykyta Shapoval advised guardedness and at least ostensible respect for Bolshevism. Still, he argued that if Bolshevism entails government by officials of the common people, then Ukraine should have its Bolshevik governors from the UkSSR.

> The Ukrainian intelligentsia should openly recognize and defend the Soviet system of government but stress that this government must be elected by peasants and workers of Ukraine. Moscow's rule in Ukraine can be undermined and finally destroyed, not by introducing separate programs and constitutions, but by demanding that the rule of peasants and workers be realized. Leninism can only be conquered with Leninism. This paradox must be understood by all those who wish to destroy Moscow's dictatorship. Moscow destroyed us by conceding "Ukrainian independence," i.e., by the very thing for which we were fighting.[22]

In sum, declarations or decrees of Ukrainian independence without allowance for the rule of Ukraine by Ukrainians, by the peasants and workers of Ukraine, was not independence. Shapoval was warning Ukrainians that there were likely ulterior purposes behind Moscow's gratuities. The aim of Soviet kindnesses was quick approbation of Soviet concessions toward nationalism, a favorable turn of attitude toward Soviet socialism, and then, most importantly, gradual assimilation and Russification of Ukraine.

Another problem concerned how Ukrainization was to occur. Ukrainian culture was developing. In which direction was it to go? Ukrainian novelist and political activist Mykola Khvylovy said that Ukraine could model itself after Russia, which "has been weighing upon us for centuries, like a master who has taught our psyche servile imitation," or the model could be the West, "the result

---

[21] Literally, indiginization of non-Russian languages and cultures.
[22] Petro Dolyna, "Famine as a Political Weapon," 20.

of the experience of many centuries."²³ Khvylovy's concern was historically always Russia's worry. Should Ukraine walk the Western, capitalist route, then that might show that the inevasible socialization of the globe, seen by Marx in the dialectical unfolding of economic history, was not inevasible. I return to the discussion of Ukrainization in chapter 10. Should Ukraine secede from the USSR, other republics might follow their lead.

When Lenin died on January 21, 1924, Joseph Stalin gradually rose to the head of the Bolsheviks after a rough political struggle with Leon Trotsky. Stalin's push to industrialize and modernize Russia with the introduction of his ambitious, even ruthless, Five-Year Plan in 1928 placed heavy demands on the peasantry to feed the laborers of those growing cities and to create a surplus of grain to be sold at market prices to other nations. To stimulate agrarian productivity, he attempted to collectivize agriculture by implementing several programs designed to keep agricultural production under the watchful eye of the State. Stalin, in effect, aimed to urbanize the countryside.

Peasant-farmers, as we shall see fully in later chapters, mightily resisted collectivization, as that entailed, at least on paper, willingly ceding their property—land, buildings, animals, and even equipment—to the State, becoming a "salaried" laborer,²⁴ and receiving few incentives for quantity and quality of work.

Why did Stalin insist on collectivizing the peasant-farmers' farms?

I spend a large part of this book aiming to answer that question. Yet, prior to addressing it, there is a need for acquaintance with the man behind the plan.

"How great was my disappointment…"

Who Was Joseph Stalin?

As undisputed head of the Bolsheviks, Vladimir Lenin aimed to make the Russian Soviet Federative Socialist Republic, the RSFSR, a global economic powerhouse after the Bolshevik Revolution ended. Something needed to be done, and quickly, as the Soviet economy was in shambles after the introduction of Bolshevik rule. Agricultural yield was poor, and the Soviets lacked the heavy industry of powerful Western nations like England, Germany, and even the United States. It also lacked the technology to develop it.

Because of the stated Bolshevik aim of global revolution, the West began to sever relationships with the Soviet Union. That led to Soviet panic about

---

[23] Petro Dolyna, "Famine as a Political Weapon," 21.
[24] With salary, often in the form of food, determined by number of full days worked.

possibility of impending war with the West, and consequently, Bolsheviks pressed for the rapid growth of heavy industry. Workers needed to be fed, and so there needed to be also a surfeit of farmed goods, and that surfeit included the exportation of grain for money to go into industry and state-owned farms. There also needed to be surplus grain to be stored in the event of a crisis. One of the most significant Bolsheviks to assist Lenin was young Joseph Stalin.

Born Josef Vissarionovich Djugashvili (1879[25]–1953, Figure 1-1)—the young revolutionary would change his name to "Stalin," with *stal* being Russian for "steel"—the ambitious Georgian was no more than 5'6" in height and unprepossessing in appearance. Stalin sported a thick and wide mustache, and had a pockmark complexion from smallpox, piercing hazel-brown eyes, and the visage of a serious, down-to-business person.[26]

Fig. 1-1. Joseph Stalin, 1920

Source: Wikipedia

---

[25] Official documents list his date of birth as 6 Dec. 1878, but his birthday was acknowledged by Stalin to be 21 Dec. 1879. For more see "Why Did Stalin Have 2 Birthdays?" in *Russia Beyond*, https://www.rbth.com/history/335676-stalin-2-birthdays-birth-date-different, accessed 21 Jan. 2023.

[26] He had a slightly deformed left hand and arm, stated officially to be due to an injury by an out-of-control phaeton that injured the joints of his left shoulder and elbow. He also had a webbed left foot, as the second and third toes were fused. Georgy Manaev, "Five Illnesses of Joseph Stalin," in *Russia Beyond*, https://www.rbth.com/history/332999-5-illnesses-of-joseph-stalin, accessed 4 Jan. 2023.

Former Soviet diplomat Andrew Barmine—for decades, an avid Bolshevik, who soured on Bolshevism because of exposure to the heavy and criminal bureaucracy of Stalin's autarchy—met Stalin on several occasions, and had this to say of the man. "He looks more coarse and common, and also smaller [than he does in retouched photographs]. His face is pockmarked and sallow. ... His eyes are dark brown with a tinge of hazel. His expression tells nothing of what he feels. There is to me a curious heaviness and sullenness about him."[27]

Stalin, Barmine continues, always dressed like a military marshal. That was for two reasons: a power-complex in compensation for physical defects (a withered left arm and webbed toes on his left foot) and a wish that the masses see him as someone superhuman, hence the need for a changeless appearance.[28]

Of the characteristics of the man, Stalin had the mark of inferiority, "which made him touchy, vindictive, and suspicious." That was expected, given Stalin's dearth of formal education, in contrast to other high officials of the Party, and his physical defects. As a man who would later wish to Russify what would become the USSR, he never fully mastered Russian, but used it "like a blunt and clumsy tool." His manner of speaking was "in a slow monotone which is tiresome to the ear." When the discussion turned theoretical at high-level meetings, "he used to sit apart, sulky and silent, unable to participate in the rapid fire of ideas and seeming to despise the whole thing as idle chatter."[29]

Stalin was a slow but patient and determined thinker, yet ruthless and unscrupulous in action and without "fellow feeling." He possessed in abundancy "strength of will, patience, slyness, ability to perceive human frailties and play upon them with contempt, and the supreme gift of pursuing a chosen goal inflexibly and without scruple."[30]

There is also Leon Trotsky's brief sketch of Stalin, the former's "attempt" at a biography. This sketch I find fascinating, because despite all through which Stalin had put Trotsky, the latter was still capable of a relatively unbiased depiction of Stalin, insofar as Trotsky's account is consistent with those of others who have met Stalin, and Trotsky knew intimately Stalin. Trotsky, careful scrutiny of his autobiography shows, also had an uncanny capacity for writing about himself, the events of his life, and others with impartiality that makes his book read more like a biography than an autobiography. When relating key events of his life, he sometimes even slips into the third-person.

---

[27] Alexander Barmine, *One Who Survived: The Life Story of a Russian under Stalin* (New York: G.P. Putnam's Sons, 1945), 157.
[28] Alexander Barmine, *One Who Survived*, 258.
[29] Alexander Barmine, *One Who Survived*, 258–60.
[30] Alexander Barmine, *One Who Survived*, 259.

Stalin's gifts, lists Trotsky, were practicality, strong will, and persistence, yet his flaws much outnumbered his gifts. He had a restricted political horizon due to a limited theoretical understanding of political philosophy. His "celebrated" *The Foundations of Leninism*, for instance, was fraught with "sophomoric errors." Outside of his clumsy mastery of his native Georgian, Stalin had no grasp of other languages. He lacked imagination and was capable merely of thinking in accord with his senses. He also lacked presence in that the leading members of the Party all thought him suited merely for third or, at best, second fiddle. Stalin was a "mediocrity."[31]

Simon Sebag Montefiore, one of the preeminent biographers of Stalin, enjoins readers to take Trotsky's view of Stalin as "colourless bureaucratic mediocrity", that is, *cum grano salis*. Stalin was instead "an energetic and vainglorious melodramatist who was exceptional in every way." He adds, "He was a mercurial neurotic with the tense, seething temperament of a highly strung actor who revels in his own drama—what his ultimate successor, Nikita Khrushchev, called *litsedei*, a man of many faces." Lazar Kaganovich, one of Stalin's most intimate comrades, said, "I knew no less that five or six Stalins." Those faces made him perfectly suited to the "conspiratorial intrigues, theoretical runes, murderous dogmatism and inhuman sternness of Lenin's Party."[32]

Yet the study of Stalin's days as a Georgian and Russian revolutionary shows the young man to be anything but a man for a third or second fiddle. He strove ever for the first fiddle.

Stalin abhorred quiet. He was only comfortable in a chaotic climate, and he was an expert in creating chaos in the service of revolutionary activities once he committed inexorably to Vladimir Lenin and Bolshevism.

Stalin was no philosopher, but a man of action—a *praktik*. His greatest expertise early in life was gleaning money for Lenin through numerous acts, often violent, of thuggery or "black work"—e.g., strikes, uprisings, kidnapping, protection-racketeering, and even murders—most of which he orchestrated. In his Georgian revolutionary days, he never had a permanent address and was adept at avoiding, escaping from, or bribing authorities.

Though short and unprepossessing, many women were attracted to him. Some found him irresistible, perhaps because of his unbridled enthusiasm for Bolshevism, evident in his "honey-colored," "burning" eyes.[33] He would have

---

[31] Leon Trotsky, *My Life: An Attempt at an Autobiography* (New York: Grosset & Dunlap, 1960), 506.
[32] Simon Sebag Montefiore, *Stalin: The Court of the Red Tsar* (New York: Alfred A. Knopf, 2005), 5.
[33] Simon Sebag Montefiore, *Young Stalin* (New York: Vintage, 2008), 208.

two wives and numerous affairs, though affairs were not uncommon in the unsettled Georgian milieu and in the chaos of the later Bolshevik USSR. Through those affairs, he sometimes had children, though, in general, he showed little concern for them. For instance, while exiled in 1914 to Kureika, far in Northern Siberia, he began a relationship with a girl of 13—Lidia Pereprygin—and twice impregnated her. The first child died, but the second, a boy named Alexander, lived, though Stalin never showed concern about his wellbeing.[34] His preference for young females, even adolescents, and peasants, reflects Stalin's crassness and need to dominate, and it intimates large emotional immaturity.

After his many early years as a Georgian revolutionary, Stalin joined the Bolshevist party and became esteemed by Vladimir Lenin, the party's leader, whom Stalin first met in 1905, because of Stalin's commitments to Marxism and to Bolshevism. Stalin would slowly earn Lenin's respect and favor—Lenin quickly recognized Stalin's dedication to the cause, his diligence, his dogged perseverance, and his willingness to do tedious but "needed" and often filthy tasks—and Stalin moved up the Bolshevist ranks to assume several significant positions in the Party and become a member of Lenin's Central Committee in 1912.

Throughout his unsettled revolutionary years, Stalin was imprisoned, double-crossed,[35] and exiled many times, and so, when he assumed dictatorship of the USSR, a position he would keep till his death in 1953, he would live, as his life and words illustrated, by certain important maxims, learned from childhood: trust no one; use any means to get done a job needing doing; when force fails, try greater force, and if greater force fails, retreat until such time that you can be assured that greater force will work; seize control when the moment is kairotic; and always repay doubly an insult. All such principles are subsumable under the Russian concept *Vlast* ("power," which implies awe, distance, and perhaps even resentment[36]). Mauserist Ivan Bokov said of Stalin: "Sentiment was foreign to him. No matter how much he loved a fellow, he would never forgive him, even the tiniest spoiling of a Party matter. He would skin him alive."[37] Stalin took seriously the task of socializing the Soviet Union of his day—he was a young man in desperate need of direction and of a mission—and he was, in the main, true to Lenin's axial vision of

---

[34] Simon Sebag Montefiore, *Young Stalin*, 282–86.
[35] An incident of betrayal by Roman Malinovsky especially scarred Stalin. Malinovsky entered the Bolshevik ranks but was eventually found to be a spy, in the service of the Okhrana, the Tsar's secret police.
[36] Victor Kravchenko, *I Chose Freedom* (New York: Charles Scrivners' Sons: 1946), 393.
[37] Simon Sebag Montefiore, *Young Stalin*, 199.

Marxism throughout his life, though Lenin's commitment toward ruthlessness in extreme cases would in time become Stalin's *modus operandi*. Millions, both within and without the Party, would be unremorsefully sacrificed under Stalin's dictatorship for the enhancement of the Party, and he, soon during his lengthy dictatorship, became the Party.

One learns much about Stalin by recounting his impression of the first time he met his hero, Lenin (Figure 1-2),[38] at a Socialist conference in Tammerfors, Finland. "I had fancied Lenin as a giant, stately and imposing. How great was my disappointment to see a most ordinary-looking man, below average in height, in no way, literally in no way, distinguishable from ordinary mortals." Stalin then goes on to express even greater disappointment that Lenin's mannerisms are ordinary. "Usually, a great man comes late to a meeting so that his appearance may be awaited with bated breath. Then, just before the great man enters, the warning goes round: 'Hush … silence … he is coming!' … How great was my disappointment to see that Lenin had arrived at the conference before the other delegates were there and had settled himself somewhere in a corner and was unassumingly carrying on a conversation, a most ordinary conversation, with the most ordinary delegates. I will not conceal from you that at that time this seemed to me to be rather a violation of certain essential rules." Stalin, however, Bolshevizes (i.e., rationalizes) his disappointment by adding that "this simplicity and modesty, this striving to remain unobserved" shows Lenin's qualifications to be a rank-and-file leader of the "simple and ordinary masses."[39]

Stalin's recollection is starkly revelatory. It shows his profound esteem for greatness, and that he has thought much and long about what greatness comprises. For Stalin, great thoughts and great words can only inhere in a physically large man: They need a large container, as it were. Furthermore, a great man must have an imposing presence that makes others cower. Yet Lenin's appearance is ordinary, not superordinary. If Lenin does not possess a physically imposing presence, he can at least act the role of a great man. Yet Lenin's actions, too, are ordinary, not superordinary. Stalin goes so far as to assert that there are, or at least ought to be, rules to which all great men must adhere, though Lenin observes none of them. The prevalent theme is a large disappointment, but Stalin cannot accept disappointment from a hero. Stalin rationalizes. Lenin's simplicity and modestly preeminently qualify him to be a great leader of the masses—that is, Lenin excels in the ordinariness of the

---

[38] Montefiore cautions that hero-worship was only deification after Stalin's death and only for political reasons. Simon Sebag Montefiore, *Young Stalin*, 211.

[39] J.V. Stalin, "Speech Delivered at a Memorial Meeting of the Kremlin Military School," in *Marxists Internet Archive*, https://www.marxists.org/reference/archive/stalin/works/1924/01/28.htm, accessed 17 Dec. 2022.

masses by being the most ordinary, or at least, that is the impression Lenin, *qua* Bolshevik, wishes to give. Still, despite Stalin's rationalizations, there is genuine disappointment.

Fig. 1-2. Lenin Speaking in May 1920 in Sverdlov Square, Moscow, with Leon Trotsky and Lev Kamenev

Source: Wikipedia.

Such disappointment was also felt in his childhood in Gori, Georgia. His father, Vissarion "Beso" Djugashvili, was a shoemaker of the lower middle class, who increasingly could not sustain his family at his craft, because his earnings continually went to wine. For the family to survive, Stalin's mother, Ekaterina "Keke" Georgievna Geladze, a devoutly religious person, had "to slave day and night" as a washerwoman. She even paid the meager rent for their dwelling—one-and-one-half rubles. His father's drunkenness was exacerbated by his cruelty. Beso, especially when inebriated, would beat young Joseph and his mother.[40] Keke would often deal with the violence by running off with the boy to neighbors. Drink would soon militate against Beso's health, and Stalin's mother, toughened by years of abuse, would then merely match her sozzled

---

[40] E. Yaroslavsky, *Landmarks in the Life of Stalin* (London: Lawrence and Wishart Ltd., 1942), 7, and Simon Sebag Montefiore, *Young Stalin* (New York: Vintage Books, 2008), 29–36.

and enfeebled husband blow for blow—the reason, says biographer Edward Radzinsky, for the emasculated Beso, permanently leaving the family for Tiflis.[41] Simon Montefiore, however, notes that Beso, on a drunken binge on one occasion, smashed the windows of Palavani Yakov Egnatashvili's tavern and then assaulted Damian Davrichewy, a policeman, who eventually ordered Beso permanently to leave Gori.[42] Stalin's lifelong push to elevate his station—to rise in the ranks of the Bolsheviks once established among them—is without a doubt an attempt to be what his father was not. Stalin could build a clear notion of what magnanimity was by seeing pusillanimity, and by avoiding it.

Young Joseph clearly went through his early life without love, which his father was incapable of giving, due to his half-seas-over disposition, and which his mother was incapable of giving, due to daily absence and a surliness of her own. She, too, sometimes beat the boy, and as he grew to young adulthood, Joseph began to grow farther from his domineering mother, especially because she ever pressed him to enter the priesthood.

Another underappreciated influence on the young boy was the bawdy, violent atmosphere of Gori, where prayers were frequent in houses and churches while drunkenness and brawling were the rules in the streets. Prayer and punishment were partners, not antagonists. At religious festivals, there was prodigious drinking, parading, and then brawling in the streets. Children of three years of age would wrestle other children, and then older children would fight, and then teens, and then men. The imbibing and fighting led to bedlam, and eventually exhaustion, early in the next day. In this milieu, young Stalin learned how to brawl, compete, and connive. Nothing good ever resulted from turning the other cheek, as it were. Blows must be met by harder blows; deceit, by larger deceit. And so, Joseph came to crave opposition and dissention, and when they did not exist, he created them. As a young man, says one biographer, Stalin was "always happiest in vigorous campaigns against internal as well as external foes."[43] Stalin would always be a fighter of windmills thought to be giants, yet he would become adept at convincing others, often through threat of physical violence, that the windmills really were giants.

Yet brawling, competing, and conniving were not their ends. Stalin brawled, competed, and connived because he craved control, complete control. He became obsessed with leading, not following, others, and those others that

---

[41] Edvard Radzinksy, *Stalin* (New York: Anchor Books, 1997), 24. One wonders here about the extent to which his father was verbally abusive, when both drunk and sober. It is characteristic of many who fail miserably at achievement to blame others for failure or see those around them as miserable failures.
[42] Simon Sebag Montefiore, *Young Stalin*, 33.
[43] Simon Sebag Montefiore, *Young Stalin*, 81.

chiefly interested him were thugs. He became aware that controlling the ruffians, criminals, and mentally maladjusted was easier than controlling the politically ambitious. In one scrap with a large safe-cracker, for instance, Stalin was beaten to unconsciousness and suffered many broken ribs. When he regained his senses, he vowed that in the future, such thugs would be working for, not against, him.[44]

When he grew to young adulthood, Stalin exhibited the tendencies, when he joined a group in his native Georgia that was to his liking, to feel out things, learn what he could of its leader(s), and then, when he thought himself to be the superior of the leader(s), aim to take control of that group. Said one young friend, "Koba [Stalin] thought it natural to be the leader and never tolerated any criticism." As a youth, he patterned himself after heroes of fiction—e.g., Rakhmetov of Nikolai Chernyshevsky's *What Is to Be Done?* and especially Koba—the Caucasian bandit and paladin of justice and truth from Alexander Kazbegi's *The Patricide*—whose name he adopted through identification as his own[45]—a practice often adopted by Bolshevik leaders. Young Stalin organized strikes, demonstrations, and riots, and he involved himself in arson, protection-racketeering, blackmail, bribery, and murder. The underground and a life of ever being on the lam suited him. He was a lifelong revolutionist who found comfort only in bedlam. Thus, when he became the autocrat of the USSR, he created crisis after crisis, and genuine crises he intensified.

Because of his obsession with complete control of affairs, Stalin never formed a deep emotional attachment to anyone—not even his first wife, Ekaterina "Kato" Djugashvili, for whom he grieved bitterly on her passing, and so much so that he leaped into her grave at her funeral. In 1907, while engaged in Bolshevik activism, "fundraising especially, he left behind Kato in a tiny apartment in Baku, Georgia, where she and her son suffered the intolerable heat, want of nutritious food, and in general the neglect of almost never having around her husband. She became ill, but Stalin, seldom at her side, offered no assistance until it was apparent that she was moribund. Seeing that she was declining, he returned her to her family in Baku, but by that time, she was severely hemorrhaging. He was with her on the day of her passing.[46]

Stalin's lack of empathy comes out in a story that he was fond of retelling while on a fishing expedition while exiled in Kureika. Thirty tribesmen went out to fish, but only 29 returned. When Stalin inquired about the puzzle, one man, unfazed, replied that he was still out there—i.e., that he drowned. Stalin was

---

[44] Simon Sebag Montefiore, *Young Stalin*, 39, 42, and 110.
[45] Simon Sebag Montefiore, *Young Stalin*, 63 and 65.
[46] Simon Sebag Montefiore, *Young Stalin*, 190–91.

taken aback by the nonchalance of all the fishermen. One replied: "Why should we have pity for men? We can always make more of them, but a horse—try to make a horse!"[47]

UPSHOT

The aim of this chapter has been to give readers a general sketch of Joseph Stalin, who during the span of time that is the focus of this book was the Bolshevik Party. Thus, any assessment of the Bolshevik attitude toward Ukraine cannot be done without the acquaintance of the dictator who was the Party.

Stalin, I have argued, lived ever by five maxims: trust no one, do whatever needs doing to do a job needing to get done, use force to overcome problems and a greater force for greater problems, take control of all matters when you can, and ever repay an insult, with interest. Though lacking large intelligence, he had much practical intelligence and cunning (street smarts), possessed diligence, and was patient and persistent. And so, with the passing of Vladimir Lenin, he was in position to vie for leadership of the Bolshevik Party, the subject of the next chapter.

---

[47] Simon Sebag Montefiore, *Young Stalin*, 289.

Chapter 2

The Death of Lenin

DESPITE STALIN'S DISAPPOINTMENT WITH LENIN'S ordinariness, Lenin would become for Stalin a quasi-father-figure. Stalin, for Lenin, would become a dutiful son inasmuch as he would attend to the dirty work of "gleaning" money for the cause and later of administrative minutiae that other prom-inent and more intellectual figures of the Party—e.g., Grigori Zinoviev, Lev Kamenev, and Leon Trotsky—found execrable. To use the metaphor of a machine, often used by the Bolsheviks, while others wished ever to tinker on paper with the design or function of the machine, Stalin was content to do the daily maintenance to ensure that the machine was running, even if not with much efficiency. Consequently, Stalin would get to know intimately the machine, and that made him dangerous. Stalin was so adept at attending to details. He soon overlorded several offices and performed several functions: e.g., member of the Central Committee (1912), editorship with Lev Kamenev of Pravda (1917), Commissar of Nationalities (1917–1924), member of the Politburo (1917), and Commissar of the Workers' and Peasants' Inspectorate (1919), Commissar of the Committee of Central Control (1920), and Secretary-General of the Party (1922).

In this chapter, I expatiate on some of those roles. I intend to show how they put Stalin in the singular position to assume leadership of the Bolshevik Party upon the death of Lenin early in 1924.

"The post of general secretary…"
The Bolshevik Factotum

In 1917, Stalin became Commissar of Nationalities. Thus, he had intercourse with Tatars, Armenians, Ukrainians, Georgians, Uzbeks, Byelorussians, Kirdghizians, Tadzhiks, Buriats, and Yakuts, inter alia. Stalin would aim to assist such republics by offering economic and material assistance as well as proffering incentives for "socializing" in the young Russian Soviet Federative Socialist Republic. The RSFSR then comprised 140 million persons, some 65 million of whom were non-Russian.

Soon overseeing the Commissariat of the Workers' and Peasants' Inspectorate (1919), the "Rabkrin," Stalin oversaw all branches of the administration and inspected them for corruption and inefficiency. This commissariat was created by Lenin, who knew that as the bureaucracy of the Party grew, there needed to be constant checks on its efficiency. He chose teams of workers and peasant-farmers, headed by Stalin, to offer a check from below, so to speak, in recognition that the machine was increasingly top-heavy. With people at the top overseeing people on the bottom and people on the bottom overseeing people on the top, the weighty bureaucratic machine quickly became even more ponderous, difficult to manage, and costly. Yet, as commissar, Stalin could see exactly how things worked, or failed to work, and he had direct input concerning changes that needed to be made concerning efficiency, and thus acquired large intra-Party political clout.

Then, in 1920, the Committee of Central Control was formed, which would oversee the moral integrity of the Party. This office aimed to purge the Party of opportunists or careerists: members of the bourgeoisie who had infiltrated the system for a career and those motivated by power (empleomaniacs), not by Bolshevik ideals. It would acquire power nearly equal to the Central Committee, the Party's main presiding body, and there was frequent political interaction between the two committees, coordinated by the Secretary-General. Stalin, as head of Rabkrin, also oversaw this office till 1923, though he was not formally commissioned as its head.

When Lenin formed the Politburo (Political Bureau) in 1917, its members included Lenin, overseeing everything; Trotsky as head of the war effort; Kamenev as Lenin's deputy; and Stalin as manager of the daily affairs. In addition to the Politburo, there was the Orgburo (Organizational Bureau), which directed the activities of the Party personnel (1919). By 1919, Stalin was the only fulltime liaison officer between the Politburo and the Orgburo. In consequence, Stalin was again privy to an extraordinary amount of information concerning the lifeblood of the goings on of the Party.

When the office of Secretary-General of the Central Committee was created on April 3, 1922, the appointment, pushed forward by Zinoviev and with the backing of Kamenev and Lenin, was Stalin's. The function of the office was "to co-ordinate the work of [the Party's] many growing and overlapping branches." Stalin would ready an agenda for each session of the Politburo, acquire data for subjects of discussion, and transmit the goings on to the lower levels of the Party. He, thus, organized and ran the meetings. No one much feared that Stalin would use the post to ill effect, for as Trotsky noted, "the post of general secretary ... could have only a technical character, never political." How little did Trotsky know Stalin.

Assignation to the sorts of roles that Stalin had shown, in keeping with Trotsky's assessment, that Stalin was not an intellect of the first rank, at least not when it came to theoretical matters, though he was trustworthy and capable, and he was willing to do the sort of menial, subordinate tasks that other high-ranking Bolsheviks found to be beneath them. Yet acceptance of those roles is indicative of Stalin's quenchless ambition. He was willing to do what he had to do to advance within the Party.

Stalin also advanced in the Party because he tended not to disagree with Lenin. That is not to say that he could not and did not think for himself. It is merely to note that Stalin was, by nature, somewhat parasitical. He needed to attach himself irretrievably to some person, or some cause, and he eventually found both person and cause in Lenin. Once attached, he was dutiful, loyal, sedulous, and persevering. Writes Isaac Deutscher, "Koba's [Stalin's early moniker] writings were neither numerous nor intellectually startling, but they were marked by fanatical devotion to the Bolshevik faction, as well as by a businesslike practical tone highly esteemed by Lenin."

Stalin was also, prior to the death of Lenin, cautiously unobtrusive. "What was striking in the General Secretary was that there was nothing striking about him." His personality was impersonal; his bearing, modest. He preferred to listen than to speak. Nevertheless, through his numerous offices, he came to know all the persons "who in one way or another made and unmade reputations." Having that knowledge, in conjunction with unobtrusiveness, callidity, and caution, made Stalin greatly dangerous, and other high-ranking Bolsheviks came to realize that much too late. Thus, Stalin slowly and invisibly rose in the ranks of Bolsheviks, upon their control of Russia, with the overthrow of the postwar Provisional Government in November 1917.

"Departing from us…"

January 21, 1924

Fate would soon provide Stalin with the opportunity to assume control of the Jejune Party. Lenin had a crippling stroke on May 25, 1922, from extreme arterial blockage and suffered paralysis in his right arm and right leg. He would have two more debilitating strokes—one in December 1922 and the third in March 1923—which confined him to a wheelchair (Figure 2-1), and he would die on January 21, 1924.

Few saw Stalin as a possible successor to Lenin. Yet Lenin himself worried prior to his death—his impression of Stalin had soured and quickly—about Stalin's limitless powers as Secretary-General and the possibility of him using them for ill. "Comrade Stalin, having become Secretary-General, has unlimited authority concentrated in his hands, and I am not sure whether he will always be capable of using that authority with sufficient caution," Lenin says in his infamous Letter to Congress, dictated by Lenin, while debilitated, from December 23, 1922, to December 29, 1922. He adds that Stalin is "too rude" and "capricious" for that office, and ought to be removed. Lenin wants someone "more tolerant, more loyal, more polite and more considerate to the comrades." Lenin has also locked horns with Stalin over the latter's bullying of other Soviet republics—Georgia especially, to be discussed in chapter 3. That spilled over into personal animosities. Lenin wrote to Stalin on March 5, 1923, concerning some foul language uttered to Lenin's wife over the telephone.

Still, Lenin did not have complete faith in other, seemingly more qualified contenders, like Leon Trotsky, as the two often disagreed about matters of the Party. Trotsky, Lenin says, "is personally perhaps the most capable man in the present CC, but he has displayed excessive self-assurance and shown excessive preoccupation with the purely administrative side of the work." Lenin's concern—and it is a fault Trotsky readily acknowledges—is that Trotsky is not a suitable face for the Party, because he is conservative, pedantic, intolerant of disorder, and a man more comfortable with the noiselessness and serenity of study than with the boisterousness and unpredictability of revolution.

Conceding Trotsky's preference for inciting the revolution through his writings, Lenin's comments are unjust. Trotsky, for instance, was a Brobdingnagian and hands-on figure as head of its military in the success of the Russian Civil War.

Fig. 2-1. Lenin, Confined to Wheelchair, March 1923

Source: Wikipedia

As he came to see just how things worked, Stalin carefully postured himself for the role of leader of the Party. As Secretary-General, Stalin wielded considerable procedural power and used it to the fullest effect with Lenin's death by isolating more worthy political contenders while jockeying for the center of the stage. Lacking Lenin's keen intelligence, Stalin did have callidity, and he used it.

For illustration, upon Lenin's passing, Stalin marketed himself as the only logical successor to Lenin. At the Second All-Union Congress of Soviets on January 26, 1924, Stalin—with vigor, confidence, and pomp which were seldom exhibited prior to Lenin's death—eulogized the former leader of the USSR. I include a large portion of that eulogy.

> Comrades, we Communists are people of a special mold. We are made of a special stuff. We are those who form the army of the great proletarian strategist, the army of Comrade Lenin. There is nothing higher than the honor of belonging to this army. There is nothing higher than the title of member of the Party whose founder and leader was Comrade Lenin. It is not given to everyone to be a member of such a party. It is the sons of the working class, the sons of want and struggle, the sons of incredible privation and heroic effort who before all should be members of such a party. That is why the Party of the Leninists, the Party of the Communists, is also called the Party of the working class.
>
> Departing from us, Comrade Lenin enjoined us to hold high and guard the purity of the great title of member of the party. We vow to you, Comrade Lenin, we shall fulfill your commandment with honor!...
>
> Departing from us, Comrade Lenin enjoined us to guard the unity of our party as the apple of our eye. We vow to you, Comrade Lenin, we shall fulfill you commandment with honor!...
>
> Departing from us, Comrade Lenin enjoined us to guard and strengthen the dictatorship of the proletariat. We vow to you, Comrade Lenin, we shall spare no effort to fulfill this commandment, too, with honor!....
>
> Departing from us, Comrade Lenin enjoined us to strengthen with all our might the alliance of the workers and peasant-farmers. We vow to you, Comrade Lenin, that this commandment, too, we shall fulfill with honor!...
>
> Departing from us, Comrade Lenin enjoined us to strengthen and extend the union of republics. We vow to you, Comrade Lenin, that this commandment too, we shall fulfill with honor!...

Departing from us, Comrade Lenin commanded us to remain faithful to the principles of the communist international. We vow to you, Comrade Lenin, we shall not spare our lives to strengthen and extend the union of the working people of the whole world—the Communist International![1]

Stalin's eulogy is perfervidly religious in structure and in tone. There are six lengthy "litanies" and six ritualized replies. Stalin is inviting members of the congress to join him in carrying through to completion the principles of the Gospel of Marx as seen through the eyes of Lenin. As the one proffering the eulogy—Trotsky was not at the funeral and said in his autobiography that Stalin deliberately did not notify him of Lenin's death in time for him to make the funeral[2]—he implicitly anoints himself as the only possible successor to Lenin as head of the Party.

Stalin hoped to become the next leader of the Party by packaged himself as the only true disciple of Lenin. He took charge of Lenin's funeral, as if he were his son. He gave, in early 1924 and a few months after the death of Lenin a series of nine lectures titled "The Foundations of Leninism" at Sverdlov University.[3] He shared pictures of himself with Lenin in an amicable conversation. Hence, it was natural for others to see him as the most reasonable successor to Lenin.

There exists no greater depiction of Stalin's awareness that his fate would be determined by the perceived closeness of him and Lenin than his "Biographical Chronicles" (21–28 Jan. 1924). It is noteworthy throughout that Stalin refers to himself in the third person, which is suggestive of objectivity.

January 21:

6.50 p.m.: Death of V.I. Lenin (in Gorki).

9.30 p.m.: J.V. Stalin with the other members of the Political Bureau of the Central Committee of the RCP(B) leave for Gorki.

January 22: J.V. Stalin makes amendments to the text of the appeal of the Eleventh All-Russian Congress of Soviets "To All the Working People of the USSR" concerning the death of V.I. Lenin.

---

[1] J.V. Stalin, "The Death of Lenin," in *Selected Works*, https://www.marxists.org/reference/archive/stalin/works/1924/01/30.htm, accessed 15 Dec. 2022.
[2] Leon Trotsky, *My Life*, 508. For more, see Ian D. Thatcher, "Trotsky and Lenin's Funeral, 27 January 1924: A Brief Note," *History*, Vol. 94. No. 2: 194–202.
[3] Stephen Kotkin, *Stalin: Paradoxes of Power, 1878–1928* (London: Allen Lane, 2014), 544.

In a telegram to the Central Committee of the Communist Party of Bukhara, J.V. Stalin announces the death of V.I. Lenin and appeals for support of Lenin's policy of strengthening the alliance between the workers and peasant-farmers, and for closer solidarity with the Soviet government.

January 23:

9 a.m.: J.V. Stalin and other members of the Central Committee of the RCP(B) carry out the coffin with Lenin's body from the house in Gorki.

1.30 p.m. 2.45 p.m.: J.V. Stalin and delegates at the Second All-Union Congress and the Eleventh All-Russian Congress of Soviets, members of the Central Committee of the Party, members of the Government, workers, and representatives of various organizations, carry the coffin with Lenin's body from the Paveletsky Railway Station to the House of Trade Unions.

6.10 p.m.: J.V. Stalin stands in the guard of honor at Lenin's bier in the Hall of Columns of the House of Trade Unions.

January 25: *Pravda*, No. 20, publishes the appeal of the Central Committee of the RCP(B), signed by J.V. Stalin, to all Party organizations, institutions and to the press to collect all documents, etc., concerning V.I. Lenin and to send them to the Leninstitute of the Central Committee of the RCP(B).

January 26:

8.24 p.m.–8.40 p.m.: At the memorial session of the Second Congress of Soviets of the USSR, J.V. Stalin delivers a speech "On the Death of Lenin" and in the name of the Bolshevik Party takes a vow to guard and fulfill the behests of Lenin.

January 27:

8 a.m.: J.V. Stalin stands in the guard of honor at Lenin's bier in the Hall of Columns of the House of Trade Unions.

8.30 a.m.: J.V. Stalin stands at the head of Lenin's bier in the Hall of Columns of the House of Trade Unions.

9 a.m.: J.V. Stalin and workers' representatives carry out the coffin with Lenin's body from the House of Trade Unions.

4 p.m.: On the conclusion of the memorial meeting in the Red Square, J.V. Stalin, V.M. Molotov and others, lift the coffin with Lenin's body and proceed towards the tomb.

January 28: J.V. Stalin delivers a speech [eulogy] at a gathering of students of the ARCEC Kremlin Military School, held in memory of V.I. Lenin.[4]

What we see often in his Chronicles is a coupling of the names V.I. Lenin (16 times) and J.V. Stalin (13 times). Other than V.M. Molotov, who would become Stalin's shadow throughout the latter's dictatorship, no other member of the Party is mentioned in the Chronicles. The most obvious successor to Lenin, Leon Trotsky, was, if Trotsky's autobiographical account is accurate, kept from the funeral. We see "others," "members," "delegates," "workers," and "representatives," but we are given no names, and no exemplary actions of others are mentioned. Stalin announces the death of Lenin to the members of the Politburo of the Central Committee, Stalin is with others carrying the coffin (mentioned four times), Stalin stands in "guard of honor" (mentioned twice) at Lenin's bier, Stalin appeals to the Central Committee to collect all of Lenin's documents for preservation, Stalin delivers "On the Death of Lenin" to the Second Congress, Stalin stands at the head of Lenin's bier at House of Trade Unions, and Stalin delivers a final eulogy for the great man to students. Although all autobiographical notes are essentially egoistic, Stalin exhibits uncannily an incapacity to recognize the existence of anyone but himself in his Chronicles.

UPSHOT

The first chapter was, in many respects, a psychobiography of Lenin. This chapter's focus has been Stalin the *Praktik*. Stalin possessed in abundancy cunning, persistence, and attentiveness to minutiae. Those characteristics, along with a profound egotism, put him in a prime position to become the leader of the Bolshevik Party. As he slowly assumed leadership, he would assume powers, through enciting fear, that no other Soviet dictator would have. Those powers would soon be exhibited in ruthless actions against his ever-present "enemies of the Party," which could be found abundantly in Ukraine.

---

[4] J.V. Stalin, "Biographical Chronicles," in *Marxists Internet Archive*, https://www.marxists.org/reference/archive/stalin/works/collected/volume6/bio.htm, accessed 17 Dec. 2022.

Chapter 3

Stalinism & Ukraine

"[Stalin's] basic idea, acquired from propagandist pamphlets as far back as Tiflis Seminary days, was that national oppression was a relic of medievalism. Imperialism, viewed as the domination of strong na-tions over weak ones, was a conception quite beyond his ken."

~Leon Trotsky

We saw in the prior chapters that Joseph Stalin was a cunning and shrewd plotter, who ever strove for power and control and who had genuine unconcern for the wellbeing of others. Early on, while shunning the Politburo's limelight, he assumed control of many significant Bolshevik offices and slowly set into place many men who were more loyal to him than to the Party or its global mission. With the death of Lenin, few saw the possibility of Stalin assuming the Party's leadership. He was too unobtrusive. Yet his unobtrusiveness and the power he had assumed through doing the dirty work of the Party made him a viable candidate, even if few recognized that.

In this chapter, I cover Stalin's rise to power, the philosophy behind his leadership, and the problem that Ukraine posed for his brand of Marxism.

"Lenin drove them with a stick"

Stalin's Machinations

Who would supplant Lenin after his death?

In answer to that question, I offer the words of Alexander Gregoryevich Barmine (1899–1987), Soviet brigadier general in the Red Army, diplomat, and later dissident, who writes in his memoirs of the uncertainty after the passing of Lenin.

> What was going to happen to us now? Who was to take the wheel of this great ship with its course set to the future through uncharted seas, with its amateur crew, its battered machinery, its young and daring engineers? A few brilliant men remained: Trotsky, Tomsky, Piatakov, Rykov, Bukharin, Radek. … [ellipsis Barmine's] I scarcely thought of

Stalin. He was very little known, and, back there in 1924, it seemed unlikely that he would ever play a leading role.[1]

Victor Kravchenko (1905–1966), captain of the Red Army but political defector to the United States in 1944, echoes the sentiment of Stalin's relative anonymity at the time of Lenin's death. In his autobiography, Kravchenko notes that he was much stirred by Stalin's eulogy of Lenin (chapter 2), yet he was relatively unaware of Stalin's existence at that time. "It [the eulogy] was a short, almost liturgical promise to follow in the path indicated by the dead leader, and it moved me as the oratory at our memorial gathering [for Lenin] had not done. Stalin was a member of the all-powerful Political Bureau, Secretary General of the Party, and had been an important figure in the new regime from the beginning. Yet this was the first time that I had become acutely aware of his existence. Strange, I thought, that his portrait was not even on our walls."[2]

The testimonies of Barmine and Kravchenko show that two prominent, in-the-know members of the Party knew little about Stalin and were likely representative of most Bolsheviks, who thought that Leon Trotsky, who was with Lenin from the beginning, was the inevitable replacement for Lenin.

Fig. 3-1. Leon Trotsky, c. 1936, Reading *The Militant*

Source: Wikipedia

---

[1] Alexander Barmine, *One Who Survived: The Life Story of a Russian under Stalin* (New York: G.P. Putnam's Sons, 1945),
[2] Victor Kravchenko, *I Chose Freedom* (New York: Charles Scribner's Sons, 1946), 40.

Though initially a Menshevik, Lev Davidovich Bronstein, better known as Leon Trotsky (1789–1940, Figure 3-1), was a brilliant theoretician and a prolific writer on Marxism who would become known for his theory of "Permanent Revolution"—the notion, roughly, that the dictatorship of the proletariat could not come about piecemeal or in stages, but that any successful Marxist revolution had to be global with a leading Western nation like Germany, the home of Marx, taking the lead. He was also a major figure in the October Revolution,[3] which overthrew Russia's Provisional Government after the World War. As People's Commissar for Military and Naval Affairs—he, in effect, founded the Red Army—Trotsky led the Bolsheviks to victory in the Russian Civil War (1917–1922) and was, with Lenin and Stalin, part of the first Politburo (1919).

Stalin, despite his post-mortem jockeying, was a dark horse. Yet he capitalized cunningly on the political pandemonium created by Lenin's death. As secretary-general, Stalin was responsible for much of that pandemonium. As the Party's "washerwoman," he surreptitiously and insidiously, but surely, had acquired control over data and over the Party's affairs both within and without Russia and from the highest and lowest levels. He knew all the duties of important members of the Party. He had control of removing and raising members of the Party. He knew how the numerous branches of the Party interacted. Most importantly, he had also stacked the Party over the years with young Bolsheviks owing him favors, as if in anticipation of his own revolution against the Old Guard of Bolsheviks (see appendix). Knowing intimately the numerous mechanisms and personages of the Party, he was in a fine spot to position himself for leadership of the Party. He surreptitiously, and slyly, did that.

There was, however, one enormous albatross—Trotsky. Stalin waited for a suitable time to attack Trotsky. To attack too soon, and unsubtly, would have been political suicide, for Trotsky was just too politically strong in the eyes of fellow Bolsheviks, and few even considered Stalin—a behind-the-scenes man, or as Trotsky said of him, "the outstanding mediocrity of the party"[4]—as a possible face of the Party. Stalin's strategy was razing. He worked toward building up himself by bringing down Trotsky as well as other contenders for the leadership of the Party. At day's end, as it were, Stalin would stand taller than all others, not through any large accomplishments, but by bringing all others so low that he would remain standing above them as the only viable alternative. That is a strategy he would use throughout his dictatorship. Vis-à-vis Trotsky, Stalin gained a loyal army of anti-Trotskyites by massaging the feet of all

---

[3] October 25 on the Julian Calendar; November 7 on the Gregorian.
[4] Leon Trotsky, *My Life: An Attempt at an Autobiography* (New York: Grosset & Dunlap, 1960), 512.

persons on whose toes Trotsky, in his efforts to win the civil war and advance issues of the Party, had stepped.[5]

Fig. 3-2. Stalin with Lev Kamenev, Alexei Rykov, and Grigori Zinoviev in 1925

Source: Wikipedia

Acknowledging Trotsky's strength prior to Lenin's death, Stalin 1923 aligned himself with Leftists[6] Grigory Zinoviev (1883–1936, Figure 3-2, rightmost) and Lev Kamenev (1883–1936, Figure 3-2, next to Stalin)—Kamenev was the acting leader of the Party during Lenin's debilitation—and he encouraged those two, more qualified in theoretical squabbles and debates, to fight with and discredit Trotsky,[7] while he, coyly, would merely refrain from the bickering.

Trotsky, probably figuring that his numerous past actions—and how great they were—on behalf of the push toward socialism would be remembered by all and would speak on his behalf, did not answer the animadversions of Zinoviev, and to a lesser extent, of Kamenev.[8]

---

[5] Leon Trotsky, *My Life*, 442 and 446.
[6] Leftists of the Party were roughly those who adopted an authoritarian, inflexible approach to solving difficulties in the move toward socialism. Rightists were more conciliatory and preferred a gradual move to socialism.
[7] Alexander Barmine, *One Who Survived*, 161.
[8] That is where he was when Lenin passed. Alexander Barmine, *One Who Survived*, 162.

Trotsky's silence—though a powerful speaker and brilliant writer, he was socially aloof and a lone wolf[9]—was taken by many members of the Party as an admission that the charges against him were not scandalmongery, but true. Soon, Trotsky and "Trotskyism," through Stalin's machinations, became anathema, and when Trotsky did attempt to parry the animadversions, it was to no avail. It was just too late. The troika of Zinoviev, Kamenev, and the "noiseless" Stalin had prevailed and would head the Party after Lenin's death.

With Trotsky humiliated and, for the most part, discredited, things quieted. Stalin, then in 1925, turned on Zinoviev and Kamenev. He distanced himself from Zinoviev at the Fourteenth Congress of the Bolshevik Communist Party of the Soviet Union (CPSU[B]) in mid-December 1925, in which he talked abundantly of Zinoviev's "deviations," his double-speak, concerning suspicions against, and then alliance with, middle peasants as well as his "unprincipled" suggestions for changes to the Politburo. Stalin also revealed that Kamenev and Zinoviev had actively asked for Stalin's assistance in ousting Trotsky from the Party, as if to appease Trotsky's remaining loyalists.[10]

Stalin would break with Zinoviev and Kamenev by 1926 and align himself with the more moderate Rightists Nikolai Bukharin, Alexei Rykov, and Mikhail Tomsky. Zinoviev and Kamenev, as anti-Leninists, were now in the Party's minority.[11]

By January 1927 and at the Fifteenth Congress of the CPSU(B), Stalin, ever cautious to enter a fray only when the time was propitious, took the offensive against Zinoviev and Kamenev.

First, new delegates had been put into place, and Zinoviev, says Stalin, had not been reelected as Chairman of the Leningrad Soviet.[12] Zinoviev was out.

Next, Stalin then turned to the issue of socialism in the USSR as it pertained to the Russian Revolution. Kamenev and Zinoviev, he says, opposed socialism in the USSR by refusing to support the October uprising of 1917 against the highly unpopular Provisional Government—just after the overthrow of the tsarist regime—to which "Lenin drove them with a stick." Stalin adds, "They

---

[9] Oleg Yegorov, "Leon Trotsky: Six Facts about the Disgraced Russian Revolutionary," *Russia Beyond*, https://www.rbth.com/arts/2016/11/07/leon-trotsky-6-facts-about-the-disgraced-russian-revolutionary_645523, accessed 26 Jan. 2023.

[10] J.V. Stalin, "Fourteenth Congress of the CPSU(B)," in *Marxists Internet Archive*, https://www.marxists.org/reference/archive/stalin/works/1925/12/18.htm, accessed 25 Jan. 2023.

[11] When the time was right—that is, with implementation of his Five-Year Plan—Stalin would also break from and turn against the moderate Rightists and assume again a Leftist posture.

[12] J.V. Stalin, "Fifteenth Congress of the CPSU(B)," in *Marxists Internet Archive*, https://www.marxists.org/reference/archive/stalin/works/1927/12/02.htm, accessed 25 Jan. 2023.

stated plainly at the time that by making an uprising we were heading for destruction, that we must wait for the Constituent Assembly, that the conditions for socialism had not matured and would not mature soon." That too was the position of Trotsky, "for he said plainly that if a victorious proletarian revolution in the West did not bring timely assistance in the more or less near future, it would be foolish to think that a revolutionary Russia could hold out in the face of a conservative Europe." Trotsky, Stalin concedes, was not goaded to the October Revolution. He went voluntarily, but "with a slight reservation, which already at that time brought him close to Kamenev and Zinoviev." That reservation was that socialism could be begun in the RSFSR, but would need quick assistance from other countries to succeed.[13]

Lenin, in contrast, eagerly faced the revolution. In contrast to Kamenev and Zinoviev, who were now linked with the falling god, Trotsky, "Lenin, on the contrary, went to the uprising without reservations, asserting that proletarian power in our country must serve as a *base* for assisting the proletarians of other countries to emancipate themselves from the yoke of the bourgeoisie."[14]

The issue is one-country socialism—that is, the possibility of socialism taking root in the USSR (formerly RSFSR) without the assistance of a strong Western nation, rebelling against capitalism. His assessment of Lenin is, in the main, correct. Lenin did think that socialism could find root in the USSR, but like Trotsky, he too believed that it would soon die, if not nurtured by growth of socialism in the West. Socialism in the USSR could not sustain itself. Stalin, however, believed that it could—at least, his Five-Year Plan, beginning in 1928, would attempt to see *if* it could. Trotsky, Kamenev, and Zinoviev would be discredited, and expelled.

In his efforts to discredit the so-called "United Opposition"—the triad of Trotsky, Kamenev, and Zinoviev—Stalin late in 1927 would introduce something that had theretofore been considered anathema in resolving issues within the Party: political ruthlessness through sanguinary violence. Prior to the death of Lenin, discord within the Party had always been settled amicably. When the United Opposition was formed to challenge Stalin for leadership of the Party, the trio appealed to the people, and that appeal was not without success. A panicky Stalin countered with thuggery to quiet the opposition. Martemyan Riutin, a Stalinist underling, gathered gangs of heavies, with whistles and truncheons, to create pandemonium at Oppositional speeches and to break up meetings.[15] By November 1927, 10 years after the October

---

[13] J.V. Stalin, "Fifteenth Congress of the CPSU(B)."
[14] J.V. Stalin, "Fifteenth Congress of the CPSU(B)."
[15] Robert Vincent Daniels, *The Conscience of the Revolution: Communist Opposition in Soviet Russia* (New York: Simon & Shuster, 1969), 303–4.

Revolution, Stalin was using the Party's police, the GPU, to "settle" intra-Party "disagreements" through the use of violence, which occurred in Moscow and in Leningrad.[16]

By the Sixteenth Congress of the Bolshevik Communist Party of the Soviet Union CPSU(B) in 1930, Stalin turned against the Rightists. He announces formally the expulsion of Bukharin, "the chief exponent and leader of the Right capitulators," from the Politburo. In his lengthy speech, Stalin mentions "Bukharin's childish formula about the capitalist elements peacefully growing into socialism"—childish, although in accord with the dialectic of Marxist materialism. Sums Stalin, "Either we vanquish and crush them, the exploiters, or they will vanquish and crush us, the workers and peasants of the USSR—that is how the question stands, comrades."[17] There is here no sense of the ineluctability of the emergence of socialism. Among the "right capitulators," he includes also Rykov and Tomsky, who too will be disgraced and dismissed from the Party. It was at this congress that Stalin was acknowledged as the sole leader of the USSR. All major contenders have been discredited, vanquished.

"I became a Marxist…"
Stalin's Contribution to Marxism

As we have seen, Stalin rose in the Party by his Georgian tactics of demolition: slander, mendacity, and psychological and physical intimidation. In such a manner, he built Stalinist Marxism on an emergent cult of personality, which he circumspectly built unhurriedly, but meticulously, over the course of decades. He lacked the presence for quick assumption of leadership of the Party. He also lacked the political backing. Writes Ian Kershaw:

> A Stalin cult had to be built carefully. This was not just because the man himself was so physically unprepossessing—diminutive and squat, his face dominated by a big walrus mustache and heavily pitted from smallpox—or that he was a secretive, intensely private individual who spoke in a quiet, undemonstrative voice, his Russian couched in a strong Georgian accent that never left him. The real problem was the

---

[16] Alexander Barmine, *One Who Survived: The Life Story of a Russian under Stalin* (New York: G.P. Putnam's Sons, 1945), 166–67, and Leon Trotsky, *My Life: An Attempt at an Autobiography* (New York: Grosset & Dunlap, 1960), 532–34.

[17] J.V. Stalin, "Report of the Central Committee to the Sixteenth Congress of the CPSU(B)" (27 June 1930), in *Marxist Internet Archives*, https://www.marxists.org/reference/archive/stalin/works/1930/aug/27.htm, accessed 28 Jan. 2023.

giant shadow of Lenin. Stalin could not be seen to be usurping the legendary image of the great Bolshevik hero and leader of the revolution. So at first Stalin tread cautiously.[18]

Though apparently unprepossessing, Stalin—perhaps because of his less-than-modest roots, his dearth of keen intellect, and his struggles with public speaking—would come to have a grip not only on the downtrodden in the USSR but also on the downtrodden worldwide. Consider this appraisal of Stalin by American civil-rights activist W.E.B. Du Bois.

> Joseph Stalin was a great man. … He knew the common man, felt his problems, followed his fate. Stalin … was a man who thought deeply, read understandingly and listened to wisdom, no matter whence it came. He was attacked and slandered as few men of power have been; yet he seldom lost his courtesy and balance; nor did he let attack drive him from his convictions nor induce him to surrender positions which he knew were correct. As one of the despised minorities of man, he first set Russia on the road to conquer race prejudice and make one nation out of its 140 groups without destroying their individuality.[19]

We have seen that Stalin was not an original thinker. I have argued that he parasitically, and unabashedly so, bound himself to Lenin, and thus saw his fate after Lenin's death to be determined by the degree to which other Bolsheviks, ensorcelled by the cult of Leninism, saw him as Lenin's favorite, or at least as the member of high-ranking Bolsheviks who was truest to the vision of Lenin. He, with an unexampled understanding of the nuts and bolts of the mammoth and inordinately complex machine of the Party, assisted fate by numerous calculated moves to convince others of his love of Lenin and unsullied uptake of Leninism. His speeches, fraught with numerous references to the Gospel of Lenin, are evidence of unbroken allegiance to his former comrade and teacher.

Of his initial attraction to Marxism, Stalin writes that he was materially and situationally disposed to Marxism. "I became a Marxist because of my social position (my father was a worker in a shoe factory, and my mother was also a working woman), but also … because of the harsh intolerance and Jesuitical

---

[18] Ian Kershaw, *To Hell and Back: Europe 1914–1949* (New York: Penguin Books, 2016), 269.
[19] W.E.B. Du Bois, "On Stalin," in *Marxists Internet Archive*, https://www.marxists.org/reference/archive/stalin/biographies/1953/03/16.htm, accessed 24 Nov. 2022.

discipline that crushed me so mercilessly at the Seminar. ... The atmosphere in which I lived was saturated with hatred against Tsarist oppression."[20]

Just how faithful was Stalin to Lenin's Marxism?

There is no consensus concerning Stalin's uptake of Leninist Marxism. Stalin was a pupil of Marx, and later Lenin, and he was committed inflexibly to the axioms of Marxism: e.g., materialism, secularism, collectivization of property, the demise of capitalism, the revolution and dictatorship of the proletariat, and inevitability of a global revolution. That comes out in his booklet, *Dialectical and Historical Materialism* (1938)—a highly unoriginal précis of Marxism, though more of a paean to Marx, intended to Sovietize Marx's principles. Lenin, following Marx, preached the "dictatorship of the proletariat"—that is, the legitimacy of there being a sovereign group of revolutionaries who, for the nonce, would rule dictatorially until such time that socialism liquidated all parties. Stalin made purchase of such a dictatorship, but as he came to relish the perks of power, he never seemed to fret much about the evanescence of that dictatorship through complete socialization. If Stalin can be deemed original in any sense apropos of socialism, his originality would be in the use of the application of forceful and extreme means to expedite Marxist socialism via revolution.

Yet Stalin was a *Praktik*, not a theoretician, for Marxism was a dialectical theory that essayed not merely to explain societies, but to change them. Thus, Marxism itself gave Stalin theoretical wiggle room for Stalinist deviations *en route* to the complete victory of the proletariat: pure global classlessness. Stalin would adopt, or abandon, almost any principle, if it should suit him in a current crisis, and many, if not most, of the crises he had faced in his life were of his making. He wormed out of crises, we shall come to see, by locating his omnipresent "enemies of the Party," who were equally "enemies of the people" and by exterminating them. It suffices to say that no one, not even his closest friends, wholly trusted Stalin. All certainly feared him.

Stalin is sometimes credited with a unique contribution to Marxism: one-country socialism. Most Bolsheviks agreed, following Marx, that Russia alone could not be socialized. Marx saw the revolution beginning in Europe. Trotsky—using a much misunderstood term, "permanent revolution"—maintained that a successful revolution needed to be firmly rooted in the socialization of Western Europe. Lenin agreed. Without the socialization of some part or all of Western Europe, Russia, even if moving to socialize, would eventually become Europeanized—that is, Russia would soon become

---

[20] Boris Souvarine, *Stalin: A Critical Survey of Bolshevism* (New York: Langmans, Green & Co., 1939), 16.

capitalistic. It was merely too much of a backwater. Trotsky writes in "Three Concepts of the Russian Revolution":

> The perspective of permanent revolution may be summarized in the following way: the complete victory of the democratic revolution in Russia is conceivable only in the form of the dictatorship of the proletariat, leaning on the peasantry. The dictatorship of the proletariat, which would inevitably place on the order of the day not only democratic but socialistic tasks as well, would at the same time give a powerful impetus to the international socialist revolution. Only the victory of the proletariat in the West could protect Russia from bourgeois restoration and assure it the possibility of rounding out the establishment of socialism. [21]

The West was key, because only there were there true proletariats—laborers, earning meager wages as slaves to capitalism.

In "The Permanent Revolution," Trotsky adds that the problem is not merely confined to Russia, but to any country wishing to socialize. "In general no country in the world can build socialism within its own national limits." Socialism, global in essence, needs to take root and quickly ratoon to other nations. "The socialist revolution ... attains completion, only in the final victory of the new society on our entire planet."[22] Lenin's view was nearly the same.

Stalin time came to disagree. By 1924, in his *The Foundations of Leninism*, he acknowledges that the "complete victory of socialism" must be global. However, Stalin now rejects the notion that there cannot be a successful, or incomplete, revolution in one country without "the combined action of the proletarians of all or at least of a majority of the advanced countries." The Russian Revolution has shown that view to be false. So too, he adds, has Lenin.

Stalin appeals to Lenin's thoughts on the subject in the latter's "Left-Wing Communism" (1920). There, Lenin writes meaningfully of a revolution taking root in one country—and he refers to the three revolutions that occurred in Russia in his day—when a nationwide crisis involves the exploited and the exploiters such that "the '*lower classes*' *do not want* the old way, and when the '*upper classes*' *cannot carry on in the old way*"—*viz.*, the exploiters are thereby rendered ineffective in further exploitation. Those things, Stalin notes, are "certain absolutely necessary conditions," which have been met in Russia. That

---

[21] Leon Trotsky, "Three Concepts of the Russian Revolution" (Aug. 1939) https://www.internationalist.org/three.html, accessed 18 Dec. 2022.
[22] Leon Trotsky, "The Permanent Revolution," in *Marxists Internet Archive,* https://www.marxists.org/archive/trotsky/1931/tpr/pr10.htm, accessed 18 Dec. 20.

conceded, Marxism demands a complete and global victory of the proletariat over the capitalist.[23]

Is Stalin's reading of Lenin tenable? Is Lenin arguing that there can be a successful and sustainable revolution in one country?

Stalin acknowledges that Lenin 1920 is merely giving needed conditions for a revolution—awareness by the exploited, a planned uprising, and installation of conditions whereby the exploited can no longer exploit—but are those conditions jointly sufficient for a successful revolution? In other words, does meeting those conditions ensure that the new socialist government will be self-sustaining? There is nothing in Stalin's quote from Lenin that shows that. Nonetheless, Stalin's nodus might be due to the poor choice of Lenin's material. The overall tenor of Lenin's argument—it concedes that since the revolutions of February and October 1917, there has been "all-round development of the Soviets on a nation-wide scale"—is consistent with one-country socialism. However, Lenin, immediately after mention of the success of socialism in the USSR in the span of over two years, states that "while the working-class movement is everywhere going through what is actually the same kind of preparatory school for victory over the bourgeoisie, it is achieving that development in its *own way* in each country" and there will soon be global contagion.[24] Lenin says nothing here that shows confidence that socialism can take root and sustain itself in the USSR or in any *one* of its republics. I am inclined to see Stalin's take as a misreading of Lenin.[25] That, of course, does not militate against the possibility of one-country socialism—especially outside the USSR.

Stalin came to believe that socialism could take root and flourish "within its own national limits" and without assistance from Western Europe—that is, that the Bolshevik Revolution does not have to be a global phenomenon with roots in the West. The keys to the uptake of that position are the enormous size of the USSR, despite its being a backwater, and its resources for industrializing, mostly untapped.

That is a radical departure from other Bolsheviks, and Marx. The secret, for Stalin, is to Bolshevize the peasant-farmers "by drawing the peasant-farmers

---

[23] J.V. Stalin, *The Foundations of Leninism*, https://www.marxists.org/reference/archive/stalin/works/1924/foundations-leninism/ch03.htm, accessed 27 Jan. 2023.
[24] V.I. Lenin, "'Left-Wing Communism: An Infantile Disorder," in *Marxists Internet Archive*, https://www.marxists.org/archive/lenin/works/1920/lwc/ch10.htm, accessed Jan. 2023.
[25] For an argument of Lenin, shifting to a defense of one-country socialism, see Erik Van Ree, "Socialism in One Country: A Reassessment," in *Studies in East European Thought*, Vol. 50, 1998: 77–117.

into the work of governing the country." That can occur only by crafting an "atmosphere of mutual confidence"[26] and collectivizing the peasant-farmers' capitalistic farms.

Stalin's deviation from Marxism and other main-line Bolshevik theorists cannot be underestimated. It is perhaps responsible for Stalin's lasting legacy among Russia's leaders. Stalin is not countermanding the Marxist view that any socialist revolution would have to be international, but merely the view that there can be no sustainable one-country revolution—especially in a boondocks like Russia. Stalin, *pace* his comrades, is emphasizing Russia's potential for greatness. In a country that occupies one-sixth of the land on the planet, there is a super-abundancy of natural resources to be tapped for expeditious development of industry in cities. In a country that occupies one-sixth of the land on the planet, there are lush and arable lands in the black-earth steppe, much of that unused, which stretches along the belly of the Soviet republics. One has only to put that arable land to efficient use—to "industrialize" Soviet farms.

Moreover, the push for one-country socialism, an inordinately ambitious task, is not as super-inordinately ambitious as the notion of global socialism through global revolution. One-country socialism is doable—or, at least, it can be tried. Moreover, in contrast to the push for Soviet socialism, there stands ominously Trotsky's "permanent revolution"—a "new society on our entire planet"—which could only have seemed to Soviets overly demanding, if not impossible, to a people, wearied and battered from years of struggle through uprisings, war, and revolutions.

Belief in one-country socialism would become the theoretical motivation for Stalin's Five-Year Plan, begun in 1928. That was an intriguing, wily maneuver, as the Soviet economy, after years of war and revolution, was in shambles, and the plan offered Soviets an occasion to turn from the unpleasantness of their lives and invest and engage in an ardent push, a sanctimonious "war," to leave capitalism once and for all behind and socialize wholly the USSR. Should the Soviet republics become fully socialized, all would awaken to a socialist Arcadia without the blights of unemployment and poverty, and then the world might be ready to follow the fine example of the USSR.

There would be one weighty albatross to attaining that Arcadia: Ukraine.

---

[26] J.V. Stalin, "The Party's Immediate Tasks in the Countryside" (22 Oct. 1924), in *Marxists Internet Archive*, https://www.marxists.org/reference/archive/stalin/works/1924/10/22.htm, accessed 18 Dec. 2022.

> "Stalin ... drove out the rural bloodsuckers"

The Ukrainian Problem

In a speech, "The Ukrainian Rada," delivered on December 14, 1917, and at the start of the Civil War, Stalin addresses the tension between the newly established Russian Council of People's Commissars (CPC), "which has always resolutely upheld the principle of self-determination," and the newly established Ukrainian Rada, headquartered in Kyiv. The CPC's refusal to acknowledge the Rada, says Stalin, concerns fundamental political differences. The Rada envisages a federal system in Russia, self-determination, and right to secession, and it maintains that the CPC, championing centralization of power, disallows all such things, which Stalin says is false. When Siberians, Byelorussians, and Turkestans asked the CPC for political directives, the CPC's response was this, "you yourselves are the authority in your localities, and you yourselves therefore must draw up the directives."[27]

Yet Russians and Ukrainians are one, continues Stalin, and he has in mind the perspective of Marxist theory. Both comprise soldiers, sailors, peasant-farmers, and laborers. Both are fighting for peace, liberty, and socialism. The conflict is between the CPC and the Ukrainian General Secretariat. The CPC aims to wrest power and give it to the people. The Ukrainian General Secretariat, quasi-feudalistic, wishes to keep landlords and capitalists—the maintain the gap between the propertied wealthy and the property-less poor.

What of Ukraine's desire to be a republic?

Stalin states that the CPC has already recognized the republic in Lenin's "Manifesto to the Ukrainian People with an Ultimatum to the Ukrainian Rada."[28] He adds, "It is prepared to recognize a republic in any of the national regions of Russia should the working population of the given region desire it. It is prepared to recognize a federal structure for our country, should the working population of the regions of Russia desire it." The Ukrainian Rada only feigns

---

[27] J.V. Stalin, "The Ukrainian Rada," in *Marxists Internet Archive*, https://www.marxists.org/reference/archive/stalin/works/1917/12/14.htm, accessed 14 Dec. 2022.

[28] Lenin says, "We, the Council of People's Commissars, recognize the people's Ukrainian Republic and its right completely to secede from Russia or to make a treaty with the Russian Republic concerning federal or other similar relations between them." Again, "Everything that concerns the national rights and national independence of the Ukrainian people is recognized by us, the Council of People's Commissars, forthwith and without reservation or qualification." V.I. Lenin, "Manifesto to the Ukrainian People with an Ultimatum to the Ukrainian Rada," in *Marxists Internet Archive*, https://www.marxists.org/archive/lenin/works/1917/dec/03.htm, accessed 3 Feb. 2023.

to be friendly to the interests of the people while being allied to the "monarchists [Alexey] Kaledin and [Mikhail] Rodzyanko as pillars of the republic," it is really a government of monarchist plutocrats—that is, "sworn enemies of the people," but friends of bourgeois.

Three issues are critical. First, General Secretariat Symon Petliura, put in charge of Ukraine's military affairs by the Rada, has issued the return of all Ukrainian units of its army and navy to return to Ukraine, which, if the issue had been followed, would have destroyed the front line of battle and have reduced to nil the possibility of "peace and armistice." Second, Kaledin, Rodzyanko, and others have ordered Ukrainian troops to fall on Soviet troops in Kyiv, Odesa, and Kharkiv to disarm them. "But the Soviets are the bulwark and hope of the revolution. Whoever disarms the Soviets disarms the revolution, wrecks the cause of peace and liberty, betrays the cause of the workers and peasant-farmers." Third, the Rada has disallowed Russian soldiers from passing through Ukraine to fight Kaledin and his counter-revolutionists, though they have allowed Kaledin and his Cossacks free passage.[29]

The three arguments are each tendentiously unpersuasive. Beyond the rousing rhetoric, the Bolshevik Revolution is not Ukraine's revolution. Ukraine sees the bedlam of World War I as an opportunity for independence and sovereignty. Stalin's gripe is that Ukraine is interfering with the Bolshevik Revolution, which is to his mind everyman's revolution.

Moreover, despite what Stalin says, Russia was never amenable to a federation of republics. It demanded for a strong federation which demanded strong centralization in Russia, and that meant Russian yoke over its "republics"—that those republics would be obedient to and of the culture of Russia. That ideal, of course, was nowise of a "federation" of republics.

Over one year later, Stalin speaks to what the success of the Bolshevik Revolution means for Ukraine. Prior to the October Revolution, Western imperialists—like Belgium, France, and England—have had "huge enterprises" in Ukraine for its coal, metals, and grains and have "proceeded to suck the blood out of the Ukrainian people in the usual, 'lawful' and unobtrusive way." With the October Revolution, the imperialists have been cast from Ukrainian soil, until the Austro-German imperialists' occupation. "Who is not familiar with the endless humiliations and tribulations undergone by Ukraine during the Austro-German occupation, the destruction of workers' and peasant-farmers' organizations, the complete disruption of industry and railway

---

[29] J.V. Stalin, "Reply to Ukrainian Comrades in the Rear and at the Front," in *Marxists Internet Archive*, https://www.marxists.org/reference/archive/stalin/works/1917/12/12.htm#2b, accessed 14 Dec. 2022.

transport, the hangings and shootings, which were such commonplace features of Ukrainian independence under the aegis of the Austro-German imperialists?"[30] The Bolshevik cause, aiming to liberate, not to subjugate, Ukraine's *hoi polloi*, ought to be Ukraine's cause.

The problem concerns Russia's role in the Bolshevik Revolution. Old Schoolers see the triumph of Bolshevism as a victory for Russia, and so Russia should be the central authority in any "federation" of states and the "republics" of Russia should be Russified. Leninists see the triumph of Bolshevism as a victory of socialism and hope fervently for contagion in Europe and a push toward secular materialism—"Russification" of a secular and economic, not cultural, sort. Lenin, for instance, always expected the excitement and success of the revolution would be a wake-up call for European nations, steeped in the abuses of capitalism.

Stalin, a Georgian, was early on sympathetic to, even insistent on, cultural diversity. As a youth, he experienced Russification in the Georgian schools, where Georgian culture was suppressed by new rules, intolerant of Georgian language and culture. Says former classmate Josef Iremashvili, "They considered us Georgians to be an inferior culture into whom the blessing of Russian civilization had to be beaten." Only the Russian language was tolerated in Georgian schools, and that posed a singular nodus for boys who knew little Russian.[31]

Yet over time, Stalin came to see allowance of cultural diversity in republics as a threat to instantiation of socialism and its growth. Marxist socialism was part of a dialectical process that was inevasibly to become global with the complete annihilation, through implosion, of capitalism. That was the end of the dialectic, according to Marx's narrative. Republics that aimed to mix capitalism and socialism would doom socialism, or at least retard much its eventuation. Like oil and water, the two were immiscible.

As Commissar of Nationalities, Stalin's view of toleration of cultural differences among republics shifted over time. Stalin was at first happy to allow for cultural variations so long as those variations were not used as goads to break from the socialist experiment or did not pose a threat to the contagion of socialism. That view, however, changed.

The break between Lenin and Stalin late in Lenin's years of moribundity was perhaps in large part because of Stalin's hardheaded insistence that any union of Soviet republics would essentially be yoked by Moscow. Stalin and Sergo

---

[30] J.V. Stalin, "Ukraine Is Liberating Itself," in *Marxists Internet Archive,* https://www.marxists.org/reference/archive/stalin/works/1918/12/01.htm, accessed 14 Dec. 2022.

[31] Simon Sebag Montefiore, *Young Stalin* (New York: Vintage, 2008), 43.

Odzhonidkidze, who headed the Transcaucasian Socialist Federative Soviet Republic (TSFSR), led a commission to propose a new model concerning Moscow's relationship to its republics—"Autonomization of the Republics." According to this model, the independent republics would be incorporated into the Russian Soviet Federation and would retain certain rights of autonomy. With inclusion, Moscow would be the central authority of the federation and that gave Moscow final say on critical political issues. Yet that autonomization was to take place *irrespective* of the consent of the "autonomous" republics: i.e., they had no choice concerning their autonomy.[32] The Soviet republics, especially Ukraine and Georgia, were incensed.

Things were especially trying in Stalin's Georgia, which having seceded from the Russian block of nations, had again been taken over by Soviet Russia in March 1922 by Stalin and Odzhonidkidze. Georgia would become with Armenia and Azerbaijan part of the TSFSR. Yet Polykarp Mdivani, a member of the Georgian Central Executive Committee, wanted Georgia to be included as a separate republic, not as a member of the TSFSR. Mdivani would not get his wish and he vehemently complained to Moscow, but to no avail. Things would come to a head when Odzhonidkidze physically abused a member of the Georgian committee, and that and other abuses were brought to Lenin's attention. Stalin accused the Georgians of being "national deviationists"; the Georgians accused Stalin of "Great Russian chauvinism."[33]

Lenin was at first perplexed, and then, furious. Unwilling autonomization was an act of imperialism, or so he stated. It is not that Lenin was so dead-set against imperialist proposals, but instead that he worried that such imperialism would diminish the prospect of the rise of the working masses in the Western capitalistic countries—in France, England, Germany, and elsewhere—by extinguishing the proletariat flame. As we have seen, Lenin was fixated on the global victory of Marxism, in accordance with Marx—neither thought that socialism could work unless on a global scale—while Stalin thought, at least hoped, that socialism could work parochially and spread gradually over time by virtue of the matchless successes in agriculture and industry in the USSR. Lenin wished to accommodate, at least for the nonce, cultural differences; Stalin, to overwhelm cultural differences by forcing republics to Russify for the sake of the rapid growth of socialism.

Lenin believed that forcing Russification would backfire and lead to failure of the revolution. He expressed that opinion in a letter he dictated titled, "The

---

[32] Serhii Plokhy, "Lenin vs. Stalin: Their Showdown over the Birth of the USSR," in *History*, https://www.history.com/news/lenin-stalin-differences-soviet-union, accessed 16 Dec. 2022.
[33] Stephen Kotkin, *Stalin: Paradoxes of Power, 1878–1928* (New York: Penguin Books, 2014), 479, and Serhii Plokhy, "Lenin vs. Stalin."

Question of Nationalities or 'Autonomization.'" Lenin attacked Stalin's Russian chauvinism, not the chauvinism, or "national deviations," of other republics. In worrying about the problem of regional nationalities for socialism, Stalin was overlooking Russian nationalism as a problem for the autonomous republics—the dictatorship of Russia and the Russification of all regional nationalities. Stalin wanted a tight union of republics; Lenin envisaged, at least at first, a "loose union of republics" in which Russian authority would be on display only for foreign policy or in times of war.[34]

Despite mouth honor to the independence of republics by Russians, on April 16, 1922, Soviet Russian Commissar Georgy Chicherin signed a treaty with Berlin that opened the way for illicit postwar relations between Germany and Soviet Russia—illicit because of the secretive military collaboration between the two nations. Chicherin attempted to sign on behalf of other republics, Ukraine and Belarus among them, and that led to tensions between Russia and its "independent" republics. Tensions led to lengthy negotiations, which led to the formation of the Union of Soviet Socialist Republics (USSR) in December 1922.[35]

On November 18, 1922, just prior to the Bolshevik conference at the Bolshoi Theatre in December, Stalin offers a sketch concerning what it will mean for any republic to become part of the about-to-be-formed USSR. He contrasts the "Far Eastern Republic" (FER)[36] of the Russian Socialist Federative Socialist Republic with the "national republics."[37] The FER is an artificial Russian construction of the "bourgeois-democratic form" to serve as a buffer against "the imperialist designs of Japan and other powers" to the East. Were that republic to be abolished, there would be no ensuing panic, and no "national interests" of that population would be harmed, for they are predominantly Russians vis-à-vis language and culture. It is otherwise with the "national republics," which are culturally distinct from Russia and could not be Russified without "reactionary fanaticism."

> This explains the fact that as soon as the Far Eastern Republic became convinced that the bourgeois-democratic form was useless as a guarantee

---

[34] V.I. Lenin, *Lenin: Collected Works*, Vol. 45 (Moscow: Progress Publishers, 1970), 756n765.
[35] Gordon H. Mueller, "Rapallo Reexamined: A New Look at Germany's Secret Military Collaboration with Russia in 1922," in *Military Affairs*, Vol. 40, No., 3, 1976: 109–117.
[36] The Far Eastern Republic was a so-called independent state, a collection of principalities, in the easternmost part of the RSFSR from April 1920 to November 1922.
[37] Over a month prior (6 Oct. 1922), Stalin headed a commission to draft the Bill for unification of the RSFSR, the Ukrainian SSR, the Transcaucasian Federation and the Byelorussian SSR into a Union of Soviet Socialist Republics. This bill was to be the focus of the first congress of the USSR.

against the imperialists, it was able to abolish itself and become a constituent part of Russia, a region, like the Urals or Siberia, without a Council of People's Commissars or Central Executive Committee, whereas the national republics, which are built on an entirely different basis, cannot be abolished, cannot be deprived of their Central Executive Committees and Councils of People's Commissars, of their national bases, as long as the nationalities which gave rise to them exist, as long as the national languages, culture, manner of life, habits and customs exist. That is why the union of the national Soviet republics into a single union state cannot end in their reunion, their merging, with Russia.

And so, the natural republics—TSFSR (Georgia, Azerbaijan, and Armenia), Ukraine, Byelorussia, Bukhara, and Khorazm—will remain outside the union "until their natural development converts them into Socialist Republics."[38] The argument is that full assimilation cannot occur until the expiration of the cultural barriers and they become Russified. There is again no intimation that full assimilation through Russification implies the superiority of Russian culture. The suggestion is that Russification must at some time occur to facilitate the spread of socialism, which requires the annihilation of cultural obstacles that are a threat to socialism.

Stalin expatiates on "the supreme organs of the Union of Soviet Socialist Republics." There are the Union Central Executive Committee and the Union Council of People's Commissars. We can sum how their formation and functions thus:

Union Central Executive Committee (UCEC)

- Is "elected by the constituent republics of the Union,"
- Has "representation in proportion to population," and
- Functions to "draw up the fundamental guiding principles of the political and economic life of the republics and federations constituting the Union."

Union Council of People's Commissars (UCPC)

- Is elected by the UCEC;

---

[38] J.V. Stalin, "Question of the Union of the Independent National Republics" (18 Nov. 1922), in *Marxists Internet Archive*, https://www.marxists.org/reference/archive/stalin/works/1922/11/18.htm, accessed 15 Dec. 2022.

- Is the "executive organ" of the UCEC,
- Has "direct and undivided control of the military affairs, foreign affairs, foreign trade, railways, and posts and telegraphs of the Union,"
- Directs "the activities of the Commissariats of Finance, Food, National Economy, Labour, and State Inspection of the republics and federations constituting the Union," and
- Directs "the Commissariats of Internal Affairs, Agriculture, Education, Justice, Social Maintenance, and Public Health of these republics and federations are to remain under the undivided and direct control of these republics and federation."

While Lenin, in convalescence, approved of the scheme for a constitution for the new USSR, Ukraine and other national republics demurred. Too many powers were given to the UCPC, and once the USSR was birthed, it also assumed control by Moscow of policing the individual republics.

UPSHOT

When the Bolsheviks took control of Russia, they incorporated other republics into the RSFSR and later into the USSR. The difficulty was Russia's role in the leadership of its republics. It was to be merely one of the many republics in the USSR, yet it was the largest nation, and the central authority of the USSR was located in Moscow. How would Moscow, the heart of the USSR, rule?

There were two nodi: entrance into and egress from the USSR and cultural differences in the various republics. Stalin early on insisted that a republic's entrance into the union was willful, and thus, it also had a right to secede and that Moscow had no right to demand that any republic become Russified. Those were promises that he could not keep and that he never meant to keep. Socialism in the USSR, for political efficiency, demanded some significant measure of cultural uniformity (e.g., common language, common economic policies, and common atheism), and nationalist "deviations" could not be tolerated without substantial risk to Stalin's socialist experiment.

Chapter 4

Collectivizing Ukrainian Farms

"Green corn waves new shoots
Though planted not long ago.
Our brigadier sports new boots
While we barefoot go.

"Oh, oh, oh, @#$%&!
Why should we lie
When we have no shoes."

~Song sung by barefoot women on a Ukrainian collective farm

Singing is something that peasants customarily do to help them get through the drudgery and arduousness of a day in the fields. It was not uncommon for peasant-farmers on a collective farm—the example above shows—to make up new lyrics for old songs or construct new songs in keeping with the nearly insufferable conditions of a workday. The song above is an excerpt from a short testimony in S.O. Pidhainy's collection of testimonies of famine-year (or nearly so) Ukrainians, *The Black Deeds of the Kremlin*—a work I have put to large use in this book. The testimony, by a certain P.V., is merely a description of the scene in a picture (Figure 4-1) on a collective farm in Ukraine. P.V. writes:

> Note the rope harness, the bent and hungry horses, a stick for a whip in the hands of the first woman, and the cows in the last plow which have to drag the plow and fulfill a milk quota as well. Women do the plowing because their husbands are "building socialism." All of them are barefoot and look wretched in their rags and tatters. The man standing apart is the overseer. He appears well off. Does he not remind you of the manager of an estate in the days of slavery?[1]

Of Pidhainy's collection of numerous "testimonies" of Stalin's sadism in the years prior to and of the Great Famine of Ukraine, this one is quite telling. It is as if P.V. is saying: "There is nothing I can write to convince you of the enormity of the push toward collective farms. One has to experience it. Barring that, a

---

[1] P.V., "Collective Farming," in *The Black Deeds of the Kremlin: A White Book*, ed. S.O. Pidhainy, Vol. 1 (Detroit: The Basilian Press, 1955), 213.

picture speaks more loudly and persuasively than words." The reference to the days of slavery is a reference to the feudalistic conditions prior to the Russian Revolution.

Fig. 4-1. Woman Goading Emaciated Horses on a Collective-Farm, Author Unknown

Source: *The Black Deeds of the Kremlin: A White Book*, ed. S.O. Pidhainy, Vol. 1 (Detroit: The Basilian Press, 1955), 213.

We have seen in the prior chapter that Vladimir Ilyich Lenin, after the Russian Civil War, assumed control of the Bolsheviks, who then gained control of the whole of Russia and several nearby republics. World War I and the Russian Revolution that began during it had brought havoc on the Soviet economy—inflation was uncontrollable—and Lenin introduced in March 1921 his New Economic Policy (NEP) as a temporary reprieve from the strictures of socialism, imposed hurriedly by the implementation of War Communism. The NEP returned domestic commerce and agriculture to private ownership while it left foreign trade, banking, and heavy industry in the hands of the Bolsheviks.

By the time of Lenin's death in January 1924, the RSFSR had become the USSR, and Joseph Stalin thereafter slyly rose to the head of the Bolsheviks through years of political maneuvering. Not intent on waiting for Western assistance to begin global socialism, Stalin, once firmly the figurehead of the Party, pushed to socialize the USSR—in effect, to leap from feudalism to socialism instead of following the blueprint of Marx, making the transition from feudalism to capitalism and then from capitalism to socialism. Stalin was aiming to do what Marx and others, like Trotsky, insisted could not be done—transition from feudalism to socialism without the intervention of capitalism to set the stage for socialism.

To socialize the Soviet Union of Republics, Stalin aimed at political and economic gigantism: to do what Western capitalistic nations were doing vis-à-vis heavy industry, but to do it larger and better by having strong central control of industry in Moscow. For heavy industry to thrive in Soviet cities, there were heavy demands for food in those cities and also for the export of food, both for money required to fuel industrial growth and to sustain the increasingly thickening bureaucratic system.

There was an immediate problem. Why would peasant-farmers cheaply sell grain to the State for the sake of industrializing it when they could continue doing what they have been doing: selling grain on the market at market prices? Moreover, there was the difficulty of collectivizing the rural farms. Collectivization meant that individual peasant-farmers would cede their lands, and other property, to the State, which would make large, more efficient—bigger for Stalin was always better—collective farms of the numerous scattered individual farms. That entailed a factory-like model of agricultural yield, hence Stalin's frequent reference to industrializing the farms of the USSR. Because of the rich black soil of its steppe, Ukraine was chiefly targeted for collective farms.

In this chapter, I examine Stalin's push to collectivize agriculture. I begin with Stalin's rescinding of Lenin's New Economic Policy (NEP) in favor of Stalin's Five-Year Plan, which aimed at breakneck improvement of Soviet industry and of agriculture, each industrialized. The goal was for laborers in cities to work conjointly with peasant-farmers in the countryside as comrades in the venture of riddance in the world of its opportunistic capitalistic vultures. The Five-Year Plan would be an inordinately ambitious plan aimed at quick socializing of the USSR. The key obstacle would be the collectivization of the countryside.

"Stalin ... drove out the rural bloodsuckers"
The Need to Collectivize

Revolutions are undertaken to escape from and change a political situation deemed overwhelmingly unjust. And so, when an "unjust" political regime has been overthrown, and numerous thousands have risked their life, with many losing it, in the cause of "justice," the leaders of the revolution ought to have political correctives to the perceived injustices of the overthrown government. Lenin proposed Bolshevism—a species of Marxism and a wholesale change of the principles of governing based on a politics of secularization, of riddance of private property, and of centralized government, *inter alia*. Stalin, who artfully schemed to the leadership of the Party upon the death of Lenin, proffered Stalinist Marxism—a commitment to Marxist principles with numerous Stalinist deviations to suit his whims when things were not going pursuant to plan.

Though both made purchase of the Marxian dialectical claim that capitalism would inevitably implode and socialism would then emerge and globally take root, both worked on the Chernyshevskian assumption[2] that revolution, not evolution, was the correct path for Russian advance on the path of Positivist, secular reforms. While Lenin worked on assumption that the provenance of the revolution had to be in a dyed-in-the-wool capitalist country of the West—Germany, the country of Marx, was generally privileged for that role—Stalin, as we have seen, pressed for the socialization of the USSR and he would begin formally in 1928 with introduction of his Five-Year Plan—a series of inordinately ambitious initiatives that marked a formal break with Lenin by overturning the NEP.

On December 27, 1929, Stalin gives a long speech on the USSR's agrarian policy at a conference of Marxist students. He begins by noting how well the movement to collectivize farms in the USSR has been going. "While we have reason to be proud of the *practical* successes achieved in socialist construction, the same cannot be said with regard to our *theoretical* work in the economic field in general, and in that of agriculture in particular." The theory is not keeping pace with practice, and that will, at some point, influence practice.[3]

Why is theory so critical?

"Theory, if it is genuine theory, gives practical workers the power of orientation, clarity of perspective, confidence in their work, faith in the victory of our cause."[4] Workers, in effect, need to know why they must work so hard if they are not working directly to advance their own material status. The argument is persuasive.

Stalin then turned to other "theories," which disfavoured communism or revolutionary efforts to begin it.

First, there is the theory of equilibrium. In a state, it says, there can be a socialist sector and a capitalist sector, and both can work in equilibrium. Thus, while the towns and cities can be industrialized in a socialist manner to maximal production, the country can remain capitalist, with peasant-farmers owning the farms, to maximize production.[5]

---

[2] For more, see William Wagner and Michael Katz, "Introduction: Chernyshevsky, *What Is to Be Done?* and the Russian Intelligentsia," in Nikolai Chernyshevky, *What Is to Be Done?* (Ithaca, NY: Cornell University Press, 1989), 1–36.
[3] J.V. Stalin, "Concerning Questions of Agrarian Policy in the USSR," in *Marxists Internet Archive*, https://www.marxists.org/reference/archive/stalin/works/1929/12/27.htm, accessed 14 Dec. 2022.
[4] J.V. Stalin, "Concerning Questions of Agrarian Policy in the USSR."
[5] J.V. Stalin, "Concerning Questions of Agrarian Policy in the USSR."

Stalin argues, "This theory overlooks the fact that behind these so-called *compartments* there are classes, and that the movement of these compartments takes place by way of a fierce class struggle, a life-and-death struggle, a struggle on the principle of 'who will beat whom?'"[6] Peasant-farmers' farms, thus, must be collectivized.

The argument, of course, is paralogistic because it begs the question. It merely follows unquestioningly the axioms of Marxist economic theory, which demands the existence of classes, and a struggle to the death between them, with eventual victory going to the masses.

Second, there is the theory of spontaneity. Capitalism has spontaneously formed in towns and has spread to the countryside. Will not the same thing happen with socialism over time? If so, why force the collectivization of farms?[7]

The reason for capitalism's growth from an "individual small-commodity economy" prior to it, says Stalin, is because both are "economies of the same type." One cannot say the say the same of capitalism and socialism, "without breaking with Marxism." Thus, "theory of spontaneity in socialist construction is a rotten, anti-Leninist theory."[8]

Here again, Stalin's objection is ineffectual because it is theory-laden, Marxistly so. According to Marx, capitalism will implode in time, and in the vacuum, socialism will take its place. Yet again, why is Marxism gospel? Nonetheless, on the assumption that Marxism is gospel, there is the remonstrance for Stalin that it cannot hurt to expedite what is better, and inevitable, through decrees to socialize the countryside and quicken the utopia of a classless global order. Nonetheless, to expediency, there is the counter-remonstrance that hurrying the inevitable might be like picking a pineapple before it is ripe.

Third, there is the theory of the stability of small-peasant farming: i.e., the advantages of socializing industry will not be had by socializing agriculture, which is economically stable. "The small peasant is enduring and patient," so goes the argument from stability, and "he is ready to bear any privation if only he can hold on to his little plot of land." Consequently, "small-peasant economy displays stability in the struggle against large-scale economy in agriculture."[9]

Against this, says Stalin, there can be no private ownership of land in Russia for a committed Bolshevik. "Our peasant-farmers do not display that slavish attachment to a plot of land which is seen in the West." Therefore, "this

---

[6] J.V. Stalin, "Concerning Questions of Agrarian Policy in the USSR."
[7] J.V. Stalin, "Concerning Questions of Agrarian Policy in the USSR."
[8] J.V. Stalin, "Concerning Questions of Agrarian Policy in the USSR."
[9] J.V. Stalin, "Concerning Questions of Agrarian Policy in the USSR."

circumstance cannot but facilitate the change from small-peasant farming to collective farming." Moreover, with State ownership of all land, there can be nothing like "absolute ground rent," which is so abhorrent to those renting plots of land.[10]

The argument for stability is also paralogistic. To say that it cannot work because Soviet peasant-farmers do not care about owning land is, as we shall see, ungrounded, tendentiously so. The peasant-farmers care greatly about both owning land and deciding for themselves how best to use that land: when to till, what to grow, when to reap, and how to sell.

Yet the question for Stalinist Marxism is efficiency: whether large State-owned farms will yield greater produce than the aggregate of small peasant-owned farms and do so efficiently, thereby at least offering peasant-farmers the reward of more leisure. Stalin offers an illustration of the collective farms of the Khopyor Region of Saratovskaya Oblast in Russia. They lack technical equipment, but through transition, they have increased crop area by as much as 50 percent. Such "dizzying" results are explicable because "the peasant-farmers, who were powerless under the conditions of individual labor, have been transformed into a mighty force once they have pooled their implements" to be able to "till neglected land and virgin soil, which is difficult to cultivate by individual labor."[11]

The problems here are several. I offer three. Increasing crop area by 50 percent, have they improved yield? Stalin here is silent. Yet, even if there has been a greater yield, is that greater yield sustainable? Moreover, there is the nodus of motivation. As we shall see, greater yield will benefit the State but not the individual farmers of collectives. Why would peasant-farmers clear more land if that yield nowise benefits them? Finally, if the collective farms of the Khopyer Region are doing well, is this illustration of success typical of other collectives of other regions? If not, how aidful is the illustration. An illustration, taken as an argument, always makes for an uncogent argument—an instance of single-shot induction: Puffin 1 is albino, so all puffins are albino.

Regardless of the uncogency of Stalin's arguments for collectivizing farms, there is the refractory fact that Marxism demanded complete collectivization of all lands—for Stalin, all lands within the USSR—and Stalin was a steadfast Marxist in that regard. Still, his arguments here are tendentious.

Stalin's plan was to focus on the maximal development of heavy industry by using the resources of Russia and Eastern Ukraine and implementing a five-year strategy—the goal being "a revolution from above" or a second Russian

---

[10] J.V. Stalin, "Concerning Questions of Agrarian Policy in the USSR."
[11] J.V. Stalin, "Concerning Questions of Agrarian Policy in the USSR."

Collectivizing Ukrainian Farms

revolution. The Five-Year Plan (1928–1932), thus, aimed to collectivize agriculture and push the development of heavy industry. In a speech in January 1928, Stalin said:

> Collective and state farms are ... large-scale farms capable of employing tractors and machines. They produce larger marketable surpluses than the landlord or kulak [wealthy-peasant] farms. It should be borne in mind that our towns and our industry are growing and will continue to grow from year to year. That is necessary for the industrialization of the country. Consequently, the demand for grain will increase from year to year, and this means that the grain procurement plans will also increase.

While the State needs an abundance of grain to feed the laborers in the developing cities, the State cannot depend on the acquisitive and capricious independent farmers, wedded to their own interests—on the kulaks (Ukr., kurkuls). There is a need for speedy development of state or collective farms.[12]

The initiative is, in effect, to urbanize the backward ruralness of individual peasants' farms through State-control. The need is twofold. First, the individual farms, Stalin thinks, cannot feed the whole country, given the rapid growth of industry in the cities, and provide needed reserves of food for export and emergencies. Second, the victory of the proletariat can never be complete if the countryside remains privatized. Following Lenin, Stalin adds that as long as the individual peasant economy is capitalist, there is the danger of "restoration of capitalism." Yet collectivization must proceed gradually, and so collectivization must at first be partial.[13] The Five-Year Plan, however, did not allow for gradualism.

Stalin saw the rapid growth of heavy industry in capitalist countries and worried that Russia and its republics, traditionally backwoods states, would be economically left behind. The tricks would be both to entice the rural peasant-farmers, especially those in Ukraine, to increase production of grain through collectivizing farms and to have the State buy the grain at a pittance of its market price and thereby offer peasant-farmers a fraction of the return they customarily received. With grain hand, the State would send grain to cities for workers and export much of the rest at market prices—there would ever be some kept in reserve—so that the State would earn the profits that peasant-

---

[12] Joseph Stalin, "Grain Procurement and the Prospects for the Development of Agriculture" (28 Jan. 1928), in *Marxists Internet Archive*, https://www.marxists.org/reference/archive/stalin/works/1928/01/x01.htm, accessed 25 Nov. 2022.

[13] Joseph Stalin, "Grain Procurement and the Prospects for the Development of Agriculture."

farmers used to get. The State would then use its heavy profits to further the aims of industrialization. In no time, the efficiency of socialism would prove its superiority to Western capitalist nations through its production.

Stalin also used the threat of another large-scale war as a motivator for laborers in factories and in fields. That was no feigned threat. Western countries knew of the USSR's commitment to Marxism, with its insistence on a global revolution and the global annihilation of capitalism, and they were concerned about Marxist mongers in their countries. And so, the USSR had to have a strong military, which demanded prodigious industrial output of both machines and weaponry for its army. If Soviet industry should lag sufficiently behind that of Western nations, the Soviet Union would be easy prey in the event of a Western assault. Heavy industry was the key.

Heavy industry—comprising the use of coal, oil, iron, steel, chemicals, transportation, lumber, machines, tools, and electricity, as well as the construction of factories—was given demands by Stalin through his Five-Year Plan for production that were absurd and unachievable. Electric companies were ordered to improve by 335 percent, iron and steel workers were enjoined to improve by 200 percent, and coal miners were told to improve by 111 percent. The overall goal was a doubling of the national income in five years and a 350 percent expansion of heavy industry.[14]

Mechanization was the key, but the USSR lacked engineers with apposite expertise. Western capitalist engineers were, thus, brought into the Soviet Union to assist the plan. Resources-rich areas of Eastern Ukraine quickly boomed into large cities with a focus on industrial output. Yet the unrealistic overall demands on heavy industry were not met, though there was a 50 percent increase in industrial output by 1932.[15] Machines at plants were worked, and overworked, to debilitation. Many laborers, overworked and overwhelmed by unrealistic demands, quit work. Many were arrested and among those adjudged guilty of "sabotage," many were exiled to gulags. The most intransigent were simply shot.

Those industrial demands placed gargantuan demands on peasant-farmers—in particular, those in Ukraine. Those demands were amplified by a shortage of farmers, as many peasant-farmers, largely dissatisfied by the demands of collectivization, left their fields for the less capricious work in the factories.

---

[14] Robert Conquest, *The Harvest of Sorrow: Soviet Collectivization and the Terror-Famine* (Oxford: Oxford University Press, 1986), 168–70.
[15] Robert Conquest, *The Harvest of Sorrow*, 170.

Fig. 4-2. Vladimir Krikhatsky, *The First Tractor*

Source: Wikipedia

The nodus for Stalin was to convince the independent farmers that collectivization was to their benefit. That would not be so difficult for the poorest farmers, for they owned little and had little to lose—especially if incentivized with governmental "gifts" of seeds, tools, and tractors to be used on collectives. Yet would the middle-income and wealthiest farmers be incentivized by the same inducements when they would be asked eventually to give up their lands, equipment, buildings, and animals?

Nodi began in 1927 with an apparent crisis of grain, which was, in effect, "a temporary disequilibrium in the grain market"—"a deficit, of more than 100,000,000 poods"[16] that were not collected by the State. Yet the harvest was said to be "a record one." Stalin adds in his speech of January 1928: "Look at the kulak farms: their barns and sheds are crammed with grain; grain is lying in the open under pent roofs for lack of storage space; the kulaks have 50,000–60,000 poods of surplus grain per farm, not counting seed, food and fodder stocks." The kulaks, the wealthy peasant-farmers, "are waiting for prices to rise, and prefer to engage in unbridled speculation" than to help the State. Moreover, they demand that the government pay them three times the price that the government has set for their grain. The poor and middle peasant-farmers have given their grain at state-fixed prices. Why are the kulaks not doing the same?[17]

---

[16] 1 pood ≈ 16 kilograms (36 pounds). Soviet assessment of yield was always projected yield, and projected yield was calculated strangely. A statistician would count the total number of hectares (1 hectare = 2.471 acres) in theory and apply the maximal yield per hectare.

[17] Joseph Stalin, "Grain Procurement and the Prospects for the Development of Agriculture" (28 Jan. 1928).

The problem was that the State had fixed prices on grain from the peasant-farmers at prices that were greatly lower than free-market prices. Thus, the disequilibrium was actually caused by state-fixed prices set too low for grain, which led to stockpiling by peasant-farmers in preference to selling to the State, and by high market prices for industrial goods, which farmers could not afford, given the State-fixed prices for their grain. Stalin blamed the wealthy peasant-farmers, whom he pejoratively dubbed "kulaks." "The kulaks organized sabotage of grain-collection in 1927–1928. Holding a great reserve of grain, they refused to sell it to the state at the price laid down by the Soviet government."[18] The crisis, however, admitted a relatively simple solution—set a higher price for grain to incentivize the peasant-farmers to purchase industrial goods to make husbandry more efficient. Stalin refused to take that route, for surplus money needed to be in the hands of the State. The goal was to maximize profits for the State so that the cities could continue to industrialize rapidly, not to make wealthy the individual farmers.

Urbanites, in the main, were not discontented with the socialist experiment, as industry in the cities had grown, by 1927, to its size pre-war. Still, ruralites, in the main, were much disinclined to collectivize, for that meant losing all that they had over the years worked to obtain, even if they were promised the use of mechanical tractors and other state-of-the-art tools or machines to make labor less grueling—a promise that could not be kept. What they were asked to give up voluntarily were "theirs," acquired by years of moil and sweat. How dear such things are to people is exemplified by a conversation between former Bolshevik Komsomol, Victor Kravchenko, and an old coachman who drove a *tachanka* (horse-drawn cart) and showed the former around a state farm. "When I had my own farm and plenty to eat, people called me Kuzma Ivanovich. Now that I am a coachman, they call me just Kuzma." His "old woman" starved to death, his daughter works in the mine, and his two sons have been exiled to Siberia. He is safe because he is old, harmless, and agreeable. "My only joy in life is these horses. I take good care of them. True, they belong to the government, but I pretend they belong to me. They are the only family I have."[19]

Ruralites were disinclined to sell their grain at the low State-fixed prices. They chose instead to stockpile it or sell it on what would become the black market. Stalin would soon decree that selling grain on the market was illegal and punishable.

---

[18] Joseph Stalin, "Grain Procurement and the Prospects for the Development of Agriculture."
[19] Victor Kravchenko, *I Chose Freedom* (New York: Charles Scribner's Sons, 1946), 115.

There was also the economic concern of inflation. If peasant-farmers did not produce at least enough to meet the needs of the growing cities, foodstuffs would be scarce, and the price for foodstuffs in the cities would inflate much. That would mean unrest of the laborers and the likelihood of strikes or uprisings.

The nodi were many and thorny. How was Stalin to deal with the nodi of rural peasant-farmers?

Stalin was bumfuzzled. Solutions required some expertise in economics, and Stalin was no economist. He turned to those men in the Party from Gosplan (State Planning Commission), the Commissariat of Inspection, and the Central Statistical Office with some apprehension of numbers and assailed them with numerous questionnaires and forms to be addressed. Yet the questions were often impenetrably opaque and poorly articulated. Said one statistician: "We cannot understand half the questions. We just put down the first thing that comes into our heads." The result was "widely conflicting figures on identical problems," based on poorly procured and ambiguous data.[20] The difficulty was compounded by fear of what might happen if an "economic expert" gave Stalin, growing ever petulant and intolerant, the sort of answer he did not want. Since his rise as head of the Party, Stalin was increasingly using coercive tactics to deal with threats to his leadership—troublesome persons would often merely disappear—and with questions concerning the soundness of his judgments. And so, there was a tendency for members of the Party to output the sort of answers that Stalin wanted if what he wanted could be ascertained.

Not fully grasping the economics of the scenario, Stalin turned away from numbers and placed blame on his ever-present figmental enemies: the kulaks. Very early in the twentieth century, "kulak" merely designated a certain type of peasant-farmer of a Soviet village: one who owned a relatively prosperous farm and, thus, was a major player in their village through being, *inter alii*, a money-lender and political leader. Hence, wealthy peasant-farmers became known as *kulaki*, Russian for "fists," as they were the peasant-farmers whose tight-fistedness kept intact the village: i.e., they formed the lifeblood of a village.

For Stalin, kulaks were a bourgeoisie *class*. He, at some point, compartmentalized the landed peasant-farmers into wealthy peasant-farmers (*kulaki*), neither wealthy nor poor peasant-farmers (*serednyaki*), and poor peasant-farmers (*bednyaki*).[21] Figure 4-3, taken from Novokhopersky County of the Voronezh Governorate, is from the Soviet magazine *Prozhektor* (31 May 1926). It aims to depict the material differences between the serednyaks (top), bednyaks (middle), and kulaks (bottom).

---

[20] Robert Conquest, *The Harvest of Sorrow*, 88.
[21] In addition, there were *katraki*, landless and seasonal, for-hire farmers.

Fig. 4-3. Serednyaks, Bednyaks, and Kulaks, 1926

Source: Wikipedia

Tripartitioning into classes was theoretically convenient, clean, and of large use for Stalin, though it did not answer to reality. While most peasant-farmers resisted collectivization, Stalin could best explain resistance to collectivization by his posit of "classes" among peasant-farmers and by the wealthiest peasant-farmers' imposition of their capitalist will on the lower classes. Yet Stalin's "kulaks," as we shall soon see, were quickly everywhere to be found, not just among the well-to-do peasant-farmers in the country. Any peasant who resisted, to any extent, the State's ownership of farms was a kulak.[22]

In 1928, there was another crisis for Stalin that demanded immediate attention. Much grain was again harvested by individual farmers, but little of that was sold to the State. The wealthy peasant-farmers were hoarding that grain for what they deemed to be a more equitable return for their labor. Their esurience and swinishness would, thought Stalin, slow the industrial output in cities and invariably lead to strikes and uprisings. There was a need for expeditious collectivization of the peasants' farms. The kulaks were greedy capitalists who would not willingly collectivize, and so they needed to be taught an unforgettable lesson.

UPSHOT

With the crisis of 1928, the State would have to step up measures to collect grain. The kulaks, continues Stalin in his speech of January 1928, are to be "ordered to deliver all their grain surpluses immediately at government prices" and those refusing to do so will be prosecuted[23] and have "their grain surpluses confiscated in favour of the state, [with] 25 per cent of the confiscated grain to be distributed among the poor peasants and economically weaker middle peasants at low government prices or in the form of long-term loans."[24] Stalin was enforcing an economic plan, designed both to reinforce the notion of classes of peasants and to create infighting among those classes, with the aim of eliminating all peasant-farmers, kulaks especially, disinclined to collectivization.

---

[22] For Bolshevik attempts to define cleanly "kulak," see Robert Conquest, *The Harvest of Sorrow*, 75–76.
[23] Under Article 107 of the Soviet Criminal Code.
[24] Joseph Stalin, "Grain Procurement and the Prospects for the Development of Agriculture."

Chapter 5

Compulsatory Collectivization

"Dialectical materialism is the world outlook of the Marxist-Leninist party. It is called dialectical materialism because its approach to the phenomena of nature, its method of studying and apprehending them, is dialectical, while its interpretation of the phenomena of nature, its conception of these phenomena, its theory, is materialistic. Historical materialism is the extension of the principles of dialectical materialism to the study of social life, an application of the principles of dialectical materialism to the phenomena of the life of society, to the study of society and of its history."

~Joseph Stalin

Joseph Stalin was inextricably committed to the socialist principles of Marx, Lenin, and Engels, which would find grounding in his *Dialectical and Historical Materialism* to be adopted fawningly later as the official Bolshevist interpretation of Marx (1938)—a rather pedestrian, unoriginal work, but it offered Stalin's justification for sanguinary means in justification of socialism. One of the tenets of Stalin, partisan indeed, was the historical "observation" of the "slow quantitative changes into rapid and abrupt qualitative changes [as] a law of development," hence, the naturalness and inevitability of "revolutions made by oppressed classes," and hence, the need of a bloody global revolution against capitalism.[1] From those who drew from Hegel's dialecticalism, in which contradictions inhere in the nature of reality (for Hegel, ideological reality; for Marx, material reality), Stalin aimed for a restructured Soviet Union, by aiming for rapid industrial production, urbanization of agriculture through modernism and collectivism, a totalitarian and centralized government deemed ineffably strong by the people, eradication of putative classes through manufactured conflict between them,[2] and an unutterably brawny head of the Party—one who certainly would show up late to meetings and speak only to significant persons.

---

[1] J.V. Stalin, "Dialectical and Historical Materialism," in *Marxists Internet Archive*, https://www.marxists.org/reference/archive/stalin/works/1938/09.htm, accessed 5 Jan. 2023.
[2] Jan Plamper, The Stalin Cult: A Study in the Alchemy of Power (Yale University Press, 2012).

"Elimination of kulaks as a class"

The Shock Brigadiers

By 1928, Bolsheviks, as they had done in 1921 with War Communism, began the aggressive policy of seizure of grain (Rus., *prodrazvyorstka*) to replace the depleted reserves of grain from the revolution and reconstruction thereafter. The Party organized activists into "brigades" comprising party members and, when possible, rural professionals such as teachers and doctors. These first brigades, however, were soft and ineffective, so they were replaced with "shock brigades."[3]

Yet so long as farmers had surpluses of grain to sell on the free market, they were not incentivized to join the Soviet collectives, and so farmers had to be forced to make "contributions" of grain, other grown foods, and even meats.[4] To incite infighting among peasant-farmers, activists, and brigadiers were drawn as much as possible from the less wealthy of the peasant-farmers.

Fig. 5-1. Ivan Vladimiro, *Prodrazvyorstka*, 1922

Source: Wikipedia

---

[3] D.T., "Grain Collection," in *The Black Deeds of the Kremlin: A White Book*, ed. S.O. Pidhainy, Vol. 1 (Detroit: The Basilian Press, 1955), 200–2.
[4] D.T., "Grain Collection," 202.

Contributions of grain were made at collection points and at specified times. They were proportioned—more appositely, disproportioned—to wealth or status. Wealthy peasant-farmers, as a tax for being efficient and productive, paid the most; unwealthy activists, the least. When farmers could not meet the demands of their contribution, they were forced to buy surplus grain at market prices, enormously larger than what the state paid farmers for surplus grain to give to the State. In that, the State used the free market to the detriment of the kulaks. That, of course, depleted any wealth peasant-farmers might have had in reserve, but that was the intendment of the State. The most troublesome wealthy farmers, Stalin's kulaks, would also receive requisitions for additional grain or even meat—this was done to ruin a wealthy farmer—and they would be resigned to sell their property or, if very obstreperous, they would be "dekulakized" and driven from their property,[5] the topic of the next chapter. That was especially practiced in Ukraine, because of the importance of Ukrainian grain. Ukrainian kulaks were called in Ukrainian kurkuls (*kurkuli*); dekulakization, dekurkulization.

Seizure of grain along with discretionary seizure of other items belonging to farmers (animals, tools, etc.) naturally led to peasant-farmers hiding grain or surreptitiously selling it to buyers other than the State when officials of the State were absent. When brigadiers overran a peasant-farmer's property in his search for hidden grain, they confiscated what grain they found, and often also they took other foodstuffs like potatoes, corn, onions, or beets, thereby often leaving peasant-farmers without any food. That additional theft was justified because of the initial deceit practiced by a peasant-farmer—that of hoarding and hiding grain. Peasant-farmers without food were forced to sell household items or clothes merely to survive.[6]

Shock brigades were unrelenting in their searches. Writes a Ukrainian going by the initials D.T: "The collectors broke insolently into [Ukrainian] houses, especially of those people suspected of being potentially dangerous to the authorities [kurkuls], or not loyal enough [semi-kurkuls], and they searched everywhere, in trunks, stoves, chimneys, shelves, in store rooms, sheds, etc. When anything was discovered, they scattered it on the floor and enjoyed the sight of weeping children gathering grains of lentils or beans from the dirt." He speaks of a certain Maria Derevyanko, a midwife, who, as an activist, was especially cruel. When D.T. asked her about her cruelty, she replied: "The Soviet government has no sympathy to waste on its enemies. I, as a Soviet citizen, am

---

[5] D.T., "Grain Collection," 201.
[6] D.T., "Grain Collection," 201.

obeying its orders." Derevyanko would report on anyone with any amount of food as if subsistence were a crime.[7]

Ukrainian Victor Kravchenko, while a young activist in the Party (*viz.*, as a member of the Komsomol), was sent to the collective farm of the Ukrainian village Podgorodnoye with two other activists, one older and one younger. While Kravchenko, sympathetic to the plight of the peasants but also loyal to the Party, used reason and empathy to encourage the collection of quotas, his older "comrade," Arshinov, used verbal and physical abuse to get grain. Said their younger comrade, Seryozha: "I have been at the hut of the peasant who was beaten up. He has a sick wife, five children, and not a crumb of bread in the house. His house reeks of poverty and despair. And that is what we call a kulak!" The family had a sumptuous supper of "a few potatoes in water." While Kravchenko reported Arshinov's cruelty to the Regional Committee in Dniepropetrovsk, the reply was that Arshinov "has his faults, …[but] he gets results!" Kravchenko was beginning to realize that the Party not only condoned such brutality, it robustly sanctioned it.[8]

Stalin would eventually, through his NKVD,[9] make it part of any Soviet's duty to report any seemingly suspicious anti-Party activities to an official of the State. Collectors received added rations for any food they gathered beyond their quotas, while peasant-farmers, without livestock, often resorted to eating their pets, hedgehogs, carrion, dried cobs of corn, and even leaves to survive.[10]

An obvious consequence of the forced "contributions" without remuneration was that farmers naturally lost any incentive to produce, and that led to low yields and fields falling follow. They too often killed their animals and ate or sold the meat; otherwise, such animals would become the property of the State. There was a marked declination in production of grain and even in number of livestock by the end of 1928. Production of grain, per capita, declined from 584 kilograms in 1927 to 484 kilograms in 1928.[11]

P. Hlushanytsya offers a list of 39 dekurkulized peasant-farmers from his Ukrainian village, Novoselytshy of Chernivtsi Oblast of Northern Ukraine, in the years 1928 and 1929. He reports that fellow villager Lukash Syrenko was put into irons, ushered barefoot to a hole in the ice of a river in which he was repeatedly dunked to force him to reveal the hiding spot of his grain. It was 22 degrees (Fahrenheit) below zero at the time. He also writes of a new wave

---

[7] D.T., "Grain Collection," 201.
[8] Victor Kravchenko, *I Chose Freedom* (New York: Charles Scribner's Sons, 1946), 101–7.
[9] See fn. 1 of the preface.
[10] D.T., "Grain Collection," 202.
[11] Merle Fainsod, *Smolensk under Soviet Rule* (Cambridge: Harvard University Press, 1958), 241–44.

of terror implemented years later in 1932, when the Great Famine of Ukraine was priming.[12]

With the reversal of Lenin's New Economic Policy in 1928 with Stalin's Five-Year Plan—just one more instance of Stalin's preference for force instead of subtlety—Stalin also reversed Lenin's Ukrainization policy, which encouraged regional succor to his policies by encouraging the growth of Ukrainian culture—covered more fully in chapter 10. Ukrainization was implemented in 1923–1924 to appease restive Ukrainian peasant-farmers and to acclimate them to Soviet rule and the gradual collectivization of their farms. Stalin was to tolerate no deviation from the socialization of all Soviet republics. Respect for cultural differences within republics was an impediment to collectivizing farms and the collection of grain. Stalin was to do away with the short-term concessions to capitalism, aimed at stabilizing an economy suffering from suffocating inflation, and prod forward with wholesale socialism, without looking back. The individual peasants' farms were to become, as quickly as possible, property of the State.

In 1929, Bolsheviks essayed to implement rural "initiatives" that went beyond the requisition of grain. The aim, overall, was to restrict the activities of the kulaks—to burke them, as it were—and thereby force compliance with Stalinist goals. Working on the presumption that the kulaks were hoarding and hiding grain, which was in large measure true, though by this time the hoarding was for the sake of survival, the government sent plenipotentiaries to villages to head meetings with officials of villages to "encourage" peasant-farmers to accept higher requisition of grain and self-taxation. Peasant-farmers, of course, stentorianly opposed such discretionary measures, but through their defiance, even if subtle, they were labeled kulaks, enemies of the state,[13] and that paved the way for extreme punishments.

By 1930, Stalin's compulsory collectivization of peasants' farms was in full effect. "The solution lies in the transition from individual peasant farming to collective, socially conducted agriculture." Collectivization, thus, must quash "the capitalist elements of the peasantry"—the kulaks.[14] The aim was to turn all non-kulaks and all other Soviets against the kulaks through a flood of published

---

[12] P. Hlushanytsay, "Kremlin's Crimes in the Village of Novoselytsya," in *The Black Deeds of the Kremlin: A White Book*, ed. S.O. Pidhainy, Vol. 1 (Detroit: The Basilian Press, 1955), 203–10.

[13] Robert Conquest, *The Harvest of Sorrow: Soviet Collectivization and the Terror-Famine* (Oxford: Oxford University Press, 1986), 94–95.

[14] H. Senko, "History of the Destruction of the Ukrainian Orthodox Church," in *The Black Deeds of the Kremlin: A White Book*, ed. S.O. Pidhainy, Vol. 1 (Detroit: The Basilian Press, 1955), 501.

propaganda that aimed to show the large successes of collectivization of Ukrainian farms,[15] to implement highly aggressive policies for collecting grain, and to encourage the non-wealthy peasant-farmers, the serednyaks, and bednyaks, to become activists and to turn against the kulaks in the clash of conflicted classes.

Fig. 5-2. Peasant-Farmers Headed for Work

Source: Ukranian World Congress

On January 21, 1930, Stalin's "Concerning the Policy of Eliminating the Kulaks as a Class" was published.[16] Kulaks are no longer to be urged by arguments or slogans at meetings or rallies. That is the policy he expressed in a 1925 speech. "A leader is one who revitalizes the Soviets and creates a peasant active around the Party in the countryside. It is impossible to lead in the old way nowadays because the economic activity of the rural population has increased, and it is necessary that this activity should assume the form of co-operation, that it should flow through the co-operatives and not past them. A leader is one who implants a co-operative communal life in the countryside."[17] And so, kulaks are no longer to be targeted and marginalized—kept on a short lease—as was the

---

[15] E.g., *Izvestia*, 4 Sept. 1929; *Izvestia*, 11 Oct. 1929; *Pravda*, 27 Oct. 1929; *Pravda*, 28 Nov. 1929; *Pravda*, 31 Dec. 1929; and *Pravda*, 13 Jan. 1930.

[16] J.V. Stalin, "Concerning the Policy of Eliminating the Kulaks as a Class," in *Marxists Internet Archive*, https://www.marxists.org/reference/archive/stalin/works/1930/01/21.htm, accessed 19 Dec. 2022.

[17] J.V. Stalin, "Results of the Work of the Fourteenth Conference of the RCP(b)," in *Marxists internet Archive*, https://www.marxists.org/reference/archive/stalin/works/1925/05/09.htm, accessed 19 Dec. 2022.

earlier policy. That policy has proven unavailing. Kulaks have been making collectivization impossible, so they need to be eliminated as a class. Figure 5-2 shows a mass of peasant-farmers marching to work early in the morning. Their sign on the bottom row says, "Liquidate the Class of Kulaks."

The key to the new plan is to go far beyond the removal of all incentives for production aimed at the market, thereby leaving kulaks with nothing but the state as their "market." That merely has led to kulaks selling on the black market. Failure to collectivize is no longer to be tolerated. The kulaks are declared to be the enemies of socialism, the enemies of the Party, the enemies of the State.

For Stalin, it is now a matter of war. As Commissar Yuri Pyatakov says: "We are obliged to adopt extreme rates of collectivization of agriculture" in a desperate manner, like the tactics of the Bolsheviks in the Russian Civil War. Bolshevik factionalism is to be turned into a war against the enemies of Bolshevism— enemies who live in the Soviet countryside. Robert Conquest states: "Party traditionalism now rallied to Stalin partly because of a belief that, however crude his methods, he was fighting the decisive battle of the regime, partly because the very dangers of the new phase seemed to demand party unity." Stalin's aggressive policy of liquidation, in effect, aimed to recreate the atmosphere of the Russian Civil War, where urgency and exigency left no room for measured actions and questioning the decisions of the Soviet State—*viz.*, Stalin. Extreme actions were needed, and justifiable. The existence of the State was at stake, so goes the argument, and with the fall of the State, the singular experiment of Marxist socialism could fail its first and most significant test. Compulsatory collectivism, thus, forced all Bolsheviks to rally foursquare behind Stalin, thereby consolidating his power to fight the enemies of the State. Refusal to rally behind Stalin at this critical juncture would be proof that one, even if a high-ranking member of the Party, was a kulak, not a comrade.[18]

Yet this compulsatory collectivization—the vile tactics employed are the subject of the next two chapters—was certainly a forced crisis of Stalin's manufacture to solidify, in some measure, his role as the Party's leader—that is, to give all Bolsheviks a common enemy, the kulaks, and thereby to divert attention from any deficiencies Stalin might seem to have as leader of the Party: i.e., the tottering economy and his efforts to harefootedly impose socialism on the countryside. Diversion was a tactic he would employ superabundantly during his tenure as an autocrat.

In such a time of desperation and cataclysm, a change of leadership could often destabilize the scenario even more. To stop and rethink, to retreat, or to consider any course other than that of Stalin's would have led, says Alexander Barmine, who fought in the Soviet Army and was a Soviet diplomat before he

---

[18] Robert Conquest, *The Harvest of Sorrow*, 96 and 111.

defected to the United States during Stalin's tenure, to "loss of everything."[19] And so, if Stalin could keep the USSR in a state of crisis—here, a crisis of the making of the kulaks, enemies of the people—it would be less likely that anyone would turn on him. Thus, Stalin created crisis after crisis, or a perpetual crisis. For instance, Stalin's Five-Year Plan, which demanded unachievably speedy gains in industrial and agricultural production, guaranteed numerous crises through mismanagement and faulty production.[20] Impossible demands for output in factories, for instance, led to hasty, panicky production. When outputs were met, the products were often defective due to overworked machines and laborers and the large number of supervisors watching and reporting on workers and watching and reporting on each other. The reason, said Stalin, for such failures, was the existence of insidious saboteurs, not a faulty plan or mismanagement. The Soviets were again at war—Stalin, at least, made things appear that that was the case—and so all true Bolsheviks needed to rally against the kulaks, who were the true enemies of the State and the true threat to socialism.

Yet it must be acknowledged that in times of crisis, even if the crisis was of his own making, Stalin was at his best. Compulsory collectivization enabled him to disregard the economic difficulties of his plan for modernizing and urbanizing the peasants' farms, and the pesky minutiae, and focus on action against counter-revolutionist saboteurs. Stanislav Strumilin, one of Stalin's economists, sums up the dictator's Marxist war whoop: "Our task is not to study economics but to change it. We are bound by no laws. There are no fortresses that the Bolsheviks cannot storm. The question of tempo is subject to decision by human beings."[21] That was the sort of vacuous, apple-polishing verbiage that Stalin typically loved to hear—that he amaranthinely encouraged. Following his cult of personality, he and those closest to him were above the rules of economic rationality and were above the social laws. The crisis demanded action, visceral action, so long as those feelings were driven by unswerving devotion to Stalin. If quotas were not being met, it was no time for panic. The plan was to up the bar, as it were, and demand results—to use greater force when force was failing.

---

[19] Alexander Barmine, *One Who Survived: The Life Story of a Russian under Stalin* (New York: G.P. Putnam's Sons, 1945), 123.
[20] In 1934, for instance, there were over 62,000 railway accidents. Simon Sebag Montfiore, *Stalin: The Court of the Red Tsar* (New York: Afred A. Knopf, 2004), 211.
[21] Robert Conquest, *The Harvest of Sorrow*, 112. Historian R.W. Davies questions whether this quote comes from Strumilin. He has combed Stumilin's works to no avail. See R.W. Davies, *Humanities and Social Sciences Online*, https://lists.h-net.org/cgi.bin/logbrowse.pl?trx=vx&list=hrussia&month=9810&week=e&msg=p85b51SJBQTh15p3TVZARg&user=&pw=, accessed 10 Nov. 2022.

"Let them freeze!"
Unhappy Dilemma

Collectivization entailed that many small peasant-owned farms would be grouped together to make a large, state-owned farm (Rus., *kolkhoz;* Ukr., *kolhosp*), and thus, the numerous scattered individual farms of peasants could be resourcefully arranged into fewer, more efficient kolkhozes. There would then be an assignation of quotas for each kolkhoz. The argument, to iterate, was that the small, peasant-owned farms could not produce sufficient grain to feed the laborers at Stalin's urban factories and produce a surplus for storage and export to bring in money for the urban factories. So, the smaller farms needed to be grouped, made larger, and come under the control and ownership of the State. There was no detailed plan concerning how that would be done, and as things would occur, urbanites with little or no experience would, in general, oversee the kolkhozes.

Why was that the case?

The notion was that if agricultural production was to be modeled after industrial production, then those with experience in the latter needed to oversee those involved in the former. It was, it seems, never largely debated if this one-model-fits-all plan was suited for agricultural yield. It was assumed by all, Stalin especially, that it must work because it was on paper attractive. Moreover, to question its viability would be to deviate from the gospel of Marx.

Collectivization entailed the eradication of the capitalist market-economy in the Soviet Union. The wealthiest and most successful farmers and any others of the peasant-farmers who might not be dyed-in-the-wool Stalinists would be forced to sell their yield at State-fixed prices,[22] and upon resisting, they risked the loss of their crops, animals, and equipment to the State. Obstreperous kulaks, as we shall see in the following chapter, were jailed, exiled, and often executed insofar as a suitable punishment might be an example for others to facilitate obedience to the State—to join the collectives. Exiled peasant-farmers, who were deemed able-bodied, were often sent to labor camps so the industrial revolution might have the benefit of free labor in coal mines or for clearing trees or making roads or canals. Others were merely sent away and put to work or left to die in places in Northern or Eastern Russia that were remote, quiet, cold, and unfriendly to human subsistence.

The so-called middle and lowest classes of peasant-farmers, serednyaks and bednyaks (often, the least productive and sometimes the least ambitious), were

---

[22] Shelia Fitzpatrick, *The Russian Revolution* (Oxford, Oxford University Press, 1994), 136.

incentivized, at least in theory, to accept collectivization because the resources of the wealthier farmers were collectivized and, so they were told, were to be distributed equally among all.[23] Yet those activists who consented to work for the State and against the kulaks, against the antagonists to collectivization, were themselves persons in need, and so they were not above "pocketing" some of the requisitioned goods. Stalin, as we have seen, talked of distributing 25 percent of collected grain to be distributed among the non-kulaks to incentivize them.[24] Yet that was, on the part of Stalin, to incite infighting among the peasant-farmers—a sort of warfare among the so-called classes of peasant-farmers. The plan overall was at least foolhardy and, at worst, insane. Any plan to maximize agricultural yield by heavily penalizing and punishing the most productive and important husbandmen was, to say the least, not well-formed. Yet Stalin persisted. The industrialization of the rural USSR through well-organized collectives would make excellent farmers of the lesser farmers.

The lower and middle peasant-farmers, especially the youths, were also bombarded with propaganda. Consider these pieces, published late in 1929.

On September 4, 1929, the Central Committee of the Communist Party issued a directive birthing "Collectivization and Harvest Day," to be held on October 14 with the aim of "a mass production campaign." Ukrainians were targeted. The directive continues, "The main purpose of this holiday will be the mobilization of the poor-middle masses for the uplifting and social reconstruction of agriculture and a continued attack on the kurkuls." To affect that mobilization there would be (1) socialist contests in villages for "conducting agricultural lectures, increasing the grain fields, collectivization and a check on agreements for socialist contests where they are already taking place" and (2) programs for inducing farm hands (*katraki*) as well as serednyaks and bednyaks

---

[23] That, at least, was Stalin's aim—a theoretical aim. There is ample evidence that bednyaks were not often persuaded by Stalinist incentives. There is a report in 1929 that states: "Many districts of the Kherson region committees of poor farmers are totally inactive in the grain collecting committees. In the Lubni region the kurkuls will not part with their grain and the committees of poor farmers remain absolutely indifferent to the problem." Also, bednyaks in villages in the Nikopol District of Southern Ukraine protested on behalf of forcing kurkuls to sell their grain to the government at State-fixed prices. *Pravda*, 30 Oct. 1929. Another report early in 1930 says that the various KNS (Committees of Poor Farmers) in the districts of Ukraine were doing little to advance collectivization. In the village Kupyansk, the village's mayor, Lisovetsky, hid kurkuls' grain his own house and militated against taxes for peasant-farmers. *Izvestia*, 7 Jan. 1930.

[24] Joseph Stalin, "Grain Procurement and the Prospects for the Development of Agriculture" (28 Jan. 1928), in Marxists Internet Archive, https://www.marxists.org/reference/archive/stalin/works/1928/01/x01.htm, accessed 25 Nov. 2022.

into the collective farms and thereby eliminating class-line distortions; and excursions and exhibitions to acquaint peasant-farmers with "concrete examples of collectivization."[25]

Two exposés in October 1929 mention the importance of activists of the Party in promoting the collectivization of Ukrainian farms. On October 8, a report concerning the Dniepropetrovsk Oblast indicates that it led all oblasts in Ukraine. The reason given is that many of the Party's activists were sent to the oblast to "encourage" collectivization." The Town Soviet sent 50 men. The Regional Council of Trade Unions sent 100 activists. The Professional Associations sent 18 brigades and 18 directors. The District Party Committee sent 230 activists. The Komosol, an organization of the Party's youths, sent numerous units of young activists.[26]

Eight days later, there was another report in Pravda about the "great service to the poor in the fall seeding and overhauling farm machinery." The All-Ukrainian Council of Trade Unions and the District Trade Unions, as well as brigades from Moscow and Leningrad, are the reason. The former has sent 120 brigades of laborers to rural Ukraine. "With their help the poor and middle elements are steadily making their attack on the kurkuls who are putting up a frantic resistance against grain collecting plans and the labor brigades."[27]

Another instance is a brief exposé, which concerns the destruction of 135,000 individual Ukrainian farms, in *Pravda* on October 20, 1929:

> Up to the present, ten regions in Ukraine—Volyn, Chernyhiw, Korosten, Proskuriw, Poltava and others—have preserved the individual farm-stead form of farming. In these regions there are 135,000 separate farmsteads and about 975 communities made up exclusively of these rural farmers.
>
> The Commissariat of Agriculture has decided to take firm measures to liquidate these relics and to bring the question up before the government to put such measures into force through legal channels.

In *Pravda* on October 27, 1929, the Soviets reported remarkable advances in collectivizing the farms in the Tilohulo-Bereziv District of Ukraine. The report begins: "The success achieved in the last few days has exceeded all expectations. Within several days, 25 per cent of the farms ... have been collectivized. Twenty villages have been collectivized 80 percent. The pull to

---

[25] Ivan Dybynets, "Collectivization Day," in *The Black Deeds of the Kremlin: A White Book*, ed. S.O. Pidhainy, Vol. 2 (Detroit: The Basilian Press, 1955), 274.
[26] *Pravda*, 8 Oct. 1929.
[27] *Pravda*, 16 Oct. 1929.

collective farms is so great that technicalities cannot be put through quickly enough. One hundred percent collectivization will be completed by the twelfth anniversary of the October Revolution." The sweep of enthusiasm is so great that "hundreds of applications are pouring in" from peasant-farmers, kurkuls among them, who are willingly "giving all their property, livestock and machinery to the collective farms." Nonetheless, the kurkuls, though eager to join the collectives, remain a potential problem. Consequently, "there is a firm resolution not to admit the kurkuls even with such generous offers. At the same time, a decision has been reached to conduct a general purge of the old collective farms to drive out the kurkuls."[28]

When one reads the exposés of September 4 and October 20, it is impossible to believe the ebullient and sanguine report of October 27 is anything but a concoction of the Party. Yet the publications were cheerleading for Stalinist initiatives. The aim was to create competition between oblasts, between districts within them, and between villages within the districts. *Izvestia* reports on August 5, 1929, "Contests must be held for the fastest completion of the grain collecting plans among districts, villages, cooperatives, and collective farms, thus encouraging more energetic action."[29] On March 18, 1930, *Izvestia* tells of a certain "collectivization fever" in Vynnytsya Oblast. "On March 10th, it had collectivized 110,688 poor and middle farmers—70 per cent—and socialized 850,000 acres of cultivated land—75 per cent." Kalynivka District leads the way with 85.3 percent, while Voroniv has only 47.3 percent. Of all livestock, 70.5 percent has been collectivized, and again Kalynivka leads the way with 92.2 percent, while Tyvriv has collectivized only 39 percent of its animals. The number of horse-machine stations—tractors were not widely available—was 182, though there were only 107 on March 1. Zhmerynka leads with 31; Kalynivka, with 23; and Turbiv, with 20. There are 34,248 socialized horses in Vynnytsya.[30]

The reality, of course, was other than the propaganda, crafted to incite complicity with Bolshevik decrees.

A certain E.M. writes of her perspective of Stalinist collectivization in the town Kobelyaky in the Poltava District of Ukraine. She writes of a parade of wagons to the town on one day at the end of November 1932. Moscow had sent 25,000 activists of the Party to promote the collectivization of Ukrainian farms.

---

[28] Ivan Dybynets, "100 Percent Collectivization," in *The Black Deeds of the Kremlin: A White Book,* ed. S.O. Pidhainy, Vol. 2 (Detroit: The Basilian Press, 1955), 276–77.
[29] Ivan Dybynets, "Origin of the Grain-Collecting 'Actives' Resolution of the Central Committee of the Communist Party of July 29, 1929," in *The Black Deeds of the Kremlin: A White Book,* ed. S.O. Pidhainy, Vol. 2 (Detroit: The Basilian Press, 1955), 144.
[30] Ivan Dybynets, "Collectivization Fever," in *The Black Deeds of the Kremlin: A White Book,* ed. S.O. Pidhainy, Vol. 2 (Detroit: The Basilian Press, 1955), 280–81.

Brigades were formed from "the poorest and most bolshevized elements" to enter the villages and persuade the peasant-farmers to eschew "the bourgeois capitalist system, built on exploitation," and to grasp that "farming in a small way was wasteful, and in a big way it exploited the poorer farmers"—that "only the nationalized, collective way of farming would bring happiness to all."[31]

The farmers of her Ukrainian village, Velyki Solontsi, were lectured on the merits of collectivized farming. The land and house of Andriy Sepity were confiscated for the good of the collective, and the landless and activists flocked to the house. Sepity was sent to Siberia, and his family disappeared. The activists formed, as had often been done, a "committee" to run the collective and to make a list of kurkuls—the enemies of the Party—and there were 52 listed. The kurkuls were collected at night and driven from the village. Their families, too, were separately taken away—"thrown out like garbage" on a sandy portion of land by River Vorskla, which from the north meets the River Dnieper. Said the communist secretary: "Those who would comfort and help the enemies of the Soviet government shall themselves be regarded as enemies. Let them freeze!"[32]

The aim was achieved. The village sums E.M., was "willfully" collectivized. Those remaining merely decided that it was preferable to "lose everything and do forced labor" than to "go to Siberia." In such a manner, she sums sardonically, happiness was brought to all.[33]

UPSHOT

As we have seen in this chapter, the initiative to collectivize all Soviet farms was undertaken in 1928, and with that push, there was the plan through large-scale propaganda thereafter to create a sort of competition between oblasts, between districts within them, and between villages within districts. Wealthy peasants, in keeping with Marxist classes, were identified and isolated, and the aim was to restrict their activities. Restriction turned into aggressive measures of collecting grain in 1930—acquisition of grain, as we shall see, would be a much greater priority than the wellbeing of the peasant-farmers—and the plan to liquidate the class of kulaks was formally put into place by Stalin.

Peasant-farmers, kulaks/kurkuls especially, unwillingly faced an unhappy dilemma. On the one hand, wholesale acceptance of collectivization meant that they would lose all for which they had ever worked but that their lives

---

[31] E.M., "Collectivization," in *The Black Deeds of the Kremlin: A White Book*, ed. S.O. Pidhainy, Vol. 1 (Detroit: The Basilian Press, 1955), 197.
[32] E.M., "Collectivization," 197–99.
[33] E.M., "Collectivization," 199.

would not be, at least, directly threatened, and they could remain in their native village. The "prize" offered such farmers was Stalin's promise of being proud contributors to a heretofore unexampled system of agrarian production, to be seen as proof of the overwhelming superiority of Stalinist Marxism, where all "comrades" were to enjoy equally the benefits of socialist production, compared to Western industrial capitalism, a system in which the many moiled while the few reaped the benefits. That, at least, was the promise. On the other hand, outright rejection of collectivization could mean dispossession, deportation, imprisonment, or even death, and death was all too common—the topics of the next two chapters. And so, even though the prize of collectivization was to most peasant-farmers a canard or hoax, the alternatives to collectivizing were wholly unattractive.

Chapter 6

The "Need" of Dekulakization

"From early morning till late at night,
We saw and split the spruce and pine,
We saw and split and pile it neatly,
And curse the GPU.

Oh, why were we born?
Oh, why were we born?
"We are doomed and exhausted,
But we believe that the time will come
When retribution finds you."

~Song sung at the Solovky Prison Camp

Ukrainian Stepan Chorny relates his story of how he was "dekurkulaized." In 1930, his hamlet, Lychmariv in Poltava Oblast, was the target of a Muscovite collectivization drive, which was not politely received by the farmers of the hamlet. Thus, a detachment of *Moskvichi* (natives of Moscow), under the direction of Commander Osipov, was sent to Lychmariv to "campaign" for collectivization. His personally trained brigadiers began that campaign of "persuasion." Persuasion entailed the imposition of ponderous taxes, which many could not meet. Yet a farmer who could meet the taxes was additionally taxed, "often greater than the value of his whole property." Chorny belonged to the latter category. When he failed to pay an impossible tax, he was arrested on December 30 and incarcerated. While in jail, Osipov confiscated all that Chorny owned and drove the latter's wife and child from his house. At some point, Chorny was released and allowed to return to his family, who now lived in a small hut with two other families—17 persons in one hut. The head of one of the other families, upon his release from prison and return to his family in the shack, died shortly after seeing the hopeless conditions to which he and his family were reduced. The head of the third family was sent to Siberia. Chorny escaped from Lychmariv to Donbas.[1]

---

[1] Stepan Chorny, "How I Was Dekurkulized," in *The Black Deeds of the Kremlin: A White Book*, ed. S.O. Pidhainy, Vol. 1 (Detroit: The Basilian Press, 1955), 211.

Chorny's fate, given that several thousands of Ukrainians suffered a worse fate, was not sadistically singular. He was neither executed nor exiled, and he was allowed the "privilege" of returning to his family, although the prospect even of subsistence was thereafter poor. His crime, given that he was overtaxed on several occasions, was that he resisted collectivization, and consequently, he was a kurkul—an enemy of the Bolshevist State.

Nonetheless, those peasant-farmers, who had a history that showed any resistance to socialism were typically not treated so leniently. Bookkeeper Mykola Prokopovich Shkuratenko of Ivankiv in Kyiv Oblast had formerly served the Union for Liberation of Ukraine, and, as was the case with so many others who had some involvement in "subversive" activities, merely "disappeared"[2]— that is, he was either taken and exiled or, most likely, shot.

In the prior chapter, we saw that Stalin blamed the insufficient harvest of grain in 1928 on wealthy peasant-farmers, the kulaks, who began thereafter aggressive policies of collecting grain. Working on the assumption that kulaks' "barns and sheds [were] crammed with grain" which they were saving to sell at market prices, Stalin began more aggressive actions, designed to empty kulaks' stockpiles for the sake of benefitting the State, not the selfish kulak capitalists. His aim soon was dekulakization, or removal of kulaks as a class. What dekulakization entailed is the subject of this chapter. Much of the focus is on dekurkulization—that is, on Ukrainians.

"We must smash the kulaks"
A Stalinist Turn of Policy

In the summer of 1929, the Soviet Communist Party demanded that some 10 percent of all Ukrainian farms be dekurkalized. Ukrainian Ivan Dubynets writes that the aims were to expropriate the possessions of kurkuls and use them to ground the collectives, to arrest or exile the most belligerent kurkuls as a lesson to other peasant-farmers, and to use the labor of exiled kurkuls to be slaves in mines, to clear forests, and to make roads, among other things.[3]

It is facile to be overly critical of what the Russian Marxist socialists— Plekhanov, Lenin, and Trotsky—were aiming to do in *fin de siècle* nineteenth-

---

[2] F. Fedorenko, "Disappeared without Trace," in *The Black Deeds of the Kremlin: A White Book*, ed. S.O. Pidhainy, Vol. 1 (Detroit: The Basilian Press, 1955), 212.

[3] Ivan Dubynets, "Dekurkulization and Deportation of the Dekurkulized," in *The Black Deeds of the Kremlin: A White Book*, ed. S.O. Pidhainy, Vol. 2 (Detroit: The Basilian Press, 1955), 151.

century Russia and after the war early in the twentieth century. It is necessary to grasp that Marxism, if we stay at a theoretical level, did offer some promise of a better life for all. One must keep in mind that the sort of socialism Lenin envisaged as a means of achieving the massive material growth of highly industrialized Western nations like America and England while eschewing the great divide between rich capitalistic industrialists—e.g., American individuals like John D. Rockefeller, Andrew Carnegie, and J. Pierpont Morgan, who monopolized on material goods and services—and the enslaved workforce of such individuals, many of whom were working long hours each day and yet living in penury, and many of whom were adolescents.

Industrialization was an extraordinary shift in the way of life for persons in highly industrialized nations like America. By the start of America's Civil War, most Americans were self-employed, yet by 1914, the American economy, industrialized, more than doubled in size and then exceeded all European economies.[4] Yet those who reaped from that arithmetical growth were not the laborers, but the industrialists, for whom there were few political obstacles. And so, Marxists like Lenin aimed to do away with free markets and *laissez-faire* capitalism, which promoted, in their eyes,[5] Darwin's principles of natural selection to economic growth—*viz.*, it allowed for economic growth at the expense of *hoi polloi*, a sort of slavery that was in respects feudalistic. What was the point of extraordinary economic growth if all too few would reap its benefits? Thus, Marxist socialism aimed to equal or exceed the growth of Western industrialized nations while distributing what was reaped to the laborers: farmers and workers in factories. That was Lenin's vision, and as a true disciple of Lenin, that too was Stalin's pledged vision. Consequently, all the roots of capitalism would eventually have to be removed from the Soviet superstructure, and that entailed the removal of the surest enemies of the State—the kulaks.

The motive force behind collectivization was "dekulakization" (Rus., *raskulachivanie;* Ukr., *rozkurkulennia*)—that is, complete riddance of kulaks, of the enterprising or disobliging peasant-farmers, as a class. Writes Lenin of the cancer of kulaks, blood-sucking vampires:

> The most bestial, coarse and savage exploiters, who many times in the history of other nations revived the rule of landlords, tsars, clergy and capitalists. There are more kulaks than capitalists but the kulaks are a minority in the nation. These blood-suckers have become rich from the

---

[4] "The Gilded Age," *U.S. History: Pre-Columbian to the New Millennium,* https://www.ushistory.org/us/36.asp, accessed 11 Dec. 2022.

[5] E.g., Herbert Spencer and William Graham Sumner.

people's poverty during war. They gained thousands and hundreds of thousands by raising prices on grain and other foodstuffs. These spiders luxuriated at the expense of the war-ruined farmers, and the hungry workers. These vampires drank the blood of the working people, growing more prosperous as the workers in the city factories grew hungrier. They grabbed the land of the landlords and grain and again enslaved the poor masses.[6]

It was the same for Stalin in the post-Lenin USSR. In all Soviet villages, kulaks were the oppressors. Whereas the plan before had been to restrict the activities of the kulaks, thereby making them less of a threat to socialism and the collectivization of farms, it was now time to eliminate the class of kulaks. In his 1929 "Speech on Agrarian Policy," Stalin begins by noting the time is ripe for aggressive, offensive measures against "capitalist elements." He adds, "We have passed from the policy of *restricting* the exploiting tendencies of the kulaks to the policy of *eliminating* the kulaks as a class."[7]

Why was there this marked shift in the Party's policy?

Stalin says that there are now "in the countryside strong-points in the form of a wide network of state farms and collective farms." The Party is now in the position "to replace the capitalist production of the kulaks by the socialist production of the collective farms and state farms." It is time to transcend declamations, phrase-mongering, and pinpricks, continues Stalin. "We must smash the kulaks.... We must ... strike so hard to prevent them from rising to their feet again."[8]

One month later, Stalin waxes philosophical. He warns against seeing the prior policy of restricting the kulaks and ousting them—that is, ousting "individual sections of the kulaks"—as essentially different. Restriction leads to ousting. "Ousting the capitalist elements in the countryside" is "restricting the exploiting tendencies of the kulaks," which is "restricting the capitalist elements in the countryside." There is but one "general policy of restricting capitalism, a component part and result of which is the ousting of individual sections of the kulaks."[9] How ousting kulaks can be a component part of restricting kulaks as well as be a result of restricting kulaks Stalin does not explain.

---

[6] From Ivan Dubynets, "The Kurkuls and the Middle Farmers," in *The Black Deeds of the Kremlin: A White Book*, ed. S.O. Pidhainy, Vol. 2 (Detroit: The Basilian Press, 1955), 155.
[7] *Pravda*, 27 Dec. 1929.
[8] *Pravda*, 27 Dec. 1929.
[9] J.V. Stalin, "Concerning the Policy of Eliminating the Kulaks as a Class," *Itrasnaya Zveda*, No. 18, 21 Jan. 1930.

Moreover, Stalin adds that the policy of elimination of the kulaks as a class is not "continuation of the policy of restricting (and ousting) the capitalist elements of the countryside." It is instead a change of the Party's policy. Collectivization cannot occur through restriction and ousting alone. There must be elimination of the kulaks, and "that is well understood by our poor and middle peasant-farmers, who are smashing the kulaks and introducing complete collectivization."[10] The logic throughout is typical of Stalin: pretzel.

One thing is worth noting in these invectives. Stalin mentions riddance of the class of kulaks, not riddance of all kulaks. To rid a class comprising persons is not necessarily to rid all the persons of that class. Stalin's aim was merely to get rid of the seemingly most disruptive members of the kulaks to serve as a dark lesson for the others to give up all capitalistic aims and become good Bolsheviks. The 1930s poster (Figure 6-1) illustrates the stage of ousting: "Remove kulaks [*kulaki* is Russian for 'fists'] from kolkhozes." A large fist is thrust into the fat "usurer's" back to force him from a village, not coming down hard on him and crushing him to death. It is the "fist" of collectivism that forces out the greedy kulak, who is a fist insofar as he holds on tightly and irrevocably to what he gained at the expense of others.

Fig. 6-1. 1930s' Poster, "Get Kulaks off Collectives"

Source: Wikipedia

The paradox, as I have noted, was this: Dekulakization of the peasantry entailed eliminating the most able, deedy, and productive peasant-farmers and then asking the remaining peasant-farmers to produce farmed goods much more than what all peasant-farmers had hitherto produced. Stalin's reply, of

---

[10] Joseph Stalin, "Concerning the Policy of Eliminating of the Kulaks as a Class."

course, was that dekulakization would remove the most obstreperous peasant-farmers and leave behind acquiescent peasant-farmers who would fit, because of their agreeableness, into the modern and large collectivized farms. It was the system, not the workers, which would make the yield: The system would mold the workers, and the results—comprising hefty increases in productivity—would reinforce in the compliant workers the notion that compliance was worth the effort. Stalin's gambit—it would be an enormous gamble because one-state Socialism was hitherto untried—required complete faith in the system. The large increase in production would win over the peasants. Yet that was not an argument suited to persuade wealthier peasant-farmers, for the yield would benefit the State, not individual farmers. To that end, those inured to the market system or those without faith in Stalinist socialism had to be nullified by branding, dispossessing, exiling, or elimination—the topic of the next chapter.

Dekulakization—for Ukrainians, dekurkulization—was enhanced by the eradication of the roots of Ukrainian villagers' culture, which was, for the most part, where Ukrainian culture and the Ukrainian language germinated. Churches and educational facilities in villages were foci.

Disrespectful protests of religious services abounded throughout Ukraine and were chiefly conducted by agents of the Komsomol—enthusiastic Soviet youths eager to do some of the blackest deeds of the Party. Smearing their faces with mud, young activists would dress as religious figures and interrupt religious services by immodest and irreverent singing and dancing in churches, especially on significant days like Easter when churches were overfull. In addition, there were anti-religious lectures "of the lowest type of ridicule and degradation of religious tradition and filthy abuse of the churchgoers." Since churches were expropriated by the State, churchgoers had to pay a rental fee, typically very large, and priests, considered worthless idlers by the godless Marxists, were forced to pay a non-worker's tax. The rationale behind the fees and taxes was to force the closure of the churches, impose atheism on the peasantry, and put the closed churches and related buildings to better use. In the village Stavka of the Kyiv Oblast, the Ukrainian church was closed and demolished, and a community center was built from salvageable materials.[11]

All manifestations of Ukrainian peasants' religiosity were eventually to be removed. And so, churches were closed and misappropriated or razed by fire, icons were removed from churches and peasants' houses, churches' bells were taken down and melted for use in Soviet industry, and priests were arrested and exiled or killed. I return to the attack on Ukrainians' religiosity in chapter 10.

---

[11] F. Pravoberezhny, "The Church and Religious Brutality Destroyed," in *The Black Deeds of the Kremlin: A White Book*, ed. S.O. Pidhainy, Vol. 2 (Detroit: The Basilian Press, 1955), 223–24.

The "Need" of Dekulakization

In conjunction with the expurgation of religiosity, Ukrainian educators too were arrested and deported, for communion of thought was needed for the uptake of Bolshevism, and educators were ever accused of having discordant ideas—of planting seeds of discontent, rebellion, or nationalism in peasant-farmers.

In typical Stalinist fashion, there was nothing subtle about the plan, which was applied in Ukraine and throughout the USSR. Dekulakization was attempted by force. From his youthful days of thuggery in Georgia, Stalin had often noticed that short-term, small aims could be quickly and satisfactorily met by force, and thus, he concluded that such coercive measures would also work in the long-term for large aims. He could not have reasoned otherwise, for he was schooled in the use of force throughout his life, and he was no stranger to sanguinary force. When force did not yield the desired results, Stalin used greater force. In a directive from June 6, 1933, for instance, he threatens secretaries of provincial, urban, and county executive committees, who have been oblivious of rotting stores of thousands of tons of grain, when "these comrades should be directed toward stocking gain and delivering the grain to the state." Repetition of that mistake will "compel the Central Committee to take even more drastic measures"[12]—the implication being that drastic measures were taken the prior year. Yet force is, psychologists have taught us, a poor motivator. It often generates compliance but seldom willful compliance, and it seldom works in the long term on large projects. When it does, it is often through fashioning a sort of learned helplessness in a target population, and a helpless population is not a productive population.

One coercive tack, I have shown, was to create the notion of distinct classes of peasant-farmers, where no clean distinctions existed, and then to set the least wealthy classes against the most wealthy—to set the serednyaks and bednyaks against the kulaks. Serednyaks and bednyaks, the middle and lower peasant-farmers, were repeatedly told that the failures of collectivization toward the end of the Five-Year Plan were due to the unwillingness of kulaks to accept collectivization. Poorer peasant-farmers were seldom persuaded, but they were incentivized by the promise of material gains.

Soviet officials created *komnezani*, committees of poor peasant-farmers, which were given privileges for breaking kulaks and for turning on any villagers who opposed in words or deeds collectivization—especially, anyone storing grain that could be used to feed laborers or for exportation. Activists of the *komnezani* would, in general, enter villages other than their own and look for

---

[12] P. Lykho, "Soviet Documents on the Famine in Ukraine," in *The Black Deeds of the Kremlin: A White Book*, ed. S.O. Pidhainy, Vol. 1 (Detroit: The Basilian Press, 1955), 232.

grain surpluses, and they were expected to find grain, for they had quotas. Leaders of activists who did not meet quotas were themselves often accused of being kulaks. For collection of grain (Rus., *prodrazvyorstka*, literally "apportionment of food"[13]), brigadiers would be rewarded with land, food, or other privileges.[14]

Yet farmers in the early years of Stalin's Five-Year Plan were unwilling to sell grain at State-dictated prices, much inferior to the prices on the market. In Ukraine, there were sent shock brigadiers—sometimes called buksyors—*buksyor* being Russian for "tugboat." A directive, published in *Pravda* on October 18, 1929, reads:[15]

> A special commission conducted an investigation into the work of the Kyiv Trade Unions in the grain collecting plan and it is found to be inadequate. It has been decided that shock brigades of professional union workers and worker's actives will be thrown into the districts. With this end in view, many workers have been mobilized, divided into groups and dispatched to the villages of the Kyiv, Bila Tserkva, Uman, Berdychiv, Shepetivka, and Pryluky regions.
>
> Most of the workers have been supplied by the metallurgical, tanners, lumber jacks and printers unions. They will all remain at their assigned places until the grain collecting plan is completed.

Buksyors were given "authority to manhandle," says Ukrainian S. Lozovy, "every farmer until he gave all his grain to the State." The men of such brigades were equipped with manufactured steel or wooden rods, some 5/8ths of an inch in diameter, up to 10 feet in length. Wooden rods would have a sharp steel point at one end, while metal rods would be sharpened at one end. Some rods had a drill bit at the end. Buksyors would poke into piles of straw, into visibly disturbed earth, and into the walls and ceilings of houses. Rods with drill bits would be used to drill into gardens to find concealed sacks of grain.[16]

---

[13] Another Russian euphemism to suit the disagreeableness of the task. The notion was that food would be taken from those who have too much and distributed to those who have too little.
[14] James Mace, "The *Komitety Nezamozhnykh Selyan* and the Structure of Soviet Rule in the Ukrainian Countryside, 1920–1933," in *Soviet Studies*, Vol. 35, 487–503.
[15] *Pravda*, 18 Oct. 1929.
[16] S. Lozovy, "What Happened in Hadyach County," *In The Black Deeds of the Kremlin: A White Book*, ed. S.O. Pidhainy, Vol. 1 (Detroit: The Basilian Press, 1955), 245–55.

The "Need" of Dekulakization 83

Fig. 6-2. Buksyors Showing their Spoils

Source: UkraineGenocide.com

Figure 6-2 depicts the spoils of a group of buksyors who have uncovered buried grain. One of the men, likely the leader, for he takes the privilege of being seated while all others stand, sits and holds in his hands a relatively short poking rod. Another stands proudly in the hole where grain was discovered. The science of collecting grain, having itself become industrialized, advanced quickly.

Collection of grain and other foodstuffs was seldom easy. Rot, as well as shortages of bags for foodstuffs, of storage facilities, and of transportation of foodstuffs, were ever a problem. Consider this report from a shock brigade that was sent to the Krasyliv District of Northwest Ukraine to collect grain and potatoes:

> The brigade came to the district under the auspices of the Grain Association. The work is difficult from every standpoint. This is our first experience with the potato-collecting plan and we find this unfavorable situation. Potatoes lie in the mud and are loaded into cars without being cleaned. 583 tons of potatoes lie out in the open and spoil as more continue to come. Lack of transportation interferes with the completion of the plan.
>
> The same situation exists with the grain collecting plan. All storage houses, makeshift constructions, are filled to capacity. Grain is piled in wet places. In the Krasyliv District 2,500 tons of grain lie at one unloading point. Railway service is irregular and one car a day leaves the

Krasyliv District. Because of this delivery of winter grains is held up by the farmers. This may result in an uncompleted grain-collecting plan.

The brigade requests that urgent measures be employed.[17]

Here, one clearly sees something typical of Stalin's directives. An order is given, and activists are enjoined to carry out that order, but there are no straightforward instructions concerning how that order is to be carried out. Activists are expected to handle problems as they surface. The result is gross inefficiency.

Given the inefficiency, it is likely that very much of what was collected was waste—unsuited for human consumption. Thus, was the aim more to keep grain and other foodstuffs away from peasant-farmers, to be a lesson to them, than to collect grain and other foodstuffs for urban workers and export?

In the western Ukrainian village Kharkivets of Lviv Oblast in 1930, only four of 780 farmers joined their collective. Then came Demen Karasyuk, an activist from the city of Tambov. He took the house of a certain serednyak named Brychko, who was sent to Siberia, where he died in six months at a prison camp. Karasyuk and his activists held rallies each day in the village square. Those rallies had no effect. So, the activists went to each house to glean signatures for collectivization. Yet, having seen peasant-farmers from collectives nearby enter their village and beg for bread, the farmers of Kharkivets were still unwilling to join. Thus, activists arrested three kurkuls each day.[18]

Soon there came buksyors, with their poking rods, to search for any grain and any food, like potatoes or beets, that might be hidden. An activist named F. Boyko then came to Kharkivets. Urging the peasant-farmers to collectivize through rallies and meetings, he confiscated grain and all the cows and sheep for taxation.[19]

Food became scarce, and so villagers foraged for acorns and other edibles in the forest till that was disallowed because the forest, socialized, was Soviet property, and peasant-farmers were forbidden to steal comestibles from the State. There was violent resistance, and at some point, almost every farmer served time in jail. Many families were exiled to gulags, where most died from hard labor.[20]

By 1932, most of the farmers of Kharkivets were collectivized through coercion. However, food was still scarce, and beggary was commonplace,

---

[17] Ivan Dybynets, "Mismanagement of Produce Seized from Farmers," *In The Black Deeds of the Kremlin: A White Book*, ed. S.O. Pidhainy, Vol. 2 (Detroit: The Basilian Press, 1955), 268.
[18] S. Lozovy, "What Happened in Hadyach County," in *The Black Deeds of the Kremlin: A White Book*, ed. S.O. Pidhainy, Vol. 2 (Detroit: The Basilian Press, 1955), 246–47.
[19] S. Lozovy, "What Happened in Hadyach County," 247–49.
[20] S. Lozovy, "What Happened in Hadyach County," 249.

especially by the elderly and children. By the next year, one-third of the villagers were starving. While some traveled to the Ukrainian cities for food, they found little, so they ventured into Russia, where food was plentiful, till travel into Russia was restricted.

Some villagers, desperate to avoid death by hunger, resorted to cannibalism. Myron and Maria Yemets had decapitated their children and salted their bodies for meat. When they were confronted and arrested, they tearfully replied that by killing and eating their children, they could remain together and at least live to have other children. They were deemed insane and shot months later.[21]

As I note above, food was ever plentiful in Russia when Ukrainians were starving from Stalin's punitive measures—especially from the years 1931 to 1933. Moreover, cannibalism was, in some measure, commonplace in Ukraine, where starvation was greatest. Agents of the Party found cannibalism disgusting, and cannibalists were usually shot. That is astonishing, for Stalin's aggressive policy of *prodrazvyorstka* made foreseeable some amount of people feeding on the flesh of other people to escape death.

"Your village is asked to give 50 kurkuls"
Finding the Elusive Kulaks

To eliminate the kulaks as a class, one first had to identify and find the kulaks. In Stalinist fashion, all peasant-farmers could be presumed to be kulaks unless shown to be otherwise. One way to show that one was not a kulak was to point out other peasants as kulaks to members of the Party. Ratting on others was a duty of all good Bolsheviks.

The poorest peasant-farmers, the so-called bednyaks, often early on willingly joined collectives, for they had little to lose by collectivizing and the promise of much to gain. They were also incentivized materially in the early stages of the collection of grain to become activists and to turn on the kulaks.

Yet poor peasant-farmers, when resistance to collectives was still strong, soon came to realize that kulaks, qua wealthy peasant-farmers, were not necessarily being targeted. Those targeted, instead, were those who owned the goods, e.g., the house, grain, animals, wagons, equipment, and tools, needed for the collective farms of the state. It became apparent that by owning too many goods, or at least goods that rightly belonged to the State, they too could become kulaks.[22] And so, bednyaks faced an unhappy dilemma. Obedience to

---

[21] S. Lozovy, "What Happened in Hadyach County," 250–53.
[22] Robert Conquest, *The Harvest of Sorrow: Soviet Collectivization and the Terror-Famine* (Oxford: Oxford University Press, 1986), 120.

the injunctions of Stalinist activists from the city won the Bolshevik favor and material gains to improve their station in the short term, but that placed them in the position of becoming the new kulaks, who next might be fleeced and persecuted.

So widespread was that worry that it found its way into the fiction of the day. In *Virgin Soil Upturned*, Mikhail Sholokhov writes of a peasant-farmer who worked assiduously to benefit the State but came to realize that through his assiduity and loyalty, he might be construed as an enemy of the State.

> I sowed twelve, then twenty and even thirty hectares....[23] I worked, and my son and his wife. I only hired a laborer a couple of times at the busiest season. What was the Soviet government's order in those years? Sow as much as you can! And now ... I am afraid that because of my thirty hectares they will drag me through the needle's eye, and call me a kulak.[24]

It was soon apparent to all, both peasant-farmers and activists, that "kulak" was a relatively arbitrary category. One female activist relates: "Who thought up this word 'kulak' anyway? Was it really a term? What torture was meted out to them! In order to massacre them, it was necessary to proclaim that kulaks are not human beings."[25] A member of the GPU said: "I am an old Bolshevik. I worked in the underground against the Tsar, and then I fought in the Civil War. Did I do all that in order that I should now surround villages with machine-guns and order my men to fire indiscriminately into crowds of peasant-farmers?"[26] Even some 40,000 Tatars in Crimea were dekulakized. When President Mehmet Kubay complained to Moscow of the Soviet Union's abuses—their thievery of goods and imposed famine in Crimea—he disappeared.[27]

At some point, the hunt for kulaks was so intense that activists were given quotas. F. Pravoberezhny tells the story of an agent from the Soviet GPU coming to his Ukrainian village, Stayky, of the Rzhyshchiv District, to gather 50 kurkuls. He met with the Village Soviet, Starovoyt, and the two, says Pravoberezhny, had the following conversation:

> "Comrade Starovoyt! Your village is asked to give 50 kurkuls."
>
> "But where will I find them? They have all been taken away already."

---

[23] One hectare equals 10,000 square meters.
[24] From Anne Applebaum, *The Red Sorrow: Stalin's War on Ukraine* (New York: Random House, 2017), 103.
[25] Robert Conquest, *The Harvest of Sorrow*, 129.
[26] Isaac Deutscher, *Stalin: A Political Biography* (London: Oxford University Press, 1945), 325.
[27] Nikolai K. Deker, *Genocide in the USSR* (Munich: Institute for the Study of the USSR, 1958), 22.

"I am not concerned with that. This is my order."

"You know very well that only the poor farmers are now left in this village. How can we find kurkuls?"

"If you do not know whom to take I shall pick them out myself, but you will be sorry."

"All right. Take them yourself. I do not know of any kurkuls."

"Well, I do. And the first one is you! The next is your father-in-law and the rest I shall soon find. Give me the list of names of the village residents. Who of these was in Zeleny's gang in 1919?"

"You already know that the whole village was with Zeleny."

"Very well. By morning I want you to have a list of 50 names ready. If you do, you may cross out your own and your father-in-law's names. If not, you will both die in Kolyma."[28]

Priests, other dignitaries of the church, and their families were too branded "kulak" and were treated in the main as kulaks of the worst sort. They were refused documents that would enable them to travel outside their village. When put on collective farms or exiled, they always got the worst jobs. It was the same with persons strongly affiliated with a church. The sons of Ukrainian Pavel Sybirny, president of his church council of a church in his village, Mykhailivka of Poltava Oblast, had each of his three sons exiled for 10 years, and the third was eventually executed. What is sadly ironic is that the surviving boys would be sent to the Russian front during World War II to fight for the government that exiled them.[29]

Stalin's general idea was to divide and conquer. He aimed to reform the peasant-farmers by classificating them into kulaks, serednyaks, and bednyaks, and then turning each class against the other, or at least the last two against the first. Infighting would, in time, lead to all being in an intolerably miserable state and create, as quickly as possible, a proletariat class against "the rule of capital" and the notion of classification by wealth. Yet implementation would occur only after all peasant-farmers learned that ownership of land was facinorous because it was against the general good, dictated by the Party, by Stalin. The

---

[28] F. Pravoberezhny, "Each Village to 'Give' 50 Kurkuls," in *The Black Deeds of the Kremlin: A White Book*, ed. S.O. Pidhainy, Vol. 2 (Detroit: The Basilian Press, 1955), 167.

[29] H. Senko, "History of the Destruction of the Ukrainian Orthodox Church," in *The Black Deeds of the Kremlin: A White Book*, ed. S.O. Pidhainy, Vol. 1 (Detroit: The Basilian Press, 1955), 499–500.

irony is that the methods of implementing this dictatorship of the proletariat were anything but anti-capitalist. Peasant-farmers were incentivized by material gain, or fear of loss, to destroy each other. Chaos could only have been the result.

That all too few peasant-farmers in Ukraine and elsewhere willingly collectivized early during the Five-Year Plan is not, as Stalin's propaganda said, a sign of gross ignorance of what was in their best interest. They knew that they would gain nothing through collectivizing and that only the State would be a gainer, and the State, while profiting on their moil, had no incentive to improve the lot of its peasant-farmers, considered collectively. The State cared least about Ukrainians.

UPSHOT

In the bedlam of compulsatory collectivization, Stalin, on November 7, 1929, announced with ebullience and optimism "a radical change."

> Our agriculture [has advanced] from individual farming to large-scale, advanced collective agriculture, to cultivation of the land in common. … The new and decisive feature of the peasant collective farm movement is that the peasant-farmers are joining the collective farms not in separate groups, as was formerly the case, but in whole villages, whole regions, whole districts and even whole provinces. And what does that mean? It means that the middle peasant has joined the collective farm movement. And that is the basis of the radical change in the development of agriculture which represents the most important achievement of Soviet power during the past year.[30]

The serednyaks had seen the light, so said Stalin. They no longer aspired to be like the kulaks, but instead, they had, with the bednyaks, collectivized. Stalin, of course, was merely reported what he hoped would soon be the case, not what was the case. Many peasant-farmers were joining collectives, but they were, in the main, given no alternative other than to join. The alternatives were dispossession, exile, and execution.

---

[30] J.V. Stalin, "To the Editorial Board of the Newspaper *Trevoga*," *Pravda*, 7 Nov. 1929.

Chapter 7

The Process of Dekulakization

"The Party has succeeded in routing the kulaks as a class, although they have not yet been dealt the final blow; the labouring peasants have been emancipated from kulak bondage and exploitation, and the Soviet regime has been given a firm economic basis in the countryside, the basis of collective farming."

~Joseph Stalin

As we have seen, by the start of 1930, Stalin upped his ante. Not only was dekulakization a desideratum of collectivization, but it was also a needed condition. "Dekulakization is now an essential element in forming and developing the collective farms. ... It is wrong to admit the kulak into the collective farm ... because he is an accursed enemy of the collective farm movement."[1] At this point, Stalin, who lacked any capacity for precise usage of words—or perhaps, who intentionally eschewed precise usage of words—was uttering a tautology: Every kulak (by definition, an enemy of the collective farm movement) was an enemy of the collective farm movement. "Kulak" has lost its categorization as an economic class, though Stalin, so wedded to Marxism with his Stalinist slant, would often continue to use it that way. At this time, anyone who posed a threat to collectivization—a bednyak, a priest, a teacher, a common laborer, a peasant who asked an ambiguous question, and even a laggard of the Party—needed to be nullified because all were kulaks. And so, all designated as kulaks were to be imprisoned, exiled, shot, or, if lucky, admitted back into the system on watchful probation. Stalin very soon would be finding kulaks within the Party—among its card-carrying workers and among its administrators and officers.

In this chapter, I critically examine the process of Stalinist dekulakization: branding, dispossession, exile or imprisonment, and execution.

---

[1] Robert Conquest, The Harvest of Sorrow: Soviet Collectivization and the Terror-Famine (Oxford: Oxford University Press, 1986), 114.

"Act like Bolsheviks worthy of Comrade Stalin!"
Branding & Dispossessing

It seems clear that if there had been much to the proposed new and scientific methods of collective farming, if the socialists could show plainly how all would equally benefit from collectivization of agriculture if only through ease of labor or greater leisure, then "kulaks" would eventually jump on Stalin's socialist wagon and might even be the staunchest advocates of the wholesale change. They did not, for there were no benefits, only deficits. Few of the peasant-farmers did unless coerced. Only among the poorest peasant-farmers did we find any purchase of the propaganda, and then, that was especially early in the propagandist campaign. Peasant-farmers who owned anything, not just kulaks, had everything to lose—all the things that they had worked for years to have—and little to gain. The State, instead, was the gainer—especially the ever-fattening agents of the State. By this point, there were classes of "comrades," and the highest officials of the Party lived lavishly.

Yet Stalin manifestly saw a necessary connection between the success of socialization and the removal of kulaks. There was Stalinist motivation for removal of all "enemies of the State"—pertaining to collectivizing farms, all who expressed the least doubt in the practicability of, as it were, urbanizing the country—and Stalin everywhere saw enemies of the State, especially in the largely inaccessible rural areas of the Soviet Union, like the villages of Ukraine. "Removal" almost always meant "exile" or "exterminate." Like a stubborn child, Stalin was mostly incapable of subtlety and unhappy with compromise. The exile of a kulak was the removal of a problem. The extermination of a kulak was the permanent removal of a problem. Those capable of hard labor tended to be exiled. The most troublesome or the infirm tended to be exterminated.

The agents of punishment were the activists, who were mainly urbanites who were deemed loyal to the Bolshevik mission and enthused about collectivization, if only because of the prospects of material gain, though bednyaks when serviceable and reliable, were also used. It would have been bootless to attempt to draw chiefly from the ruralites, for they were already victimized by the failed attempts at collectivizing their farms and, thus, hostile to Bolshevism.

In 1928 and 1929, over 27,000 urbanites, along with members of the militia and GPU from Moscow and Leningrad were sent to the farms in Ukraine to manage them. These were called the Twenty-Five-Thousanders (TFTs).[2] We find in an exposé in *Pravda*, late in November 1929: "The Central Committee considers it vital, aside from a systematic reinforcement of the collective farm movement by Party leadership, to send no less than twenty-five thousand laborers with adequate organizational-political experience to work during the coming months on collective farms, at machine-tractor stations, and in divisional boards. In picking these workers, the Professional Associations must take an active part and choose the most progressive men."[3] The rationale was twofold. First, peasant-farmers, divided into classes between which there was ever tension (according to Marxism), could not be trusted to manage other peasant-farmers. The division of peasant-farmers into classes was not so neat, and the tension between the so-called classes was not so great. Second, urbanites were selected because of some experience, whether perceived or actual, in working in factories, in management, or in affairs of the Party—skills peasant-farmers lacked. What sort of training did the TFTs receive? Each attended a two-week seminar for training before being sent to a village to "assist" it.[4] All in all, the most significant qualification for anyone sent to Soviet villages to push for the collectivization of farms was loyalty to the Party. *Pravda* publishes a directive late in 1929 that tells us of "experienced Party workers" coming to Ukrainian villages to prepare for compulsory collectivization.[5]

Peasant-farmers, unsurprisingly, reacted with hostility, for no crash course on agriculture could teach anyone anything about agricultural bounty. Consider this address to activists by an official of the Party, M.M. Khateyevich:

> The local village authorities need an injection of Bolshevik iron. That is why we are sending you. You must assume your duties with a feeling of the strictest Party responsibility, without whimpering, without any rotten liberalism. Throw your bourgeois humanitarianism out the window and act like Bolsheviks worthy of Comrade Stalin! Beat down the kulak agent wherever he raises his head! It is war! It is they or we! The last rotting vestige of capitalist farming must be wiped out at any cost! ... Through you, the party brigades, the villages must learn the meaning of Bolshevik stoutness. You must find the grain and you *will* find it. It is

---

[2] R.W. Davies, *The Socialist Offensive: The Collectivization of Soviet Agriculture, 1929–1930* (Cambridge: Harvard University Press, 1980), 297, and Ivan Trotsenko, "Ukrainians in Russian Exile Camps," in *The Black Deeds of the Kremlin: A White Book*, ed. S.O. Pidhainy, Vol. 1 (Detroit: The Basilian Press, 1955), 192–95.
[3] Pravda, 22 Nov. 1929. See also Pravda, 22 Nov. 1929; 31 Dec. 1929; and 24 Jan. 1930
[4] At first, the tenure was to be one year, but on December 5, 1930, the tenureship became by decree permanent. Robert Conquest, *The Harvest of Sorrow*, 146.
[5] Pravda, 27 Oct. 1929.

a challenge to the last whit of your initiative and to your Chekist pluck. Do not be fearful of taking extreme measures! The Party stands foursquare behind you. Comrade Stalin expects it of you. It is a life-and-death struggle. It is better to do too much than not enough.[6]

The main message was this. Whenever confronted with a choice between a measure extreme and one not so extreme, take the extreme measure, for "it is better to do too much than not enough."

There were, as I note at the end of the prior chapter, four stages of dekulakization: branding, dispossessing, exiling, or (this disjunction is used inclusively) for those deemed intransigent enemies, elimination. I cover the first two in this section.

The first step of dekulakization was to identify the kulaks, and then to brand them. Once identified and labeled "kulak," a peasant-farmer was singled out physically from others and called *odnoosibnyk* (singleton)—a term, like kulak, that quickly became highly pejorative and stuck like a tattoo. *Odnoosibnyk* was tantamount to labeling someone a selfish capitalist. It was not uncommon to depict kulaks as peasant-farmers who were lazy and fat capitalist opportunists (review Figure 6-1), usurers who lived off the labor of others by renting out land or offering loans at exorbitant rates to fellow villagers. Yet the opposite was usually the case. The kulaks were habitually the hardest working peasant-farmers, and, consequently, the wealthiest peasant-farmers—bootstrappers who rose above the common peasant-farmers through intelligent planning and hard work.[7] They were the backbone of villages in Ukraine and elsewhere. All peasant-farmers knew that.

Yet Marxism demanded that there be no vestiges anywhere of capitalism; hence, all property needed to be appropriated; hence, dekulakization was necessary. Figure 7-1 shows a propagandist parade of mostly children supposed to show villagers' enthusiastic opposition to the kulak oppressors. The signs read, "We shall liquidate the kulaks as a class!" and "All efforts toward the struggle against the destroyers of agriculture!" A commonly utilized technique of Stalin—a technique that goes back at least to Plato—was to focus on shaping the children of the Soviet Union to be fine and loyal members of the party, even if their parents were not so inclined. Slogans and propaganda were essential. Yet, as Victor Kravchenko notes in a warning given to him by his father, "No slogan, no matter how attractive, is any indication of the real policy

---

[6] Victor Kravchenko, *I Chose Freedom* (New York: Charles Scribner's Sons, 1946), 91–92.
[7] For Soviet failed attempts to define "kulak" within the confines of an economic class, see Robert Conquest, *The Harvest of Sorrow*, 74–75.

of any political party once it comes to power." He adds: "No matter what a party stands for, it will be bad if one party wins. That will only mean new masters for the old—rule by force, not by the free will of the people. It is not for this that the revolutionists gave their lives." Why was there a revolution? "They are made for people. The essence of the matter is personal rights and liberties. Without these, without human dignity, men are slaves no matter how industrialized their prison may be."[8]

The extraordinary psychological significance of branding certain peasant-farmers kulaks or odnoosibnyks—the significance of terminology, both euphemisms, and dysphemisms, in shaping Russian culture continues today (e.g., Putin's "Special Military Operation" in the February 2022 war with Ukraine)—is often overlooked. Branding is merely a special type of labeling—one that is meant to continue interminably. "Kulak" or "kurkul," as we shall later see, was a label that was meant, once given, to be forever applicable. A dekulaked kulak was still, and ever, a kulak. A poor peasant, who benefited as a pickthank, could gain materially from espionage and informing on villagers who might be enemies of the state. Thus, he might rise meteorically from his use to the Party, yet in the change of material status, he might find himself to be a kulak—a brand that he too would never lose, a brand that would be inherited by members of his immediate family. Pickthanks, too, had to exercise caution.

Fig. 7-1. "Liquidate the Kulaks" Parade

Source: Wikipedia

---

[8] Victor Kravchenko, *I Chose Freedom*, 21 and 202.

The large irony of Stalinist Marxism is that in aiming for the eradication of the bourgeoisie and supplantation of them with an amorphous group of proletariats, each presumably the equal of all others and avowedly deserving an equal share of the benefits of the state, Stalin constructed an imposing axiological hierarchy of persons of unequal status in the eyes of the Party—with axiological status, determined by usefulness to the Party, i.e., to Stalin. The Party would quickly become an enormous machine, impossible to supervise and one that drained the fiscal resources of the system. Stalin, of course, refused to see that. In his eyes, there were merely loyal members of the Party, "comrades," and each the avowed equal of all others, and his kulaks or "enemies of the state"—at least, that is the story he crafted for all others.

The next step was dispossession of property. Once dekulakized and dubbed odnoosibnyks, peasant-farmers were stripped of some or all of their property: their grain, their tools, their animals, their house, their land, and sometimes, their family. With dispossession, they were removed to a remote part of their village, usually the outskirts, where the land was scarcely arable and their "brand" would be obvious, or they were exiled or exterminated.

Peasant-farmers, as we have seen, were often dispossessed by brutal taxation—with the amount of taxation imposed sometimes rising exponentially with the appraisal of one's worth. Ukrainian Y. Maslivets writes that there were state monetary taxes and the Machine-Tractor Station Tax—a tax consisting of 25 percent of the total yield to benefit factories of tractors. The motivation here was that farmers were paying for tractors that they would soon be able to use, though that seldom occurred. Peasant-farmers who could not pay the taxes lost their farm. In the Zinkiv District of Poltava Oblast in 1932, the taxes amounted to 21.14 bushels per acre of farmed land, yet the winter's yield was 19.3 bushels/acre, and there were only 14.88 bushels of grain/acre in the spring. So, overall, 21 of the roughly 35 bushels of grain/acre, three-fifths, went to the state. Moreover, none of the surplus grain could be divided among peasant-farmers until the taxes were paid. There were years, e.g., 1932 when there was insufficient grain to pay the taxes and other requisites of the state.[9]

By 1932, the fate of most individual farmers was established. The Individual Farmer Plan was implemented, a levy of taxes on peasant-farmers who refused to collectivize that was far beyond a farmer's ability to pay. Individual farmers

---

[9] Y. Maslivets, "What Did Ukrainian Farmers Gain from Collective Farms?" in *The Black Deeds of the Kremlin: A White Book*, ed. S.O. Pidhainy, Vol. 1 (Detroit: The Basilian Press, 1955), 192–95.

were required to pay as much as 10 times what they harvested that year.[10] The aim of the "plan," of course, was dispossession.

Moreover, while the government paid up to 1.42, 1.77, and 1.5 rubles per bushel for rye, wheat, oats, and other grains, the market prices for those grains were some two-and-one-half times higher or more. By 1933, free market prices were up to 25 times more than what the State gave to its farmers. Peasant-farmers were being robbed, and yet the State's demands for grain increased arithmetically each year. The procurement of grain was almost 11 million poods in 1928–1929,[11] just over 16 million poods in 1929–1930, just over 22 million poods in 1930–1931, and nearly 23 million poods in 1931–1932.[12] And so, procurement more than doubled in a period of four years, while "remuneration" for labor was pathetically low.

The reasoning behind the successes of procurement, the Party must have thought, was that peasant-farmers were typically underperforming—that is, that they produced only to meet expectations. Raise expectations, and one would raise production, and that conclusion was given without any thought that such reasoning could only, over time, lead to catastrophe. The most absurd part of the reasoning was that demands of procurement were set by officials of the state, who knew little about farming and used crude rubrics involving available arable lands to determine demands. Disaster was imminent.

Overall, some 70 percent of income was directed to the development of the collective and to the State. The remaining 30 percent was divided among members of the collective, with each being paid pursuant to the total number of days of work. If a farmer earned anything at year's end—there were years when the demands of procurement were not met, and farmers received no pay or merely were given the promise of future pay—he was debited for things such as visits to town or to the doctor, plowing his individual plot, and kindergarten.[13]

When activists dispossessed people, it was not always clear what was to become of them. They were not only odnoosibnyks, but also, to substantivize an adjective, "obsolescents," and as obsolescents, not much consideration was given to their wellbeing. That money would be diverted to where it was most

---

[10] Y. Maslivets, "What Did Ukrainian Farmers Gain from Collective Farms?" in *The Black Deeds of the Kremlin: A White Book*, ed. S.O. Pidhainy, Vol. 1 (Detroit: The Basilian Press, 1955), 194.

[11] One pood equals 16.4 kilgrams.

[12] Robert Conquest, *The Harvest of Sorrow: Soviet Collectivization and the Terror-Famine* (Oxford: Oxford University Press, 1986), 174–75.

[13] Y. Maslivets, "What Did Ukrainian Farmers Gain from Collective Farms?" in *The Black Deeds of the Kremlin: A White Book*, ed. S.O. Pidhainy, Vol. 1 (Detroit: The Basilian Press, 1955), 192–95.

needed—the booming industrial cities—and obsolescents were exiled and put to work in remote regions of Russia or executed if deemed irremediably kulakized or too feeble for hard labor. In consequence, death rates at such remote places of exile, like in the north and northeastern regions of the Soviet Union, were inordinately high. Many died in transit.

Some dispossessed kulaks, however, escaped to the cities and found work in factories.[14] In factories often starving for laborers, it was sometimes the case that few questions were asked about one's place of origin. The deciding factors were willingness and ability to work.

Ukrainian Ivan Trotsenko states that his father, a former soldier in the Red Army, was dubbed an "under-kurkul"—an obdurate farmer who had no interest in politics, and so a not-so-immediate threat to socialization, but nonetheless obdurate. With two horses, one cow, one hog, five sheep, and 40 chickens, he was a serednyak who owned 35 acres and had six members in his family. In 1926, he and his brother sold the cattle and horses and bought a Fordson tractor, though one year later, it was taken by the Party. When he went to Kharkiv to complain about the demand for 2,500 rubles and 500 bushels of grain under the Individual Farmers Plan, his complaint was heard only by the president's secretary. On his return to his village, the chairman of the village soviet was auctioning his house, valued at some 2,000 rubles for one-tenth its price. In reply to no bids—any peasant bidding for the house would have exposed himself due to accumulated wealth as a kurkul—the chairman bid 250 rubles and took the house. The animals were sold at auction, and so too were the machines and household items.[15]

A certain E. Yemchenko, a Ukrainian girl from the village Malo Oleksandrivka, tells of her father being taxed beyond his ability to pay, the family being dispossessed, and being taken, without food or water, to a nearby railroad station to be driven to the north.

> We were all loaded on, 2,000 people, 60 to a car, mothers, fathers, children, grandmothers and grandfathers. The train headed for Moscow. During the trip some people in desperation threw themselves off the fast-moving train to kill themselves, or inflict some injury that would stave off deportation. During our whole ride to Moscow we were given no food or

---

[14] Anne Applebaum, *Red Famine: Stalin's War on Ukraine* (New York: Anchor: 2017), 154–55.
[15] Ivan Trotsenko, "Ukrainians in Russian Exile Camps," in *The Black Deeds of the Kremlin: A White Book*, ed. S.O. Pidhainy, Vol. 1 (Detroit: The Basilian Press, 1955), 138–65.

water. A great number of people died or became insane. When we reached Moscow, only half of those who started out remained alive.[16]

Once in Moscow, which was hundreds of miles from their village, they were given "soup," which was essentially warmed water with a few droplets of broth from a pail. They were then lined up outside and stripped of all clothes so activists could search for gold in pockets of clothing. Gold teeth were extracted. Victims were then taken to Vologda, over 300 miles north of Moscow, where they were herded into old churches with broken windows and cement floors. There were 47 churches acting as hostels. Most of the deportees were Ukrainians, though there were Tatars, Georgians, and Germans. As many as 50 children perished each day.[17]

They were soon transported further north via barges, where they alighted at an indistinct spot in a thick forest. The snow was deep. There, the deportees were to make a life for themselves through timbering projects.[18]

Young Yemchenko, by the age of 14 and segregated from her family, had had enough. She fled on foot. "I ... was undergoing terrifying experiences, but my intense desire to return to Ukraine persisted, and I doggedly continued." She ends her story: "When I reached my native land, it was 1933, the year of the great famine. I encountered alarming changes. It was impossible to buy bread, while stores were overflowing with goods in Russia. People were dying everywhere. There was absolutely no food; it was all taken away to the last kernel."[19]

"They threw the poor woman into a snow drift"
Exiling & Elimination

From late December 1929, when Stalin pronounced his plan of "liquidation of the kulaks as a class," to 1933, millions of kulaks, many Ukrainian kurkuls, were exiled to places such as Solovky, Ukhta-Pechora, Kotlas, Murmansk, Arkhangelsk, Mariinskoe, Karaganda, Bamlat, Shakhalin, and Kamchatka in the northern regions of the Soviet Union,[20] and there were some 600,000 deaths,

---

[16] E. Yemchenko, "From Vologda to Ukraine," in *The Black Deeds of the Kremlin: A White Book*, ed. S.O. Pidhainy, Vol. 1 (Detroit: The Basilian Press, 1955), 181.
[17] E. Yemchenko, "From Vologda to Ukraine," 181–82.
[18] E. Yemchenko, "From Vologda to Ukraine," 182–83.
[19] E. Yemchenko, "From Vologda to Ukraine," in *The Black Deeds of the Kremlin: A White Book*, ed. S.O. Pidhainy, Vol. 1 (Detroit: The Basilian Press, 1955), 183.
[20] H. Sova, "The Far Kolyma," in *The Black Deeds of the Kremlin: A White Book*, ed. S.O. Pidhainy, Vol. 2 (Detroit: The Basilian Press, 1955), 69.

many being fragile children, due to dekulakization. Up to one-third of deportees died.[21] Some deported kulaks were sent to cities and put to work in factories. The many factories of Magnitogorsk of Chelyabinsk Oblast in Russia employed some 18,000 kulaks as well as some 25,000 criminals in its mines.[22]

Ukrainian Ivan Trotsenko offers a fine account of the fate of those exiled and not executed in the numerous gulags across the Urals. His parents and brothers, along with numerous others, all half naked and nourished by some soggy black bread each day, were forced to mine coal in the Urals for 21 years. "For the past twenty years the Communists have used slave labor to cut timber, fill in swamplands and build cities like Komsomolsk, Magnitogorsk, [and] Kuzbas." Slaves built railways and roads, often in the most human-unfriendly areas, such as the railway through the swamplands between Chita and Khabarovsk and the Amur ice road. Slaves mined gold, silver, and iron ore. They built military fortifications along the Pacific coastline. While hundreds of thousands died from 1929 to 1950 from hunger, cold, typhus, and tuberculosis, and while many others continued their thralldom with missing limbs, tuberculosis, scurvy, and rheumatism, there was ever a ready supply of new recruits, newly dispossessed from their property, from Ukraine as well as Georgia and Central Asia.[23]

Prisons and forced-labor camps were disgusting. Prison cells were typically overfull with prisoners. A kurkul sent to a prison in Poltava reports that 36 persons occupied a cell meant for seven, and 83 prisoners occupied a cell meant for 20. Cells were filthy and redolent of urine and defecation. Each person was given from 100 to 150 grams of underbaked, soggy black bread. Of the 2,000 prisoners, some 30 each day died—1.5 percent each day.[24] The alarmingly high rate of death was unlikely to have been a bother to officials. It was beneficial for a prison to have the weakest and least fit for work perish and not drain the resources of the prison. There was ever seemingly an inexhaustible supply of new prisoners to replace them.

Activist Y. Maslivets was sent to Birky of the Poltava Oblast in December 1929. Birky had then some 6,000 residents and some 300 farmers and was to be arranged into four collective farms (Ukr., *kolhospi*) with a headquarters for the four. The leader was F. Kramarenko, a district judge from Zinkiv District, and who would be arrested in 1937 and exiled to Kolyma. Sixty-four peasant-

---

[21] Leonard Hubbard. *The Economics of Soviet Agriculture* (London: Macmillan, 1939), 177.
[22] John Scott, *Behind the Urals: An American Worker Is Russia's City of Steel* (Bloomington: Indiana University Press, 1973). 85.
[23] Ivan Trotsenko, "Ukrainians in Russian Exile Camps," in *The Black Deeds of the Kremlin: A White Book*, ed. S.O. Pidhainy, Vol. 1 (Detroit: The Basilian Press, 1955), 135–65.
[24] Ivan Trotsenko, "Ukrainians in Russian Exile Camps," 135–65.

farmers were deemed kurkuls by "a special brigade composed of the local dregs of humanity, such as idlers, gamblers, criminals, and other unsavory characters." The families of those men and 20 more were shortly added, were driven from their homes to the outskirts of the village to try to subsist. Imprisoned farmers who recanted—there was a need for that, for the prisons were overfull—were allowed to join the collective. Those unwilling to join were taxed in produce and money in accordance with the Individual Farmer Plan. The tax was an impossible 5,000 rubles. When the tax was not paid, farms were sold to activists for 50 to 200 rubles, and activists then resold the farms for 2,000 or more rubles.[25]

Through terror and blackmail, 75 percent of the village was collectivized by March 1930. Yet some 400 persons remained homeless, and none of the others was allowed to help them. The homeless were at some point gathered, put on wagons, and deported to a great ravine called Redkovi Pechery (Radish's Caves), where they were to subsist as cave-dwellers. "On April 18, the 200 human wretches who remained in the ravines were herded together by the police and driven to the railway station of Abazovka where trains were awaiting them. All of them, with tens of thousands of others like them, were loaded into boxcars and, under a strong GPU guard, were shipped to the far North."[26]

In 1932, Narym of Tomsk Oblast, Russia, a destination for exiles and criminals from the early seventeenth century, received 196,000 kurkuls, and that swelled the city's population to over 300,000, when its population in 1910 was under 1,000. Narym was a most inhospitable place. It was situated in a swamp, where mosquitoes thrived in the summer, and diseases were readily transferred to occupants, and temperatures in the winter had been recorded as low as -85° F.[27] Such an immediate bloating of small cities stretched impossible resources such as food and shelter, so it is likely that having the frailest perish *in transitu* was not looked upon with great regret or sorrow. As I have already noted, up to one-third of deportees died *in transitu*.

---

[25] One has today to imagine the owner of a house, valued at 200 thousand dollars, being taxed for 500 thousand dollars. Y. Maslivets, "Collectivization and 'Kurkul' Liquidation," in *The Black Deeds of the Kremlin: A White Book*, ed. S.O. Pidhainy, Vol. 1 (Detroit: The Basilian Press, 1955), Vol. 1: 187–89.
[26] Y. Maslivets, "Collectivization and 'Kurkul' Liquidation," 189–91.
[27] D.Y. Rezun, "Narym," *Concise Encyclopedia on the History of Merchants and Commerce of Siberia*, "Narym," https://ssl.translatoruser.net/officetrans/httpquery.aspx?lcidFrom=1049&lcidTo=1033&lcidUI=1033&docId=Lo3_6E7Bm4N8TKBEKoCut4J8R78cRVYEqvb8 DFbIAnuILX001DU5IWH_3fTPZ34b4Df92u0r8uGLinIJdhC2rQ**, accessed 11 Nov. 2022.

The Solovki Special [Prison] Camp (Figure 7-2) in the Solovetski Islands of the White Sea was formerly a large monastery devoted to St. Zosym and S. Savatiy. Ivan the Terrible, seeing it as a defensive structure, put a large wall around the monastery, but it was soon converted into a prison camp. Called "Solovetksy Camp of Special Assignment" in 1922 and later "Chief Camp of Special Assignment," it would become the most renowned prison camp in Soviet Russia. There was a song about the long, cold ride via train from Kem to Solovki. "Solovky, Solovky, / Where the road is long, / Pressure weighs the heart, / Fear burdens the soul." In the early years of the prison camp (1926–1927), it comprised criminals, counter-revolutionists, officials of Russia's pre-Bolshevik governments, and landlords, bourgeois, monarchists, and, of course, clergymen. With Stalin's aggressive pushes toward industrialization and rural collectivization (1928–1932), Ukrainian and Georgian peasant-farmers, clergy, and teachers as counter-revolutionists were targeted and began to fill the prisons of Solovki.[28]

Fig. 7-2. Solovky Special Camp

Source: Wikipedia

S.O. Pidhainy, who was a prisoner of the camp, notes that he and some 12,000 others labored to build a railroad track from the forest for transporting lumber to export. There was no respite during the severe and bitterly cold winter—the earth had frozen some nine feet deep, but prisoners were still enjoined to work 12-hour days—when some 10,000 Ukrainians and Dons perished. Yet the dead

---

[28] S.O. Pidhainy, "Solovky Concentration Camp," in *The Black Deeds of the Kremlin: A White Book*, ed. S.O. Pidhainy, Vol. 2 (Detroit: The Basilian Press, 1955), Vol. 2: 29–32.

were supplanted by a readily available supply of other Ukrainians. For the next three months, Pidhainy and others had to load ties onto a railroad car under the watchful eye of Cheka riflemen and then cut down trees. The quotas for trees were high. Those failing to meet the quotas, even if due to infirmity or illness, were severely beaten and punished. One such punishment was to lock an inmate into a wall cupboard used for books by the monks, and leave him for days without food or water. Many perished in that manner. Other "failures" were merely shot. Still others, broken by punishment, opted for suicide. On one day, when the temperature was -60 degrees Fahrenheit, members of Barrack 5 refused to work. The Cheka set ablaze their barrack and shot any who attempted to escape. Thus, members faced the dilemma of being burned alive or of being shot. Pidhainy, with two others, escaped the hell of Solovky on September 10, 1930, and fled to Finland.[29]

Conditions at Solovky and other camps were dreadful. Prisoners were treated "infinitely worse" than were slaves in the pre-Civil War United States. At the gulags, prisoners were not even afforded the sort of care of a pack animal. Write Victor Kravchenko: "The supply [of slaves] is well-nigh inexhaustible, and the slave-holder, the Soviet state, apparently finds it more economical to let them die in droves than to feed and clothe them."[30]

Outside of the onerous duties mentioned by Pidhainy at Solovky and its satellite camps—logging, loading, and unloading materials and building railroad lines—what other sorts of tasks were prisoners forced to execute?

Prisoners were classed into groups.

Prisoners of Group A (some 85 percent of non-invalids) were laborers and technicians. They drilled for oil and refined it, mined coal and salt, built highways, created materials for building, cleared and grubbed land for building, created electric centers, repaired instruments and equipment for building, and built houses, boats, warehouses, and even the sort of camps in which they were imprisoned. For such laborers, winter temperatures could reach as low as -90 degrees Fahrenheit, while the summer could reach 100 degrees Fahrenheit, with the added botheration of the prospect of malaria due to thick clouds of billions of mosquitoes in the swampy areas of Northern Russia. Technicians were engineers, economists, agronomists, geologists, and carpenters.

Those of Group B (some 10 percent) were administrators and servants of the camp: helpers in stores, kitchens, laundry, steam baths, and hospitals.

Group C (some five percent) comprised the unemployed: those in transit, the ill, those whose cases were being investigated, and those refusing to work and in cells of isolation.

---

[29] S.O. Pidhainy, "Solovky Concentration Camp," 29–33.
[30] Victor Kravchenko, *I Chose Freedom* (New York: Charles Scribners' Sons: 1946), 341.

The last group, Group D (under one percent), was composed of useless, unproductive, invalids (the blind, amputees, those with severe frostbite or burns, the terminally ill, and so on), who were separated from all others and given such tasks that they could perform, while they were given scant medical attention and little food. They were, in effect, left to die.[31] Because the useless were a drain a camp's resources, there were incentives for the health-squad "to hasten the demise of their sick"—that is, a competition for "camp points" for hastening the demise of the useless.[32]

What constituted the punishment of exile?

The punishment of exile was at the discretion of officials of the Party, often in troikas. Ukrainian peasant-farmers were targeted because, like other peasant-farmers, they resisted collectivization and because they were Ukrainians—that is, Ukraine was the USSR's most significant republic in terms of resources, size, and location, and Stalin could not allow any disloyalty by it to Moscow. Obstreperousness in Ukraine would send the wrong message to other Soviet republics.

We recall that grain that could not be locally sold at market prices was, early in the process of collectivizing farms, hidden in wastelands, churches, fields, haystacks, forests, and ravines in preference to selling it to the State at absurdly low prices. In extreme cases, rebellious peasant-farmers preferred to burn or dump it into rivers rather than sell it to the state at absurdly low prices. On June

---

[31] S.O. Pidhainy, "Structure of the Supreme Administration of Ukhta-Pechora Concentration Camp," in *The Black Deeds of the Kremlin: A White Book*, ed. S.O. Pidhainy, Vol. 2 (Detroit: The Basilian Press, 1955): 47–48. Pidhainy also proffers a lengthy elaboration of the living, working conditions, working quotas and wages (most of which went to upkeep of a prisoner) in such prisons: the buildings and their functions, sanitation, clothing, bedding, footwear, and food. Bread was their chief sustenance, and prisoners were afforded from 10.5 to 35 ounces, depending on the amount of completed work. S.O. Pidhainy, *The Black Deeds of the Kremlin: A White Book*, ed. S.O. Pidhainy, Vol. 2 (Detroit: The Basilian Press, 1955): 50–69. See also H. Sova, "The Far Kolyma," S.O. Pidhainy, in *The Black Deeds of the Kremlin: A White Book*, ed. S.O. Pidhainy, Vol. 2 (Detroit: The Basilian Press, 1955): 69–78.

[32] I. M***ch, "Reminiscences of Stalin's Cemetery—White Sea Baltic Canal," in *The Black Deeds of the Kremlin: A White Book*, ed. S.O. Pidhainy, Vol. 2 (Detroit: The Basilian Press, 1955): 87. Stalin in time came to see the value of having prison camps filled with relatively healthy and productive laborers. During his Great Purge of 1936–1938, he said in reply to the possibility of the early release of those prisoners who have distinguished themselves by exemplary work. "Can we not fond some other way of showing appreciation of their work? From the point of view of the economy it is a bad idea. The best people would be freed, and those left would be the worst." Edvard Radzinsky, *Stalin* (New York: Anchor, 1997), 414.

14, 1929, hiding grain was by law decreed to be a crime punishable by exile, according to the North Caucasus Committee. Yet in practice, only one or two peasant-farmers per village were to be exiled, so as to serve as an example for and deterrence to disobedience to the Party. Two weeks later, a law was passed such that kulaks who had not delivered their quota of grain, even if they were not hiding grain, could be penalized, even exiled.[33]

Exile as punishment was soon doled out to intransigents who resisted collectivization. When the TFTs entered Ukraine in 1929 and "campaigned" for collective farming, they organized daily meetings with peasant-farmers to "persuade" them of the desirability of collectivized farms. "They pleaded, ranted, promised paradise, and threatened with their revolvers, but the farmers remained obdurate." The most obdurate were placed on lists of kurkuls to be rounded up by the GPU and imprisoned or exiled. Under-kurkuls, obdurate farmers who were politically harmless, were harassed by the Individual Farmer Plan. Their land was then confiscated, the owner and his family were evacuated, and everything was sold at prices rock-bottom, usually to activists, for, as I have already noted, other peasant-farmers feared that purchase of anything of worth would brand them kurkuls, and they too would be dispossessed of what they just purchased and exiled.[34]

Finally, and this does not need descant, those peasant-farmers deemed most fractious were left to die or were exterminated, usually *en route* to some destination. Stalin even passed a law on July 14, 1932, when the famine was surging, that any peasant-farmer caught stealing grain could legally be shot. I offer a few illustrations, some stark.

In the Ukrainian village Velyki Solontsi of Poltava Oblast, the house and land of Andriy Sepity were confiscated. They were to be the center of a collective farm to be called "Granit." That excited the poorest peasant-farmers and activists, who were convinced that new farming practices would be good for all peasant-farmers. Sepity was "banished to Siberia," and his wife and children, driven from the home, merely "disappeared."[35]

Even with the panic caused by the confiscation of Sepity's property, only some 20 of the 500 farmers of Velyki Solontsai joined the collective. A troika was formed. The three officials of the Party prepared a list of "kurkuls," and then 52 kurkuls were removed. Once removed, their wives and children were gathered into wagons at night, taken to a sandy patch along River Vorskla, and merely

---

[33] Robert Conquest, *The Harvest of Sorrow*, 103–6.
[34] Ivan Trotsenko, "Ukrainians in Russian Exile Camps," 136–38.
[35] E.M. "Collectivization," in *The Black Deeds of the Kremlin: A White Book*, ed. S.O. Pidhainy, Vol. 1 (Detroit: The Basilian Press, 1955), 198.

left there. "Tired and terrified, they were thrown out like garbage, in the hope that they would perish there from cold and hunger."[36]

Next, K. Shvets was preparing to remove from his pillaged house in Hrushka in Kyiv Oblast to a house in Kyiv. The hamlet had been razed to accommodate a *radhosp*—a large State farm. Before leaving, he took a picture of his family before the decimated house. A member of a shock brigade nearby watched Shvets taking the picture, and Shvets was accosted by a soldier and several young activists of the Komsomol. Shvets was shot that evening as an enemy of the people. His wife, upon hearing of his arrest, died from cardiac arrest, and the children were taken by the State.[37]

Again, there is the fate of Petro Grigorenko's Uncle Alexander. Grigorenko was told that his uncle was arrested for "economic sabotage," as he was accused of being "an owner of gold"—a most serious charge. Since all property formally belonged to the State and gold was property, gold formally belonged to the State. While under arrest, his uncle was said to have died from heart failure. Yet many years later, Grigorenko met a man at Serbsky Institute for Psychological Disorders—the man had been imprisoned for 34 years prior to entering the institute—and the man told Grigorenko of the interrogative process for anyone accused of owning gold. If one accused did not admit to having gold, even if he really had no gold, he was beaten with felt boots, filled with bricks. If during his beating he admitted to having gold, if only to stop the beating, he immediately had to find gold, or the beating would continue till death. If he refused to admit to having gold or admitted to having no gold, he would be beaten to death.[38] The process, of course, worked on the assumption of the infallibility of the Party concerning its accusation.

Finally, F. Fedorchenko tells of the sorry fate of Ukrainian Danylo Artemenko, who belonged to the collective called Snizhne of Novo-Mykolayivske of the Kyiv Oblast. Artemenko was one of the district's best farmers. Though illiterate, he was deedy, and he became quite prosperous, though he had a family of 13 for which to provide.[39]

Artemenko suffered more than his share of tragedies prior to being killed.

First, there was the suicide of his son, who died from smoking tea leaves in 1927 in preference to being drafted into Russia's Red Army.[40]

---

[36] E.M. "Collectivization," 198.

[37] I. Antonenko, "Devastation of the Hamlet of Hrushka," in *The Black Deeds of the Kremlin: A White Book*, ed. S.O. Pidhainy, Vol. 1 (Detroit: The Basilian Press, 1955), 267.

[38] Petro Grigorenko, *Memoirs* (New York: W.W. Norton, 1982), 41.

[39] F. Fedorchenko, "Tragedy of Danylo Artemenko," in *The Black Deeds of the Kremlin: A White Book*, ed. S.O. Pidhainy, Vol. 1 (Detroit: The Basilian Press, 1955), 214.

[40] F. Fedorchenko, "Tragedy of Danylo Artemenko," 214.

Next, there was the arrest of his entire family in 1931. They were exiled to Izkevk, Russia, for hard labor. Daughter Anna and her husband escaped the camp. They were found and arrested in the village of Domanivka. While her husband was sent to a concentration camp, Anna was stripped of all clothes and thrown into a cold, water-filled basement for a day as a form of torture. When released, she was voiceless and insane. She died from pleurisy a few days later.[41]

Third, another daughter, Natalia, and her three small children were tossed from her house.

> Her household effects became the booty of the raiding party of communists, windows were boarded up, and the house locked. Then Natalia went to her father's house, which stood empty in the forest. But the communists found her there. A drunken communist gang broke into the house one winter night, tied Natalia's hands behind her back and beat her mercilessly. After this, they threw the poor woman into a snow drift. Her children were also thrown after her through the broken windows.

The house was set ablaze.[42]

To save her children, Natalia quietly returned to her former house. She was there discovered and killed along with one of her three children. Ten years later, her husband, Petro Sydorenko, returned home and found his two remaining children. He was arrested, and activists found a Bible and other religious books in his possession. "This 'crime' required special punishment. He was led into the forest, his eyes gouged out, tongue and nose cut off, hands broken, and then shot at close range. When people found his body on June 1, 1943, they could hardly recognize their good neighbor."[43] For the activists, it seems, there could not have been execution without some "friendly" foreplay.

Danylo Artemenko's other children all died in the Izhevsk Gulag.[44]

UPSHOT

In this lengthy chapter, I have focused on Stalin's policy of dekulakization—his commitment to the riddance of the kulaks as a class—and the various, often violent means of implementation. This was, in some sense, the beginning of Stalin's cruelties, as leader of the Party. By the late 1930s, he would customarily remove anyone, even those of significance in the Party, execute them, and

---

[41] F. Fedorchenko, "Tragedy of Danylo Artemenko," 214–15.
[42] F. Fedorchenko, "Tragedy of Danylo Artemenko," 216.
[43] F. Fedorchenko, "Tragedy of Danylo Artemenko," 215–16.
[44] F. Fedorchenko, "Tragedy of Danylo Artemenko," 215

replace them with others willing to please him, but knowing little of the history of Stalin's rise to power and the abuses of his titanolatry.

Biographer Isaac Deuscher, who is by no means a Stalinist apologist and who writes in the middle of the twentieth century, offers this defense of Stalin's ruthlessness:

> It [Stalin's industrial revolution] has perpetrated cruelties excusable in earlier centuries but unforgivable in this. This is a valid argument, but only within limits. Russia has been belated in her historical development. In England serfdom had disappeared by the end of the fourteenth century. Stalin's parents were still serfs. By the standards of British history, the fourteenth and the twentieth centuries have, in a sense, met in contemporary Russia. They have met in Stalin.[45]

Though an apology, it is a strange argument for several reasons. First, an argument's validity is cut-and-dry. It cannot be conditioned or qualified. Yet that is a criticism that will have little appeal to those other than mavens of logic. Second and most significantly, Deutscher cites economic backwardness as a justification for numerous acts of extraordinary cruelty. Stalin was, after all, aiming to bring his country into the twentieth century by improving its industry and thereby (in theory) improving the country's standard of living for its population, so his unconcern might be pardonable.

Yet the first edition of Deutscher's book was published in 1949; the second, 1966. Thus, he was not privy to the plethora of data (testimonies, accounts, Soviet documents, etc.) during his Five-Year Plan concerning Stalin's atrocities, directed especially at Ukrainians, which has been readily available to later scholars—especially at the fall of the USSR in 1991. Nonetheless, he was privy and did write about the numerous executions at the behest of Stalin later in the 1930s, covered in the afterword, to eliminate the hundreds of thousands of "spies," "counter-revolutionists," and "conspirators"—the Bolsheviks of Lenin's day, members of the NKVD, members of the Red Army, and anyone who merely knew too much about just how Stalin went about his business. Only a few, like Stalin's right-hand man Vyacheslav Molotov, a lifelong committed Stalinist who quietly did whatever he was told and never asked questions, were not put to death at the behest of Stalin. Any argument that excuses the deaths of numerous hundreds of thousands of persons, many of whom were Stalin's Bolshevik's comrades, to justify the promise of a better future for others can only be justified by the most nearsighted, ruthless utilitarian.

---

[45] Isaac Deutscher, *Stalin: A Political Biography* (London: Oxford University Press, 1945), 343.

Chapter 8

Ukrainians' Resistance to Dekurkalization

"Trotsky was asked to answer four questions. 1. What does the Party mean to the workers of the USSR? 2. What does agriculture mean to the state? 3. What is Trotskyist opposition likely to bring the Soviet nation? 4. What does the present rule according to Stalin's general line mean?

"Trotsky replied that he must give a talk (doklad) in order to answer the questions. He was told that there was no time for that and that his answers must be as brief and possible. He thought for a while and said: "To the first question you may obtain an an-swer by omitting the first letter from my speech: doklad—oklad (burden), To the second question by omitting the first two letters: doklad—klad (hoard), To the third question by omitting the first three letters: doklad—lad (order), To the fourth question by omit-ting the first four letters: doklad—ad (hell)."

~R. Kiyanyn

In a booklet titled in translation *The Golgotha of Ukraine: Eye-Witness Accounts of the Famine in Ukraine Instigated and Fostered by the Kremlin an Attempt to Quell Ukrainian Resistance to Soviet Russian National and Social Enslavement of the Ukrainian People*, published in 1953, Dr. Luke Myshuha begins in the foreword: "The dedication to this booklet could well be: 'To the millions of Ukrainians who died in 1932 and 1933 of hunger, of a famine arranged purposely by the Kremlin regime to suppress the opposition of the liberty-loving Ukrainian peasants to collectivization.'"[1] Myshuha refers to a sad event that is called by Ukrainians *Holodomor*, or death by starvation.

Myshuha is clearly coming from a Ukrainian perspective, but his assertion is, in the main, correct. Ukrainian farmers, especially the so-called kurkuls, objected strenuously to collectivization. To be told after years of hard and efficient work that your land and your labor were no longer your own could only have been crushingly overwhelming. Resistance to the plan was not

---

[1] Dmytro Solviy and Stephen Shumeyko, *The Golgotha of Ukraine: Eye-Witness Accounts of the Famine in Ukraine Instigated and Fostered by the Kremlin an Attempt to Quell Ukrainian Resistance to Soviet Russian National and Social Enslavement of the Ukrainian People* (New York: Ukrainian Congress Committee of America, 1953), 3.

tolerated by the State and was met with brutal, often inhumane force—branding, imprisonment, confession through torture, exile, and execution—and that brutality, of course, decupled the difficulties.

As we have seen, persons generally unfamiliar with farming were managing collective farms. Overseers were chosen mostly on account of their fealty to the Party and their willingness to employ extreme measures to collectivize peasants. That was part of what would quickly become an enormous bureaucracy with overseers overseeing overseers, with Soviet police with a global presence eying anyone who might be suspected of being an enemy of the Party, with numerous others eying those eying, and mountains of paperwork. The "system" was thus grossly inefficient and inexpressibly costly.

Collectivized and individual farmers—with impossible quotas, crippling taxes, a promised "return" for their produce much less than standard market prices, and the threat of exile or even death for showing any hint of opposition to collectivization or the Party's discretionary directives—were disincentivized to produce. Many became rebellious; others, inactive through lethargy or exhaustion. Much grain was not harvested, and much harvested grain was lost due to poor means of transportation, bad processing, or neglectful storage.

Theft, especially of grain, by peasants, was commonplace. Some peasants told themselves that they were stealing food or other items that were rightfully theirs. Others told themselves that what they stole belonged to no one but to some "State": an invisible thing by invisible figures that had assumed ownership of everything.

Peasants often responded by revolts, often sanguinary. It is not difficult to grasp why there was resistance. Peasant-farmers who owned anything lost almost everything. Most importantly, they lost their independence—their ability to direct their own affairs. They were no longer in charge of what to sow and reap and when and to whom to sell. That, too, was to be determined by the invisible State, whose members seemed to be ubiquitous.

Party representatives, removed to and living in villages or in kolkhozes were execrated, and so they were sometimes beaten or killed, especially in the early stages of the Five-Year Plan. Yet resistance by peasant-farmers was met with greater force. Party-loyal activists stormed the farms to prod for hidden grain, and, in the process, confiscated other foods (e.g., beets, sunflower seeds, and potatoes), livestock (e.g., cows and pigs), farming equipment (including tractors), and even clothing and household items. During the critical years of 1932 and 1933, when all foodstuffs of any kind, even orts, were taken from Ukrainian farmers, those farmers were still required to meet state-imposed and absurdly high quotas. Whatever grain was collected was sent to Russian cities to feed laborers and exported to grain-needing nations for money to maintain and improve industry. Worst of all, "surplus" grain was kept in granaries, guarded by armed officials of the State, and potatoes were kept at distilleries, and both granaries and distilleries were often in plain sight of starving Ukrainian peasants. Victor Kravchenko reports that there was always sufficient food for members of the Party in villages suffering from want of food. In the village of Logina, there was a butter plant where butter was made, packaged, and exported to English-speaking countries, while the villagers nearby starved. He also discovered near at the railroad station near the village a brick building with thousands of poods of grain from the year prior.[2] From his observations as an activist, starving Ukrainian peasant-farmers were, consequently, not deemed a sufficient reason for the surcease of exporting and surplusing grain. Thus, rioting to get at the grain and potatoes was common, and many peasants lost their lives in a desperate effort to get food for themselves and their families.

In this chapter, I examine the methods of resistance by peasant-farmers as well as Moscow's responses to such resistance. The focus is, of course, on Ukraine.

"Fight for grain, fight for socialism!"
Shift to Compulsory Collectivization

Aggressive measures of collecting grain and other foodstuffs (*prodrazvyorstka*), Soviet collection of grain, began early in 1929—a year noted for the celebration of Stalin's fiftieth birthday. That was the year of Stalin's apotheosis. He had attained god-like status—Soviet atheists, starving for worship of some sort, could now look upon him as their savior—and thus, Stalin could take his place on the Olympus of Marxism along with Marx and Lenin. With the inpouring of congratulatory messages from all worshippers, Stalin replied succinctly, "I regard your greetings as addressed to the great Party of the working class which bore me and reared me in its own image and likeness."[3] The language was meant to appear as if his successes were derivative. He was merely the largest beneficiary of the successes of the Party. The "humility" is manifestly immodest. Moreover, the language was intentionally Biblical. He was born of the Party— an idea of Marx that was birthed by Lenin, and he was the rightful heir of Leninist rule—but he was reared in the "image and likeness" of the Party. Stalin proclaims himself to be the new, secular Christ.

The year 1929 was also noteworthy because that year, Stalin put into law stricter measures for collecting grain. The People's Commissar of Trade, Israel

---

[2] Victor Kravchenko, *I Chose Freedom* (New York: Charles Scribners' Sons, 1946), 121 and 129.
[3] Edvard Radzinsky, *Stalin* (New York: Anchor: 1997), 245.

Veitser, offered this account of the plan on January 5, 1929, for the collection of grain for the year 1928–1929 to the Presidium of the Ukrainian Central Committee:

> Last year's grain collecting plan for 65 million bushels was completed 80 per cent on the whole, 77 per cent on wheat and rye and still less on corn and sunflower seed.
>
> An obstinate resistance to the collecting plans is made by the kurkul who stubbornly refuses to sell his grain to the state.
>
> Complying with the wishes of the farmers the grain collecting plan will be carried to every village.
>
> The grain collecting plans have been handled by Ukrainian organizations: the Grain Association and the Consumers' and Farmers' Co-operatives.
>
> [Grigory] Petrovsky[4] suggests that children under government maintenance in children's homes should be given more and better food.
>
> In its resolution, the Ukrainian Central Executive Committee confirms that last year's grain collecting campaign was conducted in difficult circumstances which arose because of the poor crop on the Ukrainian steppes, the wide gap between prices on the free markets and the contracts and the resistance of the kurkuls.
>
> The Presidium of the Ukrainian Central Executive Committee further confirms that this year's campaign will also be difficult. Therefore, it proposes that the Regional Executive Committees, District Executive Committees, and villages' Soviets draw into the grain collecting campaign and the execution of the plan all the village social organizations and all organizations of the poor and middle-class farmers in order to defeat kurkul resistance.
>
> The Presidium proposes that 75 percent of the plan be completed by January 1, 1930, and the whole plan for February or March.

---

[4] Chairman of the UkSSR.

The Presidium considers the main undertaking of all Soviet and cooperative organizations to be the completion of grain collecting plans on time.⁵

The directive mentions no coercive measures, but it is significant because it marks a change of plan concerning the collection of Ukrainian grain by the Soviets. The plan of collection prior to this time has been in the hands of Ukrainian cooperatives, subordinate to the Ukrainian Central Government in Kharkiv. Yet Ukrainian farmers have been reluctant to sell all their grain for the paltry prices that the State has offered, so now there must be Soviet control of *prodrazvyorstka*, and the State will now do all that it can to force key concessions from the Ukrainian kurkuls. That comes out in a directive about centralization on November 1, 1929, which demands that all farms be collectivized and that "national state organizations" are to be eliminated in favor of "a union of all branches of agriculture in the whole of the USSR." The reason is that "all-Union management" has proven that only in such a manner can there be a scientific approach to agriculture and can organizations such as the Central Farmers' Bank, the Grain Trust, the Collective Farm Center, the Tractor Center, the Farm Supply, the Cattle Ranch, and the Sheep Ranch, *inter alia*, get corralled and made efficient.⁶

The Central Committee of the Ukrainian Communist Party replied to the January directive with this plaint on November 6, 1929:

> The individual farmer's plan can be relied on for 25 to 30 percent of the food produce plan. The remaining 70 to 75 per cent will have to be taken from the middle and poor farmers, in which case a seed shortage might occur for that group. The central grain collecting plan will not leave a single pound of grain for the people's own consumption.
>
> In some places protests are heard that the grain collecting plan is too big and cannot be completed. Ukrainian Party organizations are waging an intensive struggle with different forms of resistance to the plan. Actively assisting the government with its grain collecting plan in Ukraine are 6,500 Communists, hundreds of labor brigades and the middle-class farmers.

---

⁵ R. Kyanyin, "The Gap Between Market Prices and Contracting," in *The Black Deeds of the Kremlin: A White Book*, ed. S.O. Pidhainy, Vol. 2 (Detroit: The Basilian Press, 1955), 263–64.
⁶ *Izvestia*, 21 Nov. 1929.

The reply is a polite statement concerning the impossibility of meeting January's directive. If the plan is to be met, then the people will starve.

Yet Stalin is neither amused nor placated, and he enjoins that the demands for grain be met. The Party needs money for the sustenance and growth of its industries, and it cannot affect loans from capitalistic countries, so a war begins between the Party and the rural peasant farmers for Stalin. Says Ukrainian Y. Bondar, "Half a bushel of grain was of more value then, according to Communist calculations, than a human life which could have been saved by that half bushel." Stalin's focus was on the amount of grain collected, not those who harvested the grain. It matters little if Ukrainian harvesters suffer, even die of starvation, in the process of *prodrazvyorstka*. The socialist experiment is in a stage of crisis. The kulaks as a class, especially the kurkuls, must now be taught an unforgettable lesson through liquidation. It has become a matter of war. The Party will promote the slogan, "Fight for grain, fight for socialism." It is facile to see that the famine some years later was inevitable.[7]

An exposé in *Pravda*, early in 1930, mentions mildly aggressive measures of grain collection. In the village Oleshky of the Kherson Oblast of Southern Ukraine, there arrives a certain Korol, who bullies himself into the village and greets peasant-farmers with this message, "Those who do not [collectivize] will be deported to the Solovky Islands with the kurkuls." The farmers, afraid, sign up for collectivization.[8] There is also mention of coercion in two districts of the Vinnytsia Oblast of Western Ukraine. "Everything was subject to collectivization even the women's hope chests. All clothing, household goods and women's chests were taken to the collective farm general collection and then divided equally among everybody."[9]

W. Slobidsky gives an account of the village Vesela, near Kharkiv, which has been fully supportive of the Bolshevik Revolution, and so the Party has been favorably treating it until peasant-farmers, at the bidding of a veterinarian who arrives at the village and speaks to them of the pitfalls of collectivization, take a stand against collectivizing. During the speech, GPU activists surround the building, arrest all in attendance, and exile them to the Urals. Slobidsky adds that he once met one of the exiled members of that meeting. The man's feet and hands were severely distorted because they had been frozen while he was in exile. The man also mentioned that he once chanced upon the veterinarian,

---

[7] Y. Bondar, "Grain Collecting," in *The Black Deeds of the Kremlin: A White Book*, ed. S.O. Pidhainy, Vol. 2 (Detroit: The Basilian Press, 1955), 261.
[8] *Pravda*, 12 Mar. 1930.
[9] *Izvestia*, 18 Mar. 1930.

Ukrainians' Resistance to Dekurkalization 113

"who was moving about in freedom."[10] The implication is that the veterinarian had been working as an agitator of the Party who stirred up the farmers in the village.

A woman from the village Fediyivka of Poltava Oblast tells how aggressive brigadiers destroyed her life. Left with five children after the arrest and exile of her husband, this independent farmer had whatever food she grew—grain, beets, and potatoes—confiscated by young brigadiers. She and her children survived due to hidden grain. That still was insufficient. Three of her children swelled, died, and were buried. When brigadiers noticed the disturbed earth near the house, they suspected buried grain, even though the woman told them it was a grave. In digging for grain, they found the corpse of her boy, Oleksa, whose body they badly mutilated from the digging. The buksyors, frustrated, left without covering the corpse again with soil.[11]

In spring 1933, when the State effectively returned seed-grain to the collectives so that there could be a spring harvest, the woman, much emaciated from want of food, was given rye seed-grain by the State. That she could not plant due to her debilitated state, so she entered into an agreement with the nearby collective. It would till and seed her land in return for some percentage of the crop. When the woman and her 14-year-old boy went into her field to clip some heads of grain, they were beaten and then jailed. Yet the peasant and her boy escaped. She then gathered her other son, moved to a thicket in the forest, and lived there for a few months. She returned to her farm without incident. However, when the grain quota for her farm and for those of other individual farmers was not met, she and other independent farmers were sentenced to three years of imprisonment. To eschew imprisonment, she writes, "I was compelled to join the collective farm where I worked and cursed all those who compelled me to join this chain gang, toil there, and keep my children undernourished."[12]

Peasant-farmers came to recognize in time that the push to collectivize Ukrainian farms was a war that they could not win. The Party's fight for grain was motivated by the directive to local activists and buksyors to collect as much grain, and other foodstuffs, as rapidly as possible, and the means of carrying out that directive were left to the heartless buksyors, and they were encouraged to use the most drastic, contemptible measures.

---

[10] W. Slobidsky, "Driven into Collective Farms by GPU Provocations," in *The Black Deeds of the Kremlin: A White Book*, ed. S.O. Pidhainy, Vol. 2 (Detroit: The Basilian Press, 1955), 282–84.
[11] H.F., "Nearly Shot for Taking Stems of Grain from Her Own Field," in *The Black Deeds of the Kremlin: A White Book*, ed. S.O. Pidhainy, Vol. 2 (Detroit: The Basilian Press, 1955), 450–52.
[12] H.F., "Nearly Shot for Taking Stems of Grain from Her Own Field," 451–52.

The Party also commercially blockaded villages that could not meet their quota. On December 15, 1932, the Party decreed that Ukrainian villages undersupplying the State with grain would lose "the supply and sales of commercial goods." The decree was to apply to individual peasant-farmers and collectives. From the oblasts of Dniepropetrovsk, Don, Chernyhiv, Odesa, and Kharkiv, there were limned respectively 27, 10, 8, 15, and 6 villages on that blacklist.[13]

"The crime of 'gleaning'"
Peasant-Farmers' Resistance

Compulsatory collectivization began in the middle of 1929, when Stalin decided that the class of kurkuls had to be eliminated. Peasant-farmers were not willfully joining collectives, so there had to be a radical shift in the Party's policy. "In district after district, the voluntary principle has been replaced by coercion through threats of dekurkulization, disfranchisement, and other repressive methods." Official data of the Party proclaimed enormous successes in collectivization, but the reality was otherwise.[14] There was stout resistance to the oppressive measures of *prodrazvyorstka*.

Resistance took the form of hiding grain, slaughtering livestock, focusing on private plots in preference to the kolkhoz's fields, lethargy or refusing to work the fields and violent uprisings. I proffer several illustrations of each.

The most common form of resistance was hiding away grain. "Seeing that there was no way to satisfy the exorbitant demands of the authorities, and as a sort of passive resistance to robbery," writes the Ukrainian going by D.T., "the people began to conceal their grain. Suitable hiding places were found in gardens, fields, behind false walls, under stoves, or in sheds, leaving in the house a small quantity, sufficient only for a few days."[15] Hiding grain quickly led, as we have seen, to buksyors who were schooled both in finding hidden grain and, over time, in meeting out beatings to peasants hiding it. Collectors were given quotas to meet and rewarded for exceeding their quotas.[16] So collectors, eager to be rewarded, took everything that they could take, and Ukrainian farmers were often left with nothing to eat. Lack of emaciation to buksyors was concerning. Families that were not emaciated from starvation

---

[13] *Izvestia*, 15 Dec. 1932.
[14] Ivan Dubnyets, "Why Retreat in Collectivization Was Necessary," D.T. "Grain Collection," in *The Black Deeds of the Kremlin: A White Book*, ed. S.O. Pidhainy, Vol. 1 (Detroit: The Basilian Press, 1955), 292.
[15] D.T. "Grain Collection," in *The Black Deeds of the Kremlin: A White Book*, ed. S.O. Pidhainy, Vol. 1 (Detroit: The Basilian Press, 1955), 201.
[16] D.T. "Grain Collection," 202.

were exposed as kurkuls—enemies of the state. The logic was again pretzel. Ukrainian farmers could prove their allegiance to the State, it seems, only by a willingness to starve for it.

In Ukraine, sunflower seeds were an item commonly confiscated. Ukraine was and still is noted for its abundance of sunflowers and its sunflower oil. In the Dniepropetrovsk Oblast, as reported in *Pravda* in 1929, there was expectancy of 25,000 bushels of sunflower seed, but only 6,500 bushels were collected. The kurkuls, as private speculators, were shipping oil in packages through the mail to the towns and cities, instead of to the State. "Measures have been taken against the speculators. The number of oil mills is limited, and the amount of sunflower seed milled is restricted. Only four to five pints of oil per month is allowed for each farm family."[17]

Things worsened in 1932. In the Ukrainian town of Novoselytsia of the Chernivtsi Oblast, a decree issued on August 7 "called for the summary execution of persons committing the 'crime' of gleaning." Those who gleaned were generally imprisoned or exiled, but many were executed. Many who were imprisoned or exiled died while away. Ten persons who were sent to labor on the White Sea-Baltic Sea Canal died. Opanas Berezovsky was found, by his daughter of 10, to have 25 pounds of wheat "gleaned." He was arrested and shot.[18]

A second form of resistance was the slaughter of livestock on peasants' farms. That form of protest was natural since Ukrainian peasant-farmers were forewarned that the State, upon collectivization, would confiscate their livestock, hogs, and chickens without compensation. Consequently, many Ukrainian farmers in 1929 slaughtered their livestock and ate, salted, and hid, or sold the meat and other byproducts. Peasant-farmers flooded the markets of nearby towns with meat as well as their own tables. Many, unaccustomed to the luxury of eating meat, became ill.[19]

Early in 1930, *Pravda* notes, "Before entering collective farming the middle, and even the poor farmers try to get rid of their livestock, hoarding the money from the sale." Who is responsible for such villainy? "Under the influence of kurkul agitation—that in collective farming, their property will be taken away to make everybody equal—the farmers are not only slaughtering their beef

---

[17] *Pravda*, 24 Nov. 1929.
[18] P. Hlushanytsya, "Kremlin's Crimes in the Village of Novoselytsya," in *The Black Deeds of the Kremlin: A White Book*, ed. S.O. Pidhainy, Vol. 1 (Detroit: The Basilian Press, 1955), 205.
[19] "Ukrainian farmers, although raising livestock and fowl, rarely ate meat. Their main diet was bread and vegetables and meat was something they had for holiday dinners only. They used milk liberally but the eggs were all sold. When a hog was full-grown it went to the market. Only for Christmas and Easter holidays would a Ukrainian farmer allow himself to butcher a hog, the fat from which was made to last the year round." I. Medvynets, "We Will Kill Them and Eat Them Ourselves," in *The Black Deeds of the Kremlin: A White Book*, ed. S.O. Pidhainy, Vol. 2 (Detroit: The Basilian Press, 1955), 237.

cattle but even the milch cows and sheep and are selling their horses for half their value."[20] Some two weeks later, *Pravda* reports, "In the Blahosloyev District [of Ukraine], the number of horses has been reduced by 14 percent, sheep by 39 percent, oxen 84 percent, grazing cattle 70 percent, milch cows 13 percent." The newspaper continues: "In the village Zavadiwka, Odesa region, the blockheads announced socialization of livestock without previously preparing the farmers and on the following day out of 400 sheep only 167 were left. The rest were killed. Out of 600 cows, 200 remained and it is not known what became of the missing."[21]

A third form of resistance through protest was a partial or complete refusal to work. Although many Ukrainian farmers soon joined collectives—most had no choice—there was little enthusiasm to produce pursuant to the increasingly ambitious aims of the Party. There was, in general, no reward for increased production, only punishments for failure to meet quotas. High production was rewarded with even higher goals of production. Ukrainian farmers, thus, often merely refused to work the farms. Many focused on their private plots, which were granted to farmers as some concession to their loss of property, not the government-owned fields.

Petro Grigorenko, the only Russian general to be exiled by Stalin—many were shot—relates in his *Memoirs* that when he went to the Ukrainian village Archangel, a village of some 2,000 farms, he discovered only eight men working the fields and no overseer. When he confronted some of the laggards about not harvesting the grain, they acknowledged that the grain would rot. Their apathy was not a form of protest. They were merely pococurante: They had been pushed to complete indifference. "The people were so repulsed by the forced collectivization of farms that they were consumed by apathy."[22] At some point, many became too weak to work.

Yet peasant-farmers, even those enfeebled by hunger, were often forced to work the fields of their collectives. In many instances, shock brigadiers, who infiltrated Ukrainian villages, roused the peasant-farmers each morning for work, though the farmers took their time in readying for work, and those brigadiers oversaw production.

---

[20] *Pravda*, 11 Jan. 1930
[21] *Pravda*, 24 Jan. 1930.
[22] Petro Grigorenko, *Memoirs* (New York: W.W. Norton, 1984), 39.

Fig. 8-1. Exiled Female Kulaks Deforesting, 1930

Source: Wikipedia

Nonetheless, without incentives to work in the collectives and incensed by the ignorance of managers of the collective from cities, farmers dallied in the fields, and yield by Ukrainian peasant-farmers in 1931 was some 40 percent less than the year prior. Throughout 1931 and early 1932, *Pravda* published numerous exposés on a dearth of production in Ukraine in 1931.[23] Conditions in 1932 would be worse. Sowing and reaping lagged behind expectations in all parts of the USSR, but lagging was greatest in the Caucasus and especially in Ukraine. On March 2, 1932, *Pravda* noted, "Ukraine is in the last ranks of grain collections."[24] The farmers by that time had become just too starved to farm.

Rebellions or uprisings were the fourth sort of resistance. When Ukrainian peasant-farmers were not so starved in the early years of collectivization that they still had pluck and pride, they rebelled. Such jacqueries ranged from mild protests apropos of the injustices of collectivization to arson and sanguinary uprisings. There were thousands of such uprisings in Ukraine.

Hnat Sokolowsky mentions an uprising that began in the hamlet Osadchg of Dnipropetrovsk Oblast. As many of the insurgents were in sympathy with the League for Liberation of Ukraine—*viz.*, they were Ukrainian nationalists—the insurgency quickly spread to nearby oblasts. On one occasion, a large band of insurgents—armed with scythes, pitchforks, and old firearms—rushed toward

---

[23] Petro Dolyna, "Introduction," in *The Black Deeds of the Kremlin: A White Book*, ed. S.O. Pidhainy, Vol. 2 (Detroit: The Basilian Press, 1955), 25–26.
[24] *Pravda*, 2 Mar. 1932.

Pavlohrad, where the 30th Division of the Red Army was stationed. The insurgents' leader had communications with Commander Myasoyedov of the division and in sympathy with the insurgents, and urged him and his men to join the insurgency. Myasoyedov and his staff were arrested, and GPU troops came and quashed the rebellion and imprisoned and executed many of the participants.[25]

The harsh measures of the GPU in Osadchg led to further resistance. Farmers burned grain-yards and other significant buildings. There were more arrests. Sokolovsky was arrested and thrown into Cell 6, in which he was crammed with 82 other men such that no one could lie down. The prisoners were "interviewed" in the typical Soviet manner: torture. Those who confessed to crimes did so only to stop being beaten. "After a month of such 'examination' in the Vasylkiv Prison, we were taken to a provincial penitentiary in Dnipropetrovsk and from there, with broken ribs, teeth knocked out and jaws split, we were sent to concentration camps."[26]

What is remarkable is the valiant role women played, especially Ukrainian women, in resistance. Women's uprisings (*babski bunty*) were common and often effective, perhaps because it took an especially hardened buksyor to beat or kill a woman.[27] Women fought dispossession by aggressively confronting, sometimes attacking, activists. Gen. Petro Grigorenko states that there was a clever method to those rebellions. The peasant women of the villages would assault the young activists of the Komsomol and other agents of the Party at the collectives. Because only women were the assailants, the activists at first seldom asked for military backup. If the activists, however, attacked the women, then the men would intervene.[28] In Odesa Oblast, for example, in February 1930, women confronted local activists, disbursed them, and regained lost property. In the village Vizirka of Odesa Oblast, a certain Rashkov came and spoke menacingly of the need for Ukrainians to form a kolhosp (Ukr. for kolkhoz or collective). The men listened in silence and with unconcern, but the women set upon the Bolshevist, tore off his clothes, and thrashed him. The State then sent members of the Twenty-Five Thousanders to terrorize the village, but even that was to no avail.[29]

---

[25] Hnat Sokolowsky, "Anti-Collective Unrest in Ukraine," in *The Black Deeds of the Kremlin: A White Book*, ed. S.O. Pidhainy, Vol. 1 (Detroit: The Basilian Press, 1955), 217–19.
[26] Hnat Sokolowsky, "Anti-Collective Unrest in Ukraine," 218–21.
[27] Robert Conquest, *The Harvest of Sorrow: Soviet Collectivization and the Terror-Famine* (Oxford: Oxford University Press, 1986), 157.
[28] Petro Grigorenko, *Memoirs*, 36
[29] Hnat Sokolowsky, "Anti-Collective Unrest in Ukraine," in *The Black Deeds of the Kremlin: A White Book*, ed. S.O. Pidhainy, Vol. 1 (Detroit: The Basilian Press, 1955), 217.

Not all women's jacqueries were successful. In February 1930, in a collective in the Ukrainian village Viknyna, a few hundred kilometers to the south of Kyiv, the collectivized cattle were dying, and the plows and other instruments were decaying from rust; there rose a women's rebellion. "Desperate women armed with pokers, hay forks and oven irons fell upon the collectives with great shouts, tongue lashings and curses addressed to the Russian occupants and in a moment the collective ceased to exist." The GPU came in a few days, arrested many, exiled some, and executed others. Order was restored to the collective, but with the loss of laborers, the collective's land was mostly fallow.[30] In the village Pleshy of Poltava Oblast in the spring of 1933, starving women rushed to the store of grain and stole much grain. A GPU detachment fired on the women, and many were killed.[31]

UPSHOT

In this chapter, I have shown how peasant-farmers resisted the aggressive Stalinist measures to collectivize and urbanize the Soviet countryside. Peasant-farmers, recognizing that there was nothing substantive to gain by collectivizing and quite much to lose, resisted collectivization through hiding grain, slaughtering farm animals, hebetude, and even violent uprisings. Stalin would respond at first by relaxing compulsory measures and next by even more aggressive measures of forcing collectivization that would soon lead to widespread famine in Ukraine.

---

[30] Oleksader Hai-Holowko, "The Tragedy of Viknyna," in *The Black Deeds of the Kremlin: A White Book*, ed. S.O. Pidhainy, Vol. 2 (Detroit: The Basilian Press, 1955), 292.
[31] Hnat Sokolowsky, "Anti-Collective Unrest in Ukraine," 218.

Chapter 9

Respite & Resumption

"Successes have their seamy side, especially when they are attained with comparative 'ease'—'unexpectedly' so to speak."

~Joseph Stalin

Joseph Stalin, as Leon Trotsky noted, was a highly unimaginative thinker. He ever tended to approach difficulties with force, often violent force. When force met with failure, as it often did, he then tended to explain it by recourse to saboteurs, who sometimes forced for him a change of plan. Yet, the adoption of a change of plan was often a stopgap measure—a temporary reprieve as if to catch one's breath—before implementation of more forceful measures. That was the case with the failure of collectivizing farms. He began in 1928 with willful collectivization, shifted to compulsory collectivization in 1929, and then to the elimination of kulaks as a class early in 1930.

Yet early in March 1930, there was, for the nonce, a radical shift in policy due to over-excited activists and the resultant rebellions of peasant-farmers.

"Dizzy with success"
Halting Aggressive Activists' Actions

On March 2, 1930, Stalin gives a speech, "On Questions of the Collective-Farm Movement," better known as "Dizzy with Success." The speech, later published, is typical of many of Stalin's most singular speeches. He starts by underscoring several unqualified successes of his Five-Year Plan. He here begins by citing the enormous successes of collectivizing farms. "The Soviet government's successes in the sphere of the collective-farm movement are now being spoken of by everyone. Even our enemies are forced to admit that the successes are substantial." Thus, "a radical turn of the countryside towards socialism may be considered as already achieved."[1]

Then enters pandemonium, as Stalin turns to reasons for panic. There are dangerous enemies lurking. The unqualified successes, it seems, are to be

---

[1] Joseph Stalin, "Dizzy with Success," *Pravda*, 2 Mar. 1930.

qualified. They have made members of the Party "dizzy with success"—one of the most quote-worthy of Stalin's lines. Activists have become vain and conceited, hence lightheaded. In such dizziness, they have lost "all sense of proportion and the capacity to understand realities." In such a manner, "they show a tendency to overrate their own strength and to underrate the strength of the enemy." Activists, wallowing in confidence, expect the impossible, and that has become a detriment and danger to the Party and to the collective farm movement.[2]

Stalin focuses on two points. First, the successes of collectivizing the farms are due to "the voluntary character of the collective-farm movement" and "taking into account the diversity of conditions in the various regions of the USSR." Second, the Party has identified "the main link in the movement" toward collectivization as the agricultural artel: the socialization of labor, usage of land, machines and tools, livestock, and agricultural buildings.[3] The first point, we have clearly seen, is an obvious yarn and requires no amplification. The second point is procedural. Stalin argues: "The [agricultural] artel is the main link of the collective-farm movement because it is the form best adapted for solving the grain problem. And the grain problem is the main link in the whole system of agriculture because, if it is not solved, it will be impossible to solve either the problem of stock-breeding (small and large), or the problem of the industrial and special crops that provide the principal raw materials for industry." So, the agricultural artel is best suited to solve the problem of grain, and a solution to the problem of grain allows for stock-breeding, food for laborers in cities, and money from exported grain to improve the industry in cities.

Activists, dizzied by success, have put the cart before the horse, as it were. They want to socialize dwelling houses, small livestock, dairy cows, and poultry without solving the grain problem, and they want to do so "when the artel form of collective farming is not yet consolidated." Moreover, they aim to socialize what should not be (at least, not yet) socialized: household gardens and orchards, dwelling houses, dairy cows, and small livestock. It is as if one were to build a house without establishing a suitable foundation. "Where artels are not yet consolidated, attempts are being made to skip the artel framework and to leap straight away into the agricultural commune. The artel is still not consolidated, but they are already 'socializing' dwelling houses, small livestock and poultry; moreover, this 'socialization' is degenerating into bureaucratic decreeing on paper, because the conditions which would make such socialization necessary do not yet exist."[4]

Stalin is reacting to overly zealous attempts to enforce collectives on peasant-farmers. He is plainly aware of problems with quotas and collectives. It is likely

---

[2] Joseph Stalin, "Dizzy with Success."
[3] Joseph Stalin, "Dizzy with Success."
[4] Joseph Stalin, "Dizzy with Success."

not so much that he objects to the means of enforcing *prodrazvyorstka*, but instead that those means are having deleterious effects: resistance, not compliance. He mentions one "socializer" who demanded that an artel register all poultry in three days and have special commanders both for registration and supervision of that task and for occupying key positions in the artel—i.e., to have all aspects of the artel under the strictest control. He mentions certain "revolutionaries" who begin collectivization by removing the bells from churches. He sums rhetorically, "How could there have arisen in our midst such blockheaded exercises in 'socialization,' such ludicrous attempts to overleap oneself, attempts which aim at bypassing classes and the class struggle, and which in fact bring grist to the mill of our class enemies?"[5]

Some accounts of overly aggressive measures of collecting grain have been published in the Soviet papers. In October 1929, *Pravda* mentions drunkenness and thievery in the village Lukobarske of the Proskuriv District of Ukraine. The collectors there comprise a Polish officer and several kurkuls, hooligans, and drunkards. For those refusing to hand over grain, the collectors are confiscating peasants' property—they bought (stole) a fanning mill for 1.1 rubles, which they sold for 60 rubles—and spent their profit on drink. There were no repercussions.[6]

Stalin's speech comes not long after a speech on January 21, 1930, in which he argues dynamically for the elimination of the class of kulaks. The means are not to be mere restrictions to their activities, such as taxations, for such means are only partly effective as long as kulaks are allowed to own instruments of production and have the right to free use of land. Kulaks "must be smashed in open battle."[7] The implication seems to be that anything goes.

Yet on March 2, Stalin backsteps. He now argues that collectors must be sensitive to the resistance of peasant-farmers to collectivize and to differences in circumstances and culture.

What the speeches of January 21 and March 2 show is Stalin's now somewhat "compliant" commitment to socialism. He was never averse to the use of harsh, extreme measures to its implementation and to the use of even harsher, more extreme measures if the harsh, extreme measures were not working. Yet he was also willing to adopt radically different measures, even measures inconsistent with socialism in the short term, to advance socialism.

Those speeches also show that Stalin's "programs" of collectivizing and then of compulsatory collectivization through dekulakization were not smartly

---

[5] Joseph Stalin, "Dizzy with Success."
[6] *Pravda*, 22 Oct. 1929.
[7] J.V. Stalin, *Intrasnaya Zveda*, No. 18, 21 Jan. 1930.

designed. In short, there were no programs. Stalin proceeded *au pied levé*.[8] He gave activists no rubric. Instead, they were given goals, and they were enjoined to meet those goals.

Stalin's policies through his directives were reactive, not proactive. He issued directives, as we have seen, for collectivizing the peasants' farms and bringing in urbanites with the scantest training, to direct those affairs with the implicit order, "You know what to do, so get it done." The lack of a rubric was intentional. Failure then could not be directed at Stalin, but on his agents. No one could counter, "But the plan was defective," for there was almost always no plan.

Moreover, Stalin probably never expected such inflexible resistance to his plan for "industrializing" the countryside. His belief was that the advantages of State-owned collectives for all would be obvious—modern machines for ease of labor, more efficient use of land, greater yield—and that peasant-farmers, seeing those advantages, would merely willfully collectivize. Only when there unexpectedly was heavy resistance by peasant-farmers to collectivize did Stalin come up with an "inarticulate" plan.

That is large evidence that the theory behind attempts at implementation—e.g., forced integration of kulaks by severe restrictions on their activities, then compulsory collectivization, and later dekulakization—was defective, perhaps severely flawed. That socialization seemed to be working in urban areas was used as evidence that it would also work in rural areas. Part of the theoretical difficulty was Stalin forcing "facts" to confirm his theory—Stalin's uptake of the Gospel of Marx despite incommodious facts.

No finer illustration of the inefficiency of dekulakization exists in the amount of manpower needed to oversee collectivized farms and the prodigious financial cost. There was, I reiterate, an ever-growing political bureaucracy. There was amaranthine resistance to collectivization because it was immediately seen that peasant-farmers were asked to give all that they had to the State, and they were threatened with alienation, dispossession, exile, and even death, if noncompliant with collectivizing. With continued resistance to Soviet decrees and with the continual occurrence of often violent revolts, there needed ever to be in villages activists to propagandize, GPU members to spy for the Party, a police force, a mobile force of the GPU to quash uprisings, and then a large number of GPU spies to ensure that the activists, GPU spies, and police were doing their job. There were also the "rewards," costly when added up, given to spies and pickthanks among the Soviets—the sycophantic informers.

---

[8] Says Conquest: "No such programme existed. … Stalin and his closest associates hustled the part step by step into the full campaign without having any established plan on which argument might take place." Robert Conquest, *The Harvest of Sorrow: Soviet Collectivization and the Terror-Famine* (Oxford: Oxford University Press, 1986), 144.

Information was funneled up to the Party's Central Committee, whose job it was then to issue decrees to identify the poisonous kulaks. One can readily see that the cost of running a collective farm was extraordinarily exorbitant when compared to the cost of individual peasant-farmers, each running his own farm. The cost of proving correct Marxism was exorbitant and cripplingly so, and here I have merely sketched the heavy bureaucracy involved with the countryside. It was worse in cities. As Stalin's paranoia grew, so too did the network of activists, police, spies, and uber-spies.

Stalin's Marxism, his revolution from above, failed in kolkhozes because the enormous system with its abundance of channels—where managers of farms knew little about farming, where different answers to questions were put forth by different offices, where data were poorly procured or procured to satisfy Stalin's whims, where the process of readying for procurement of data was complex, where proposals needed to be vetted and revetted before they got to Stalin, where all issues deemed important needed Stalin's approbation even if he was not readily available, and where all agencies and agents, even the police, needed to be policed, *inter alia*—disallowed anything like efficiency. It was literally a Hydra's head. Yet the official Soviet data, unsurprisingly, belied the reality. It was manufactured to show the efficiency of a well-designed and well-oiled governmental machine—the triumph of Stalinist Marxism and the moribundity of capitalism.[9]

The collectives could not grow and flourish, as any growth and prosperity would be funneled upward to keep alive the prodigious and ever-bloating bureaucracy needed to keep in check the peasant-farmers of the kolkhozes. Whenever there were seen to be problems, the solution was always the ever-expensive greater checks and controls from above, when the farmers, if left to themselves, could have managed their affairs suitably well, without the implementation of laws upon laws. Further laws meant further restrictions on peasant-farmers and that, of course, disincentivized those who were not dispossessed of property, exiled, or killed from working hard. Again, the more peasant-farmers produced, the more the State would take. The ever-increasing intrusiveness of the State fattened the system, thereby making it increasingly expensive and thereby alienating ever more the farmers from their produce. It was ever more difficult to imagine how this "revolution from above" would someday liberate the peasant-farmers and create a thriving mass of fattening proletariats. The peasants of farms quickly saw that only the Party was getting fat.

Yet there were attempts at sustenance and growth of Ukrainian kolhosps. Y. Maslivets says that of the total income of a Ukrainian kolhosp in 1932, up to 35 percent was targeted for a reserve fund, some 15 percent for a "cultural fund,"

---

[9] Merle Fainsod, *Smolensk under Soviet Rule* (Cambridge: Cambridge University Press, 1958), 265, and Naum Jansy, *The Socialized Agriculture of the USSR* (Stanford: Stanford University Press, 1949), 451.

some 10 percent for a "relief fund," and another 10 percent for "other funds." The remaining, some 30 percent, was relegated to the farmers, and each was paid at year's end pursuant to his "work days." A kolhosp would make extra money by encouraging members to grow other crops—e.g., sunflowers for their oil—and sustain livestock—e.g., pigs for their meat—so that members could buy oil and meat, though at inflated prices (4–5 rubles for a pound of sunflower oil and 3.6–6.8 rubles for a pound of pork, while members were paid 0.1–1.2 rubles per day). The Soviet papers published hyperbolized accounts of how kolkhozes throughout the USSR flourished, but "Ukrainian farmers fell prey to Russian imperialism, a form of material misery and lawlessness hitherto unknown."[10] In sum, the promised prosperity they never saw.

And so, being dizzied with success, Stalin, on March 2, 1930, is euphemistically and elliptically saying that collectivization is not working because the activists have been trying too forcefully and irrationally to convince peasant-farmers to collectivize. Thus, Stalin returns to—at least, he here pays mouth honor to—his early view that collectivization must be a willful process and must be sensitive to cultural or regional differences. He is wholly unconcerned that the notion of compulsatory collectivizing, a "life-and-death struggle," is a policy he has advocated some months earlier.[11]

Thus, at some point, Stalin throws the peasant dogs some bones to placate them, at least for the nonce.

First, as noted above, he allows for peasant-farmers of collectives to have small "private plots" (Figure 9-1), which are to be granted to farmers who put in all their labor days and remain committed first to the goals of the State. Private plots, of course, are much inferior to the collectives' plots and difficult to farm; the richest soil is for the kolkhoz. Some of the plots awarded to peasant-farmers were not grubbed or arable and thus were of little worth or worthless and refused.

Second, Stalin announces that those unsatisfied with collectivization can leave. In April 1930, Stalin says in *Pravda*: "We are dividing the land into individual farms for those who do not wish to farm collectively, and then once more we shall socialize and rebuild until kulak resistance has been broken once and for all."[12] What he fails to say is that those departing will be generally given

---

[10] Y. Maslivets, "What Did Ukrainian Farmers Gain from Collective Farms?" in *The Black Deeds of the Kremlin: A White Book*, ed. S.O. Pidhainy, Vol. 1 (Detroit: The Basilian Press, 1955), 194–95.

[11] J.V. Stalin, "Concerning Questions of Agrarian Policy in the USSR" (27 Dec. 1929), in *Marxists Internet Archive*, https://www.marxists.org/reference/archive/stalin/works/1929/12/27.htm, accessed 19 Dec. 2022.

[12] Joseph Stalin, *Pravda*, 17 Apr. 1830.

less land than they owned prior to collectivization, that that land will be on the outskirts of the collective, and that that land, perhaps because it has never been grubbed, will also be inferior in quality.

Fig. 9-1. *Haymakers,* Volodymyr Orlovskyi, 1878

Source: Eurmaidon Press

Third, on May 20, 1932, the Central Executive Committee and Sovnarkom decrees that peasant-farmers who have met their quotas can sell the surplus on the free market. The idea again is to quell the peasants' increasing discontent.[13] There is little risk here by the State. Scant few of the kolkhozes and individual farms will be able to meet the exorbitant quotas.

And so, those were the generally meatless bones that Stalin was throwing at peasant-farmers. They were temporary concessions—"we are really for you, not against you"—an effort to appease disgruntled peasant-farmers. Those meatless bones, as they were *prima facie* attractive, also allowed for easy identification of kulaks. Anyone leaving a kolkhoz for an individual farm, for instance, could be readily identified as a kulak. Anyone focusing too much on a private garden was also a kulak. Those anti-Leninists would have to be crushed.

---

[13] Stanislav Kul'chyts'yi, "The Holodomor of 1932–33: How and Why?" in *East/West: Journal of Ukrainian Studies,* Vol. 2, No. 1, 2015: 105.

"A Mortal Blow against the Class Enemy"
Resumption of Aggressive Activism

Throwing meatless bones to the peasant dogs was evidence of Stalin vacillating on his policies, which were never well articulated. Stalin would put into place a directive without instructions, order subordinates to implement that directive, issue plenty of pro-directive slogans for the masses, and, if it did not work, place blame on those "enemies of the Party" who were coordinating or implementing the directive.

For Stalin, resistance to collectivization would eventually be overcome—especially among Ukrainians. Independent farmers would be burked through heavy taxes and quotas until many gave up the dream of farming their own plots and collectivized.[14] In Ukraine, peasant-farmers would, in time, be starved into submission—at least, those farmers who did not perish from want of food. That is the story of subsequent chapters.

Though the rural kolkhozes did poorly, the urban factories produced much, though there was little grain for the cities.[15] The Party vaunted that laborers earned a handsome wage, yet the money had no purchasing power. Inflation was rampant in the USSR. The ruble in 1932 was almost one-fifth its market value in 1927, and so workers could buy little with their money. Goods were too pricey. Nonetheless, laborers in factories enjoyed much greater "prosperity" than collectivized farmers, inasmuch as the farmers, given Stalin's always present concerns for dekulakizing the collectives, not only had problems meeting quotas and paying taxes but also, especially in Ukraine, merely staying alive. There was scant food in Ukraine early in the 1930s. Thus, many flocked to cities to find work, thereby exacerbating the problem of insufficient grain for the cities and for export.

Despite the decree of May 20, 1932, the collection of grain in Ukraine in 1932 was off. The head of the Soviet government in Ukraine, Vlas Chubar, writes to Stalin and Viacheslav Molotov to warn them of impending disaster. "In order to better secure themselves for the winter compared to last year, [the peasant-farmers] will begin the mass theft of grain." On the same day, Hryhorii Petrovs'kyi, head of the All-Ukrainian Central Executive Committee, writes to Molotov and Stalin, "Because of starvation the peasants will be gathering

---

[14] Yet many other individual farmers persisted, despite the taxes, and in the main and despite their disadvantages, tended to fare better than collectivized farmers. Robert Conquest, *The Harvest of Sorrow*, 267.

[15] Robert Conquest, *The Harvest of Sorrow*, 169.

unripened grain, and much of it may perish in vain."[16] Ukrainian peasant-farmers, remembering the lack of grain during the winter of 1931, were cognizant that they could perish if they did not keep some grain for their own consumption. Stalin responded by rescinding the pledge of May 20, 1932. He instead aggressively proposed what would be dubbed the Five Ears of Grain Law (18 Nov. 1932), which declared that all property of collectives was State-owned and that theft of any such property would be punished by ten years of imprisonment or, in some instances, death.[17] There were, in addition, meat (25-month quota of meat) and potato (one-year quota of potatoes) penalties for independent and collective farms that did not meet government-given quotas.[18] The presumption again was that those farmers not meeting quotas were hoarders, not that they had no grain for the quotas.

Having encountered difficulties in procuring grain from Ukraine in the summer of 1932, the deputy head of the GPU, Vsevolod Balyts'kyi, was sent to Ukraine. There, he discovered "organized sabotage of state grain deliveries and the fall sowing, organized mass thefts on collective farms and state farms, terror toward the most steadfast and staunch Communists and activists in the countryside, the influx of dozens of Petliurite emissaries (see chapter 3), and the distribution of Petliurite leaflets." He advocated trenchantly "exposure and smashing of the counterrevolutionary, insurgent underground and the infliction of a decisive blow at all counterrevolutionary, kulak-Petliurite elements" that were corrupting the Ukrainian peasantry.[19] Balyts'kyi was telling Stalin just what Stalin wanted to hear.

As if there were not enough fetters on Ukrainian farmers, the Party introduced another fetter, designed chiefly to keep Ukrainian peasant-farmers on the farms and under the keen vigilance of the State: The Internal Passport. This law, formalized in December 1932, decreed that no peasant could move to a city without the Party's approbation. Months later, the confinement was tightened. Peasant-farmers were not allowed to leave a collective farm without the consent of those overseeing their collective. Individual farmers needed the consent of some representative of the Party. Prior to those laws, peasant-farmers, especially in Ukraine, had been highly mobile. They migrated to cities or other areas for work when the conditions for profitable farming were poor.

Those laws severely restricted their mobility by tying farmers to their farms, both independent and collective farms. Their fate, thus, was the fate of their

---

[16] Stanislav Kul'chyts'yi, "The Holodomor of 1932–33," 105.
[17] Stanislav Kul'chyts'yi, "The Holodomor of 1932–33: 105–6.
[18] Anne Applebaum, *The Red Sorrow: Stalin's War on Ukraine* (New York: Random House, 2017), 227.
[19] Stanislav Kul'chyts'yi, "The Holodomor of 1932–33": 106–7

farm: produce or perish. The intendment of the law was also, perhaps chiefly, to track "migrating" kurkuls—to keep them in Ukrainian villages where there was widespread famine at the time, as we shall see in chapter 11.[20] It is impossible not to see those directives as punitive measures, given their timeliness. Ukrainian Semen Modul writes of numerous posters to which he was privy after the directives. One read: "Passportization—A Mortal Blow against the Class Enemy."[21]

With that noted, the psychology of these restrictions for members of collectives was evident. A peasant could not merely pick up and move to a place where his options for material success were best. He was now willy-nilly wedded to his collective, for the option to withdraw came with even further albatrosses that made the possibility of sustenance—of continuing to live-unlikely. Many peasant-farmers saw this as a return to the serfdom suffered prior to the Russian Revolution. What, then, was the point of the Russian Revolution?

UPSHOT

In the end, collectivization was a victory for the Party. By June 1929, just over one million holdings were on collective farms. By March 1, 1930, that number jumped geometrically to 14.26 million, and it continued to rise due to punitive measures.

That victory, however, was Pyrrhic. Agrarian production was off, and the number of livestock by 1934 was reduced by over 60 percent. Robert Conquest sums:

> Not a superior agriculture. Not a contented peasantry. On the contrary, agricultural production had been drastically reduced, and the peasant-farmers driven off by the million to death and exile, with those who stayed reduced, in their own view, to serfs. But the State now controlled the grain production, however reduced in quantity. And collective farming had prevailed.[22]

Thus, Stalin's victory was one of forcing collectivization on the peasant-farmers of the USSR—Ukrainians being especially targeted because of their fecund, black-soil steppe. The will of the Party, Stalin's will, had been imposed on, and had quashed, the will of the peasantry.

---

[20] H.M., "Passports—A Blow against Class Enemies" and "The Single Passport System throughout USSR," in *The Black Deeds of the Kremlin: A White Book*, ed. S.O. Pidhainy, Vol. 2 (Detroit: The Basilian Press, 1955), 457–60.

[21] Semen Modul, "Passportization—A Mortal Blow against Class Enemies," in *The Black Deeds of the Kremlin: A White Book*, ed. S.O. Pidhainy, Vol. 2 (Detroit: The Basilian Press, 1955), 461–63.

[22] Robert Conquest, *The Harvest of Sorrow*, 159 and 187.

Chapter 10

The Problem of Nationalization

"It is terrible to lie in chains,
To rot in dungeon deep,
But it is still worse, when you are free
To sleep, and sleep, and sleep."

~Taras Shevchenko

Resistance to collectivization was Stalin's largest challenge of his Five-Year Plan. Resistance, we have seen, was firm and immediate. Ukrainian ruralites posed a hefty problem. Ukrainian peasant-farmers were fiscally prudent and of an independent disposition, and so they wanted no part of socialization.

There was another nodus for Stalin. Many peasant-farmers in Ukraine resented the interference of Moscow, a Russian city, in their affairs, which they considered to be, if not distinctly Ukrainian, at least non-Russian. Over time, the Ukrainian intelligentsia drew from the culture and stories of the peasants in the villages of Ukraine and began to concretize a social and political identity that in some measure to be centered on stories, more fantastic than factual, of Ukrainian Cossacks' push to be independent of Poland and Lithuania to the west and Russia to the east.[1] The end of World War I and the tohubohu of the Russian Revolution offered an ideal opportunity for actions directed at independence and perhaps even nationhood, but as we have seen in Chapter 1, those efforts failed due to incapacity to support political ambitions with military might.

Stalin always saw any advocacy for a Ukrainian nationality, distinct from Russia, as a threat to his one-country socialism. In this chapter, I cover Stalin's actions to quash any attempt to craft a sense of Ukrainian identity. My account, limited to one chapter, is necessarily selective.

---

[1] Serhii Plokhy, *The Cossack Myth: History and Nationhood in the Age of Empires* (Cambridge: Cambridge University Press, 2012).

"Kulak arithmetic"
The New Kurkuls

In his address of April 2, 1930, on the progress of the collective-farm movement, Stalin's first point concerning the unmatched success of collectivization is dual: It has succeeded so well because the collective movement has been voluntary, not coerced, and because the collective movement has taken into consideration regional material and social variations, before implementation.[2] The falsity of the first statement concerning the voluntariness of this compound sentence has been shown in the prior chapter. The second statement, concerning the accommodation of regional variations, too is false but requires amplification—especially as it relates to Ukraine.

The largest malfunction of collectivization was a social failure, failure of neglect, which had both regional and cultural components.

Concerning the regional disregard, Stalin could not see—and perhaps this incapacity was merely refusal to see—that the atmosphere of the country was much unlike the atmosphere of the cities. In aiming to introduce urban methods of agricultural production—that is, to model agricultural production after production in the factories of Russian cities—he failed to realize that the urbanite manner of living was drastically different from, and, in the eyes of the peasants, inferior to, the ruralite manner of living. Soviet farmers, once "formally" freed from the serfdom under the tsars (1861) and again with the chaos of the Russian Revolution, were experiencing a second serfdom, for they were chained, often broken, by cumbrous taxes, quotas, and albatrosses of other decrees in the effort to collectivize farms, which would be in the main overseen by urban incompetents. Stalin faced amaranthine resistance by the peasant-farmers because he was taking away a manner of living freely—the freedom that existed in the peasantry after the Revolution.

There was also cultural disregard. His notion of the ideal Soviet culture—godless, materialistic, technological and scientific, industrial, progressive, "urban," and equalitarian (at least in theory), and there is overlap in these categories—was appropriate to all Soviet republics and was to be a model (again, at least in theory), established by the future successes of the Soviet Union, for all nations of the globe, regardless of culture, and region. The potential reward of such socialization was a secular utopia, covered more fully in the last chapter, so worthwhile and humanly desirable that all means, even

---

[2] Joseph Stalin, "Dizzy with Success," *Works*, Vol. 12 (Moscow: Foreign Languages Publishing House, 1955): 199.

the extermination of a significant percentage of the people in the USSR, were deemed apposite for its fruition. There was ultimately—despite his claim that socializing other republics entailed due consideration of soil, climate, culture, and so on—no tolerance of deviations from that model, and more significantly, no tolerance of deviations from Stalin's discretionary directives.

Cultural disregard manifested itself in Stalin's plan to Russify all the Soviet republics, even republics where the culture was radically different from that of Moscow.

Yet kolkhozes failed miserably in Islamic republics. In Kazakhstan, for instance, well over 40,000 households were dekulakized, as Moscow tried to introduce collective farms on a culture—nomadic, with poor soil, and accustomed to herding and pasturing animals—and so the enterprise could only have been abortive. There was no sensitivity to the Kazakhs' way of life over the centuries, their wishes, the nature of the soil and the nature of the climate. Stalin wanted uniformity with the Party's aims. Hence, he aimed to fix the nomads into "arable" plots of land so they could be collectivized—to liquidate "the *bai* semi-feudalist [and] tribal attitudes."[3] In 1926, 80 percent of the population of Kazakhstan lived through herding; by 1930, that number had been reduced to 27 percent, though cultivated lands increased only by 17 percent—a trifle.[4] Those new kolkhozes were unproductive due to poor soil, dry conditions, and nomads who were disinclined to be farmers. Livestock that was not intentionally slaughtered by Kazakhs was gathered and put into the collectives. Of 117,000 gathered and put into the giant State farms, there were only 13,000 by the end of winter.[5]

The Party's failure to accommodate the nomadic nature of its Islamic republics was no isolated incident of oversight. It was the Party's policy. Stalin was invariably a Procrustean figure. He was not merely the head of the Party; he was the Party. No republic of the Great Union was to have an identity independent of the mother republic, Russia, because Moscow was the political center of the great USSR. Russification of other republics would facilitate ease of communication, and Marxism as a political philosophy aimed at economic industrialization of the globe, and the science of economics, which spoke a language universal to all, was to be the sole "cultural" glue.

---

[3] S.K., "The Kazakhs Slaughtered their Cattle," in *The Black Deeds of the Kremlin: A White Book*, ed. S.O. Pidhainy, Vol. 2 (Detroit: The Basilian Press, 1955), 243–44, and Robert Conquest, *The Harvest of Sorrow: Soviet Collectivization and the Terror-Famine* (Oxford: Oxford University Press, 1986), 191.
[4] Martha Brill Olcutt, "The Collectivization Drive in Kazakhstan," in *Russian Review*, Vol. 40, 1981, 133–34.
[5] S.K. "The Kazakhs Slaughtered their Cattle," in *The Black Deeds of the Kremlin: A White Book*, ed. S.O. Pidhainy, Vol. 2 (Detroit: The Basilian Press, 1955), 243.

Thus, Stalin thought nothing of cultural differences between Ukrainian and Russian peasants. Like Russians before him, Stalin did not consider Ukraine to be culturally unique and distinct from Russia. Ukraine was "Little Rus"—a term, long in usage, that could be taken pejoratively or diminutively—and differences in the two cultures—differences in language, especially noticeable in the rural villages—were due to the vulgarity of Ukrainian peasants whose distance from the progressive Russian cities like Moscow and Petrograd militated for their Russian Philistinism.

Yet Ukrainians, especially to the east of the Dnipro River, were corrupted even more by exposure to the capitalistic West and by Ukrainian pundits who sought ever to Westernize or "derussify" Ukrainians. Russians throughout the centuries were very chary about the contaminative influence of Western countries like Poland and Lithuania on Ukrainians. Situated neatly between the West and the East, Ukraine was the gateway between the capitalist Western nations and Russia to the East. It was thus an admixture of Western and Eastern ideals as well as Scandinavian and Islamic ideals from the North and South, respectively. Many of those situated in what would be Ukraine of Stalin's day over time came to see themselves not as Little Russians, not as Poles, not as Scandinavians, and not as Turks, but as a people with their own stories, their own foods, their own religious rituals, and their own heritage. Evidence of that was that they were formally recognized as a republic of the USSR and not as part of Russia. In the chaos after World War I, as we have seen, Ukrainians nearly formed their own nation. The Bolsheviks kept that from occurring.

Once he eventually established himself as the Boss of the Party—he was commonly referred to as *Vozhd*—after the death of Lenin in 1924, Stalin had a watchful eye on Ukrainians' push for independence and saw it as the major threat to Soviet socialism. It was the largest of the Soviet republics, had fecund black soil that was ideal for grasses of all sorts, offered Russia access to the Black Sea, and was a buffer between Russia and the capitalist West. Thus, as early as 1928, when Stalin reversed Lenin's Ukrainization policy with the advent of his Five-Year Plan, the issues of dekurkalization and denationalization of Ukrainian peasants were seen to be dependent, not insofar as the one materially entailed the other—Stalin wrote as if it did—but insofar as kurkuls were seen increasingly to harbor notions of nationalism and insofar as nationalists were increasingly seen to be friendly to kurkuls. And so, for Stalin, the Ukrainian nationalist question became the kulak question.

The Problem of Nationalization

By 1932, the year when the famine in Ukraine began to rage, Ukraine had been much more collectivized (70 percent) than Russia proper (59 percent).[6] If the success of collectivization was due, as Stalin said early in 1930, to willful integration and sensitivity to material and cultural regional differences, how could Ukrainian nationalism to Stalin be a threat?

By 1933, kulaks, Stalin thought, had insidiously entered the Soviet kolkhozes to destroy the system while inside the system. Stalin was committed to the sinister infiltration of a new sort of kulak—nationalist kulaks, who had entered the kolkhozes not to facilitate and assist the aims of the State, but to destroy the State. The kulaks were now *in* the kolkhozes, as card-carrying members of the Party, where they could work most inconspicuously to undermine the system. The kulaks as a class had been exterminated, but numerous individual kulaks remained and entered the system to devastate the system.

Fig. 10-1. Bourgeoisie, Priest, and Kulak Pulling Alexander Kolchak, Viktor Deni, 1919

Source: Brown Library

What led Stalin to that remarkable conclusion?

Stalin addressed that question in a speech titled "Work in the Countryside" on January 11, 1933.[7] He answers, "The face of the class enemy has changed of

---

[6] Robert Conquest, *The Harvest of Sorrow: Soviet Collectivization and the Terror-Famine* (Oxford: Oxford University Press, 1986), 220.
[7] Joseph Stalin, "Work in the Countryside," in *Marxists Internet Archive*, https://www.marxists.org/reference/archive/stalin/works/1933/01/11.htm, accessed 17 Nov. 2022.

late." The kulak "has changed his tactics—has passed from frontal attacks against the collective farms to activities conducted on the sly." He continues:

> People look for the class enemy outside the collective farms; they look for persons with ferocious visages, with enormous teeth and thick necks, and with sawn-off shotguns in their hands. They look for kulaks like those depicted on our posters. But such kulaks have long ceased to exist on the surface. The present-day kulaks and kulak agents, the present-day anti-Soviet elements in the countryside are in the main "quiet," "smooth-spoken," almost "saintly" people. There is no need to look for them far from the collective farms; they are inside the collective farms, occupying posts as storekeepers, managers, accountants, secretaries, etc.

These on-the-sly kulaks were outwardly in favor of collectivization, yet on the inside, "they carry on sabotage and wrecking work." These on-the-sly kulaks were outwardly in favor of procurements for grain, yet on the inside, they seditiously asked for "a fund for the needs of livestock-raising three times as large as that actually required" and for "six to ten pounds of bread per working member per day for public catering."

By aiming to implement a plan that wholly disincentivized laborers in the country, by using coercion and a one-size-fits-all method and culture for all regions in the union of republics, by introducing urban methods to enhance bucolic production, and by building an overstuffed bureaucratic machine that was impossibly expensive, incapable of efficiency, and increasingly paranoid, collectivization of the farms could not work.

Stalin could never accept that conclusion, however strongly supported by the available evidence. The countryside had to be collectivized, for Marxism disallowed private ownership of property. To allow for rural farms to remain privatized while the cities were collectivized would be an admission of the failure of Marxist socialism, which could not tolerate any amount of capitalism. And so, when he encountered the failure of his Stalinist Marxism in the kolkhozes, Stalin marshaled forth his enemies of the Party, and they were everywhere, and everyone, even the staunchest Stalinist, was a suspect. Nevertheless, perhaps the biggest saboteurs were Ukrainian kurkuls, the new kulaks, who seemingly eagerly collectivized but did so, in Stalin's mind, to obliterate socialism in Ukraine and push for a separate Ukrainian identity.

When confronted with statistics concerning the heavy demands for Ukrainian grain at the plenum of the Ukrainian Central Committee in February 1933, it was acknowledged that the supply of grain was reported to be low, but those reports were based on biased evidence. Pavel Postyshev, head of the

Organizational Instruction Department of the Central Committee and an official of the Party close to Stalin, reports:

> The officials begin to show you statistics and tables on the low harvest which are compiled everywhere by enemy elements in the kolkhozes.... But these statistics say nothing about the grain in the fields or that which was stolen or hidden. But our comrades, including various plenipotentiaries, not being able to understand these false figures thrust upon them, often become champions of the kulaks and defenders of these figures. In countless cases, it has been proven that this arithmetic is purely kulak arithmetic; according to it we would not even get half the estimated amount. False figures and blown-up statements also serve, in the hands of enemy elements, as covers for thefts, for wholesale stealing of bread.[8]

The official position of the Party was ever that low reported yields benefitted kulaks, working from within to destroy the kolkhozes by failing to reap all grasses or stealing and hiding grain that belonged to the state. Many of the saboteurs were Ukrainian nationalists, so the nodus now was Ukrainian nationalism.

"Without the right to correspond "
"De-Ukrainizing" Ukrainians

Stalin was ever against the independence of any Soviet republic, especially Ukraine. In "Marxism and the National Question," written in 1913 and a famous early publication, Stalin acknowledges that Russia at the time is in a transitional stage of development. The aim is "the complete democratization of the country," and to that end, all reasonable means must be considered. Despite the "imperialism" of the West, "Russian Marxists cannot dispense with the right of nations to self-determination." Yet nations may, for whatever reasons, wish to "remain within the framework of the whole." Ought such nations to be culturally and nationally autonomous? In other words, can there be a political whole, a super-nation, comprising culturally independent nations—a form of federalism?[9]

---

[8] Robert Conquest, *The Harvest of Sorrow*, 242.
[9] Joseph Stalin, "Marxism and the National Question," in *Marxists Internet Archive*, https://www.marxists.org/reference/archive/stalin/works/1913/03.htm, accessed 22 Jan. 2023.

There cannot, says Stalin. First, it is artificial and impracticable to make a whole nation of "people whom the march of events, real events, is disuniting and dispersing to every corner of the country." Second, "it stimulates nationalism," "national curiae," or "national peculiarities," each of which is incompatible with socialism.[10] In short, if the satellites of the whole are to be nationally distinct, their unity will be nominal, not actual.

The solution, he asserts, is "*regional* autonomy" for entities like Poland, Lithuania, the Caucasus, and Ukraine, but wholesale political integration into the whole. The benefits are chiefly four. "It does not deal with a fiction bereft of territory"—*viz.*, it deals not with theory, but reality. Next, it breaks down national barriers and focuses on unity, not division. Third, it utilizes the natural resources of a region and develops its productions without recourse to the directive of a common central authority. Last, regional autonomy will not be threatened by "oppressed" minorities—e.g., the Poles in Ukraine or the Jews in Poland—so long as the "old order" is supplanted by "complete democratization." The new order must be sensitive to the pockets of minorities and the possibility of their discontent, but that is readily alleviated by allowance "of use [of] its native language." And so, to incorporate, as it were, regions of former nations, like the Caucasus and Ukraine, into a national whole, there must be "equal rights of nations in all forms (language, schools, etc.)."[11]

To the difficulty of "organizational federalism and cultural-national autonomy" of other nations—that for Stalin is a problem in that "unlimited federalism leads to complete rupture" or separatism—the only cure is the internationalization of "Social-Democracy." The first step is for Russia to unite all nationalities into "single, integral collective bodies" and those collective bodies into "a single party." Stalin is introducing a top-down theoretical policy to address the evils of liberalism.

There are, Stalin adds, two ways of achieving functional political unity. There is the federalism of the Bund, which entails the demarcation of workers according to nationalities, and there is an international organization with territorial autonomy. Both, however, entail a compromise of principles, and there can be no compromise. Stalin sums tellingly, "Principles triumph, they do not 'compromise.'"[12]

Some 12 years later, Stalin again addresses the national question as it relates to the Soviet Union and the problem of the peasants. There is, unsurprisingly, a sea change of stance to the Bolshevik Left. He adds on March 30, 1925, that the

---

[10] Joseph Stalin, "Marxism and the National Question."
[11] Joseph Stalin, "Marxism and the National Question."
[12] Joseph Stalin, "Marxism and the National Question."

peasant question is the national question, but the "is" here is not the "is" of identity, in the sense of "Everything flawless is perfect," but the "is" of predication, in the sense of "Every lime is a fruit." The peasant question is part of the larger national question, but it constitutes the core of it. Stalin elaborates:

> It is quite true that the national question must not be identified with the peasant question, for, in addition to the peasant question, the national question includes such questions as national culture, national statehood, etc. But it is also beyond doubt that, after all, the peasant question is the basis, the quintessence, of the national question. That explains the fact that the peasantry constitutes the main army of the national movement, that there is no powerful national movement without the peasant army, nor can there be. That is what is meant when it is said that, in essence, the national question is a peasant question.[13]

There can be no push for independence without a peasant army, so the national question is reducible to the peasant question. The national question is much larger than the peasant question, considered a problem, and the latter is wholly a part of the former.

There is, expectedly, confusion in the argument. Stalin argues, in effect, that a nation's push for independence cannot succeed without an army of peasants. If one prevents the peasants from rising in revolt, if one solves the peasant question, then there is no possibility of a republic attaining statehood.

According to this argument, the peasant problem here comprises *solely* the nodus of peasants striving for statehood, independent of the USSR. So, if we can prevent the peasants from uprising, we solve the national problem, or so goes the argument.

Yet, as we have seen, the peasant problem, identical to the kulak problem, is much larger. It includes peasants who are uninterested in nation-building but hostile to collective farms. Thus, the national problem seems to be part of the peasant problem, not the converse.

Still, it does follow that if we solve the peasant problem, then the national problem disappears because the peasant problem consists of (1) peasants unhappy with collectivization, (2) peasants committed to independence, and, of course, (3) peasants both unhappy with collectivization and committed to independence. Thus, neither can be reducible to the other.

---

[13] Joseph Stalin, "Concerning the National Question in Yugoslavia," in *Marxists Internet Archive*, https://www.marxists.org/reference/archive/stalin/works/1925/03/30.htm, acessed 18 Nov. 2022.

Notwithstanding Stalin's paralogisms and despite his avowed commitments both to voluntary acquiescence to collectivization and to consideration of regional variations when collectivizing, he has never had any interest in allowing any republic to have any sort of culture independence to that of Russia, and he has never cared for voluntary acceptance of Russification. He has tolerated notions of cultural identity independent from the mother country only inasmuch as his resources have demanded that he has had, for the nonce, to tolerate them. And so, all satellite republics, willy-nilly, are to be collectivized.

The most problematic nodus always concerned Ukrainians. Ukraine was ever the USSR's plumb. Rich in soil and replete with other natural resources, Stalin refused to allow Ukrainians to see themselves as culturally distinct from Russia. Moreover, the secession of Ukraine could speedily snowball and lead to the secession of other, lesser republics. In a December 1932 letter to Lev Kaganovich, who at the time was a member of the Politburo and headed other significant offices, Stalin says, "We should set ourselves the goal of turning Ukraine into a real fortress of the USSR, a truly model republic." The aim is to set into place new cadres to supplant current leaders of the Ukrainian Soviet and the Ukrainian government. Stalin accuses Ukrainian Soviets in the letter of mechanically implementing Ukrainization, "without taking account of the concrete particulars of each district, without careful selection of Ukrainian Bolshevik cadres." That made it easy for counter-revolutionists, the bourgeois, to flourish.[14] This comment is just over two years after his speech concerning the dizziness of many incautious activists of the Party.

In the North Caucasus Territory to the east of the Black Sea, there were over three million Ukrainians, and Ukrainian culture therein was in frondescence. With Lenin's about-face with the New Economic Plan in the early 1920s, there were Ukrainian primary schools as well as prominent institutes such as the Ukrainian Pedagogical Institute in Krasnoda and the Ukrainian Pedagogical Technical School in Poltavkaya. By 1929 and after the demise of Lenin, however, Stalin began the expurgation of Ukrainian culture. Most of the professors of the two institutes had been arrested on trumped up charges, along with other literary and political Ukrainian figures. By 1937, all 746 Ukrainian primary schools in Kuban were Russified.[15] Literary figures were especially attractive targets, as many were in the process of creating a Ukrainian culture—a culture distinct from that of Russia. Nearly 250 literati disappeared; so too did 62 linguists. "Nowhere do repression, purges, subjection and all types of bureaucratic hooliganism, in general, assume such deadly proportions as in

---

[14] Serhii Plohky, *The Gates of Europe: A History of Ukraine* (New York: Basic Books, 2021), 252.
[15] Robert Conquest, *The Harvest of Sorrow*, 278–79.

Ukraine in the struggle against powerful subterranean striving among the Ukrainian masses toward greater freedom and independence."[16]

Political expurgation in Ukraine began at the top. As famine raged in the countryside, many key figures within the Ukrainian Communist Party were accused of pushing toward nationalism and arrested. Three key figures were Mykola Skrypnyk, Matvii Yavorsky, and Mykhaylo Yalovy.

Fig. 10-2. Mykola Skrypnyk

Source: Encyclopedia of Ukraine

Mykola Skrypnyk (1872–1933, Figure 10-2) was a lifelong communist and activist who, by 1917, had been exiled seven times. Skrypnyk would hold many important Soviet posts. In March 1918, he was appointed by Lenin as the Peoples' Secretariat of the Soviet Government of Ukraine. As a member of Russia's Cheka, he oversaw the section for fighting counterrevolution. As commissar to Ukraine, he performed many vital Bolshevik functions and earned membership to the Central Committee in April 1920 of the Ukrainian Communist Party and the All-Union Communist Party. One of the foremost scholars of his day, he directed the Ukrainian Institute of Marxism-Leninism (1928–1930) and oversaw the Ukrainian Society of Marxist Historians from 1928. As the Ukrainian Commissar of Education (1927), he worked to advance Ukrainian culture and to improve literacy among Ukrainians. At the Orthographic

---

[16] Robert Conquest, *The Harvest of Sorrow*, 272.

Conference in Kharkiv in 1927, he worked toward formalizing the first standardized Ukrainian alphabet, which was adopted the next year.[17]

While he strived for Ukraine's cultural autonomy from Russia, Skrypnyk was never an advocate of Ukraine leaving the Soviet Union and forming an independent nation. He was too much of a committed Bolshevik for that. Nonetheless, as a Ukrainian and adherent of the Ukrainization of the UkSSR, he often, and understandably so, encountered Russian hostility, as attempts to preserve or promote Ukrainian culture were adjudged contrary to Stalin's socialization of Russia's many republics.

While Lenin saw Skrypnyk as someone who advanced Soviet interests in Ukraine—Skrypnyk, to ingeminate, never advocated for Ukraine being independent of the Soviet Union—Stalin wanted nothing to do with the preservation of Ukrainian culture. He replaced Skrypnyk in January 1933 as Ukrainian Commissar of Education with Pavel Postyshev, who had an adversarial relationship with Skrypnyk and who claimed falsely that Skrypnyk made Ukrainian nationalism the "cornerstone" of his ideology—"an end in itself." Thus, Skrypnyk was not a committed Bolshevik but a Ukrainian nationalist. Skrypnyk saw his liquidation was to be soon, and so he committed suicide in preference to receiving a bullet to the back of his head.[18] His suicide was officially declared by the Party to be "an act of faintheartedness particularly unworthy of a member of the Central Committee of the All-Union Communist Party."[19] "Faintheartedness" was a euphemism for saying that Postyshev and Stalin were disallowed the pleasure of knowing Skrypnyk had died from a Soviet bullet.

Matvii Yavorksy (1885–1937) graduated from Lviv University in 1910 with a degree in law. A disciple of Marx, he became a member of the Ukrainian Communist Party in 1920 and headed the history section of the Ukrainian Institute of Marxism-Leninism as well as Ukrholovnauka—an institution that supervised scholarship in Ukraine. He wrote much on the history of Ukraine, but his works smacked of a Marxist slant. Nonetheless, he was attacked by Russian Bolsheviks for being more of a nationalist than a Marxist. He was removed from the Ukrainian Communist Party in 1930 and arrested in March 1931. Exiled to the Solovets Islands, he was killed in 1937.[20]

---

[17] "Mykola Skrynyk," in *Internet Encyclopedia of Ukraine,* http://www.encyclopediaofukraine.com/display.asp?linkpath=pages%5CS%5CK%5CSkrypnykMykola.htm, accessed 21 Nov. 2022.
[18] "Mykola Skrypnyk," in *Internet Encyclopedia of Ukraine.*
[19] Robert Conquest, *The Harvest of Sorrow,* 268.
[20] "Matvii Yavorsky," in *Internet Encyclopedia of Ukraine,* http://www.encyclopediaofUkraine.com/display.asp?linkpath=pages%5CY%5CA%5CYavorskyMatvii.htm, accessed 21 Nov. 2022.

Mykhaylo Yalovy (1895–1937) was a novelist, poet, playwright, and editor of the Ukrainian State Publishing House. A committed communist, he also worked assiduously to promote an independent Ukrainian culture through unabated wit in his publications. He was arrested on May 13, 1933, and charged with aiming to overthrow the government. He was summarily executed on November 3, 1937.

Removal of such key figures—thousands more can be listed—was merely a small part of Stalin's push to expunge any notion of an independent culture in Ukraine. Ukrainian nationalists, to any degree, were enemies of socialism. Thus, Ukrainian academies, institutes, and learned societies were not institutions of socialism to Stalin, but institutions of "class-enemy ideology" that needed expurgation. That ideology was nationalism, which kept those Ukrainians from joining "organically with the Party." Targeted institutions were the Agricultural Academy, the Shevchenko Research Institute of Literary Scholarship, the Ukrainian Institute of Eastern Studies, the Ukrainian Chamber of Weights and Measures, the Ukrainian Film Company, the Ukrainian Institute of Philosophy, and even the Karl Marx State Institution in Kharkiv. Ukrainian institutions of the arts were also purged. On November 19, 1933, Postyshev vaunted that 2,000 nationalists, 300 scientists, and writers among them, had been "cleaned out." Eight Soviet institutions were purged of 200 nationalists. Of those working in the cooperatives, 2,000 were found to be nationalists through the Party's inimitable means of disclosure and removed. The motivation for this expurgation of thousands of Ukrainians in key positions in Ukraine was "nationalist deviation."[21]

Fig. 10-3. Ukrainian Kobzars Mykhailo Kravchenko and Petro Dravchenko, Old Postcard, 1902

Source: Encylopedia of Ukraine

---

[21] Robert Conquest, *The Harvest of Sorrow*, 269–70.

In 1933, Ukrainian kobzars (e.g., Figure 10-3) were invited to a congress by Stalin Kharkiv in 1932. In the manner of Homer, kobzars were itinerant musicians, often blind, who were established in the sixteenth century in the Zaporozhian Sich. They sang Ukrainian epics, religious songs, and folk songs and did much over the centuries to establish, create, and preserve a Ukrainian identity independent of Poland and Russia. While they sang, they played a bandura or kobza. Once assembled in Kharkiv by Stalin, all were arrested and taken outside the city, where they were executed.[22]

"Instead of the bells we shall enjoy the hum of the tractors"
Stripping Ukrainians of their Right to Worship

"Communism and religion are mutually exclusive," said T. Samsonov of the Soviet Cheka. "No machinery can destroy religion except that of the [Cheka]."[23] Marxism was an ideology, wholly material, that praised man, not God, and thus, peasants had to be stripped of their belief in an otherworldly God before there could be complete faith in the Party. For Stalinist Marxism to take root, Ukrainian godliness had to be supplanted by Marxist godlessness, and the febrility of religious worship had to be supplanted by the febrility of Stalinism. Consequently, the question of God was at the heart of the Stalinization of Ukraine.

What struck most the hearts of Ukrainians was the attempt to remove their religiosity, which was the heart and soul of most villagers' lives. After the mayhem following World War I and with the introduction of Lenin's New Economic Policy, by 1923, there were 2,000 Orthodox churches in Ukraine, with 2,500 priests and 36 bishops.[24]

Religious toleration began in 1918 when a new law placed religious propaganda on a par with non-religious propaganda. Each was allowed free expression. Yet the Party controlled the printing presses, and religious buildings, like monasteries or churches, belonged to the state and could be used for secular functions. Priests not only had no special status, they were, in Stalin's time, generally singled out as counter-revolutionists and enemies of the Party (e.g., review Figure 10-1).

---

[22] Dmitriy Shostakovich, *Testimonies* (New York: 1979), 214–25.
[23] Edvard Radzinsky, *Stalin* (New York: Anchor: 1997), 244.
[24] Yewhen Prirva, "The Ukrainian Autocephalous Orthodox Church," in *The Black Deeds of the Kremlin: A White Book*, ed. S.O. Pidhainy, Vol. 1 (Detroit: The Basilian Press, 1955), 488.

In 1923, however, the USSR began a sustained assault on the Ukrainian Autocephalous Orthodox Church—religious freedom being an important part of Ukraine's push for independence after World War I.[25] More than 1,000 priests, 28 bishops, and numerous thousands of others of faith were put to death.[26] The State used the Famine of 1921–1922 as an excuse to confiscate silver and golden objects and those with precious stones. There was rioting and consequently, there were arrests and executions. The "League of the Godless" was formed in 1925 to promote the atheism of the Party—especially members of the Komsomol. By 1929, to the secular education of schools, there was added instruction in anti-religion.[27]

The Party placed burdensome, usually crippling so, restrictions on churches and parishioners. A member of a church was at some point barred from office work and governmental positions. Priests' children could not attend school. Churches were confiscated; priests were persecuted. Religious materials could not be published. Metropolitan Vasyl Lypkivsky was arrested in 1923 and, in 1925, forbidden to leave Kyiv. Other restrictions were placed on bishops and other dignitaries. Lypkivsky was eventually replaced and forced to live in a solitary manner, for all visitors were forthwith arrested. He would later be again arrested and then murdered in prison. By 1932, 30 bishops, 2,000 priests, and other significant members of the church were exiled or killed by gunfire or torture.[28] Churches were looted, taxed, and misappropriated or razed, and those who protested disappeared.

All the time, the Party pushed atheism on the young of the UkSSR. Newspapers offered a flood of testimonies of young Ukrainians warming to atheism. *Izvestia* reports late in 1929: "Clubs and Red centers industries of Kyiv are preparing for an anti-Christmas campaign. An all-Ukrainian anti-religious museum will open soon in St. Volodymyr's Cathedral. An anti-religious exhibition will be held, a stage show, etc. The clubs are holding special anti-religious evenings." Again, "The Kharkiv Komsomol Organization has formed a special brigade which travels to rural areas holding meetings and aiding the anti-religious movement." Also, in Kharkiv, there were plans by young activists for a "mammoth carnival on December 25 and discussion of plans for turning Christmas into a special industrial holiday. In the Ukrainian village Zimeniv of

---

[25] For more, see Mytrofan Yavdas, *Ukrainian Autocephalous Orthodox Church, 1921–1936* (Munich: Ingolstadt, 1956).
[26] Ivan Dubynets, "Annihilating the Church and Destroying Religious Life" and "The Ukrainian Autocephalous Orthodox Church," in *The Black Deeds of the Kremlin: A White Book*, ed. S.O. Pidhainy, Vol. 2 (Detroit: The Basilian Press, 1955), 206.
[27] Yewhen Prirva, "The Ukrainian Autocephalous Orthodox Church," 488.
[28] Yewhen Prirva, "The Ukrainian Autocephalous Orthodox Church," 488.

Tsebrykiv District of Odesa Oblast, activists campaigned to remove churches from religious fantasts and to turn them into educational institutions. "Nearly the whole population voted in favor of this idea"[29]—a typical Bolshevik hyperbole. Committees of youths even took it upon themselves "to prevent prayer meetings in private homes."[30] The village Kryvychky of Ulyaniv District has symbolically left behind their religiosity. "Instead of a cross, a [Soviet] red flag is at the top of the church."[31] Shock brigades of the Komsomol in Kharkiv Oblast collected religious relics—icons, lamps, crosses, and Bibles—to be burned at a "mass anti-religious gathering." One member of a shock brigade has said, "We, the workers, are appealing to the Ukrainian people to take down the church bells not only in Kharkiv but in all of Ukraine."[32]

In Deimanivka of Poltava Oblast, Ukraine, St. Nicholas Church was "assaulted." Several members of the village's council broke through the doors of the church early in 1930. They took the crosses and bells, removed the icons and books and burned them outside, seized the rugs for their offices and the elaborate vestments and silken altar cloths, which were ripped into small pieces to become useful as tobacco pouches, and mostly destroyed the inside of the church in what they called an "Anti-Religious Carnival." The church would later be "usefully" appropriated: It would become a granary for wheat.[33]

In Pisky of Staroblisk District, Ukraine, the church was heavily taxed, but the parishioners rallied to pay that tax. Orders from Regional Headquarters then came to close the church. The first step was the removal of its priest, Father Makedonsky. He was given a ponderous tax of meat, but again the parishioners rallied. Yet he was again taxed for meat with a demand for an impossible quantity. Failing to pay the tax, he was arrested for "subversive activity" and exiled to the mines of Kuzbas for five years. He was presumed dead years later, as no one from the village ever again heard from him.[34]

There was also appropriation of religious buildings. H. Senko mentions that in his Ukrainian village, Mykhailivka, the church-owned building next to its

---

[29] *Izvestia*, 14 Dec. 1929.
[30] *Izvestia*, 5 Jan. 1930.
[31] *Izvestia*, 4 Jan. 1930.
[32] *Izvestia*, 7 Jan. 1930.
[33] H. Senko, "History of the Destruction of the Ukrainian Orthodox Church," in *The Black Deeds of the Kremlin: A White Book*, ed. S.O. Pidhainy, Vol. 1 (Detroit: The Basilian Press, 1955), 500–1.
[34] E. Mury, "The Communist Dictatorship in Practice," in *The Black Deeds of the Kremlin: A White Book*, ed. S.O. Pidhainy, Vol. 1 (Detroit: The Basilian Press, 1955), 458–59.

church, was used to interrogate and imprison counter-revolutionists.[35] In Polova Village of Chernyvtsi Oblast, Ukraine, in 1928, Fr. Pylyp was arrested, exiled, and shortly murdered. It was decided by local activists to appropriate the church as a prison for "kurkuls."[36] The same people who used the building as a house of worship would now be many of its prisoners.

In the village Klushnykivka of Poltava Oblast, Ukraine, Holy Mother of God Church had its only priest, Fr. Vasyl Vasylenko, arrested and exiled. Villagers were forced to sign petitions to convert the church into a community center. The church was ransacked on February 15, 1930, and its icons, books, and archives[37] were collected and burned. Several dashed into the blaze to rescue certain sacred items. The next day, the metal crosses and bells were removed for scrap iron to be used for Soviet industry. Yet when the Bolsheviks pushed for the community center in 1932, many villagers resisted such a sacrilegious conversion. They were collected and tortured by having their fingers broken or being placed into sacks and being kicked around the ground. They were then exiled for ten years "without the right to correspond"—a common Bolshevik euphemism for being shot. With the final renovations to the church for its use as a community center finished, the regional Communist authorities ordered that it be used as a granary.[38]

Activists of the Party who did the sacrilegious work were usually and unsurprisingly young men of the Komsomal. The most fervent Bolsheviks seemed to take special pleasure in desacralizing a church in a village (e.g., Figure 10-4). It was one thing to try to set villagers Stalin-straight by stealing grain or even exiling or killing a few peasants of a village, but quite another to break the will of numerous villagers at one time by gutting or razing their church. If the people of a village might be considered to constitute a body, then their church was its soul. The religious holidays of the year—e.g., Yordan (Jesus' baptism), Masnitsya (beginning of spring), Easter (resurrection of Jesus), Kupala Night (summer solstice), and Christmas (Jesus' birth)—marked times of respite from work and celebration. They concomitantly defined the

---

[35] H. Senko, "History of the Destruction of the Ukrainian Orthodox Church," in *The Black Deeds of the Kremlin: A White Book*, ed. S.O. Pidhainy, Vol. 1 (Detroit: The Basilian Press, 1955), 499.

[36] H. Senko, "History of the Destruction of the Ukrainian Orthodox Church," in *The Black Deeds of the Kremlin: A White Book*, ed. S.O. Pidhainy, Vol. 1 (Detroit: The Basilian Press, 1955), 506–7.

[37] Archives often contained valued information concerning the history of a village over the centuries.

[38] H. Senko, "History of the Destruction of the Ukrainian Orthodox Church," in *The Black Deeds of the Kremlin: A White Book*, ed. S.O. Pidhainy, Vol. 1 (Detroit: The Basilian Press, 1955), 503–4

agricultural season. To destroy the church of a village was, in effect, to destroy the village. For most villagers, work and worship were bedfellows. It is no wonder that many willingly faced exile or death in defense of their church.

Ukrainian priest Rev. M. Yavdas mentions his arrest by the GPU on September 8, 1929. He was a priest for only four years and only 26 years of age. He, judged to be a murderer and thief, walked some 65 kilometers to Uman. All the while, Yavdas was treated as a criminal much lower than the others. In Uman, he was enjoined to recant his religiosity. He did not, and thus was beaten. Thrown into a cell with 34 others, Yavdas mentions the daily routine: the hot black liquid in the morning, 200 grams of very soggy black bread later, a walk after the meal for 15 minutes, and then return to the cell, where the preoccupation was killing lice. After one week, he was transferred to Poltava, where he joined other priests and was again interrogated, asked to recant his religiosity, and beaten. From October 29, 1929, to February 1930, 28 priests were jailed. Five were shot, one went insane, and the others were exiled to the North. Yavdas was sent to the coal mines of the Suchan Tributary, where he, for six years, picked for coal. Some 300 persons from the more intelligent of the camp were culled to be shot. Some were burned alive. Yavdas survived his 10 years, and thereafter roamed Ukraine and beyond for odd jobs. Because he was a priest, he was denied the benefits of Soviet citizenship.[39]

Fig. 10-4. Ivan Vladimirov, Confiscation of Church Property in Petrograd, 1922

Source: Wikipedia

---

[39] M. Yavdas, "How Communists Persecute Clergymen," in *The Black Deeds of the Kremlin: A White Book*, ed. S.O. Pidhainy, Vol. 1 (Detroit: The Basilian Press, 1955), 492–96.

Confiscation of the bells of churches was especially rewarded by the Party. From the Pervomaysk District of Odesa Oblast of Ukraine, two carloads of bells were removed from churches and sent to a nearby factory. "Telegrams of congratulations have been sent to Comrade Yaroslavsky and the Central Council of Atheists."[40] In the Ukrainian village of Lysa Hora, the people overwhelmingly voted to remove all church bells. Said one villager, "Instead of the bells we shall enjoy the hum of the tractors."[41] In the Zhytomyr Oblast of Ukraine, 8,000 pounds of bells had been collected after the poor and middle-class peasant-farmers voted to close all churches.[42] "The administrative division of the City Soviet of Kharkiv," reports *Izvestia*, "has decided to close a few churches in the city. It has also decided to take down all the church bells and give them to industrial needs."[43] In subsequent months, there were many more reports of villagers all over Ukraine who had "decided that the bells [of churches] should go to help industrialization." Chepayivtsi of Zolotonosha District of Ukraine alone donated 5,000 pounds worth of bells.[44]

Why was there such a push to remove bells from churches?

The ringing of a church's bells marked the time for parishioners to be ready for service on Sunday. It also marked singular events such as the arrival of a bishop or prince, a baptism, the start or conclusion of a time of prayer, and a funeral. They were also used at times for secular purposes, such as the provenance of war, general public mourning, or to announce a fire or a flood. Soviet dissident Petro Grigorenko, though a lifelong atheist, talks of a moving aesthetic moment while imprisoned in Lefortovo. "I did not believe in God, but in my heart that church [Church of Peter and Paul] was a living being emitting a living voice. Right then, I decided that if I was freed, I would go there. ... I had come to know when the bells would ring and would put everything else aside to listen. The first chime always brought blessedness to my soul, and each time the ringing stopped I was terribly sad."[45] Removal of bells from a church was the signal, above all, that it was no longer a church. That, for many villagers, was comparable to the removal of the heart of a living being. The fact that the metals of bells would be melted and used in factories was the great victory of Marxist atheism. It also, for the Soviets, signaled victory of the hum of the tractor to the pealing of bells.

---

[40] *Pravda*, 27 Nov. 1929.
[41] *Pravda*, 30 Nov. 1929.
[42] *Izvestia*, 22 Dec. 1929.
[43] *Izvestia*, 5 Jan. 1930.
[44] *Izvestia*, 5 Feb. 1930.
[45] Petro G. Grigorenko, *Memoirs* (New York: W.W. Norton, 1982), 292.

UPSHOT

Despite insistence that collectivization of farms needed to be done both willfully and with respect for cultural differences in different republics and regions of republics, in Ukraine there could be for Stalin no respect of cultural differences. Ukraine was the most significant of the republics of the USSR, and respect for Ukrainian culture as distinct from Russian culture ever posed the threat of the possibility of Ukraine seceding from the USSR and even partnering with Western capitalist nations. Ukraine was the USSR's breadbasket, and its farms, Stalinized, would be collectivized with or without the consent of Ukrainian peasant-farmers. Moreover, the Party's avowal of respect for diversity could never be respected. Stalinist Marxism ever meant strong, central authority over all Soviet republics, and with authority in Moscow, the culture of Moscow would have to be the culture of the USSR, and Russian would have to be the language of the USSR. Otherwise communications from and to the Central Committee would be hampered greatly.

Chapter 11

The Great Ukrainian Famine of 1932–1933

"One day in May I travelled for two kilometers through the hamlets of Reshetyliv District, on the way to Doctor Podolsky. I counted eleven corpses of all ages and sexes lying by the wayside. I also saw the remains of Kolisnyk's children. Kolisnyk was at one time a well-to-do farmer, but he and his wife had died of starvation a week before.

"A few days earlier the Kolisnik's girl had gone to the chair-man of the village soviet, Mykola Zinenko, to beg for food because her parents had died, but the chairman told the child: 'To hell with you. You can all die.'"

~P. Reshetylivsky

As a result of the War Communism imposed by Lenin on the Russian Soviet Federative Socialist Republic and the aggressive *prodrazvyorstka* (collection of grain/food), issued on January 11, 1919, and applied to Ukraine, the RSFSR suffered a severe famine in the years 1921 to 1922. Russia was in shambles. It had suffered from over three years of participation in World War I, and thereafter, there was the overthrow of the tsarist regime and the lengthy Russian Revolution. During the revolution and as part of the Bolshevik decree of War Communism, grain was requisitioned from peasant-farmers throughout the RSFSR to feed the soldiers participating in the chaos. Imposition of War Communism during the Civil War was a means of state control of all major aspects of the Russian economy, inasmuch as that was possible, in an effort for Bolsheviks to sustain their revolution. The State, mostly under the rule of the Bolsheviks, assumed control of industries, foreign trade of goods, and the railways, and it forbade private enterprises. The State expropriated whatever grain it could glean from peasant-farmers and distributed it to the starving urban areas and to the Red Army.[1] At first, *prodrazvyorstka* entailed grain and fodder, but later in 1919, activists were purloining meat and potatoes, and in 1920, almost any foodstuff that could be expropriated. While 108 million poods of grain and fodder were collected in 1918–1919, that number jumped to 367 million poods in 1920–1921. Expropriation of grain, it comes as no surprise, led to marked reduction in the production of grain

---

[1] Robert Himmer, "The Transition from War Communism to the New Economic Policy: An Analysis of Stalin's Views," in *The Russian Review*, Vol. 53, No. 4: 515–29.

because all surplus grain would be seized and, consequently, there was no incentive for peasant-farmers to produce in surplus. By the end of 1922, as many as five million people in the RSFSR had perished from want of food.[2]

The famine was needlessly severe in Ukraine.[3] A brutal drought had reduced the crop in 1921 to about one-third of the normal yield, and the crop of 1922 was again poor. Yet there were sufficient reserves to see Ukrainians through the crisis; however, those reserves were expropriated by the Soviets. The grain that was not funneled to the Red Army in their civil war and to Soviet cities was sold abroad for money to sustain the war. Moreover, Ukrainian peasant-farmers were heavily taxed to support the Bolshevik cause. Though the Soviet government, once aware of the acuteness of the famine, initiated famine-relief in 1921 and sought help from abroad, those efforts were directed to the hard-hit Volga River region of Russia, not to Ukraine. International efforts for relief reached Ukraine only in 1922. Though there are no official documents to assist them, researchers have concluded that as many as one million Ukrainians died in this famine. The disinclination of Russia to assist Ukraine could have been the result of a deliberate effort by Lenin to punish Ukrainians for anti-Bolshevist, nationalist sentiments.[4]

From the years 1932 to 1933, there would be another famine, one of greater severity and scope, to hit Soviet Russia and its republics—most notably Ukraine. That famine would result in the deaths of some four million Ukrainians, though the real number was perhaps much larger. While Moscow seemed to show concern for Ukrainians in the Famine of 1921–1922[5] insofar as they needed Ukrainian grain for their needs and they needed Ukrainian peasant-farmers because they needed Ukrainian grain, the Famine of 1932–

---

[2] Veryha argues that the Soviet attitude toward Ukraine was genocidal. Wasyl Veryha, *A Case of Genocide in the Ukrainian Famine of 1921–1923: Famine as a Weapon* (Lewiston, NY: Edwin Mellen Press, 2007).

[3] For American assistance, see H.H. Fisher, *The Famine in Soviet Russia: 1919–1923* (New York: Macmillan, 1927).

[4] Adrij Makuch and Vasyl Markus, "Famine of 1921–3," *Internet Encyclopedia of Ukraine*, http://www.encyclopediaofUkraine.com/display.asp?linkpath=pages%5CF%5CA%5CFamineof1921hD73.htm, accessed 6 Jan. 2023.

[5] Kravchenko offers a first-hand account of the famine of 1921–1922. Hunger and cold predominated. Money was valueless. Typhus spread and there were daily funerals. "A thousand simple things that had been taken for granted—street cleaners, telephone service, the water supply, transport-suddenly became difficult, precious, sometimes unattainable." He adds: "Men eyed every living thing—horses dogs, cats, house pets—with greedy despair." People made soups from tree-bark and chewed on untanned leather. Every blade of grass was eaten. Even the dead were eaten. Victor Kravchenko, *I Chose Freedom* (New York: Charles Scribner's Sons, 1946), 22 and 31.

1933 was distinctly genocidal. The large-scale deaths of numerous Ukrainian peasant-farmers might prove a valued and lasting message to those remaining Ukrainians.

Dying is what Ukrainians did. The Famine of 1932–1933 is the topic of this chapter.

"Brigadiers of the Red Broom"
Inevitability of Widespread Famine

While numerous thousands of Ukrainians were moribund, the "Brigadiers of the Red Broom"—so-called because they swept clean villages of all grain and other foodstuffs—continued unabated their heartless actions. At first, such collectors comprised local communists and even criminals, but those collectors proved undependable, and so urban communists, by the thousands, the "Thousanders" or "Twenty-Five Thousanders" were sent to the farms. So well did the Thousanders do their work that they became the governing officials of the collectives.[6]

Yet there was little "surplus" grain to be found by 1932 and little grain to be found by 1933—mainly in Ukraine.[7] Still, Red brigades were enjoined to collect grain and other foods. If there was no food, they collected anything of worth, or anything deemed of worth to the peasants—samovars, rugs, utensils, and even pictures—to break the people. All peasants suffered except those engaged in brigandage.

By the year 1932, Soviet peasant-farmers, Ukrainians especially, were in trouble. Lack of incentives to work collectives or individual fields due to crippling taxes, poor pay for grain sold to the State, collection of "surplus" grains, unenthusiastic overseeing of collectives, and confiscation of other property by Soviet agents led to lethargy—unsown lands and disincentive to reap what had been sown. Still, the Party's expectations for the collection of grain were unabated and annually increased. Soviet authorities, under Stalin's orders, tightened the screws, and had activists search for grain or food of any sort that might be stored. Those with hidden grain or even any food, as we have seen, were punished severely.

---

[6] Ivan Dubynets, "The Village 'Active' and the 'Thousanders,'" in *The Black Deeds of the Kremlin: A White Book*, ed. S.O. Pidhainy, Vol. 2 (Detroit: The Basilian Press, 1955), 143.

[7] Robert W. Davies, Mark B. Tauger, and Stephen G. Wheatcroft, "Stalin, Grain Stocks and the Famine of 1932–1933," in *Slavic Review*, Vol. 3, No. 54, 1995: 645.

Confiscated reserves were sometimes kept nearby in granaries that often were overfull as if to tantalize sadistically the peasants.[8]

The Red Brooms worked so thoroughly that activists, by 1932, expected Ukrainian peasants to be bloated from starvation (Figure 11-1)—to be moribund. Peasants who were not dying aroused suspicion. That meant that there was food somewhere on the premises. It was thus proof that a family was a family of kulaks. Dmytro Soloviy mentions an incident of one member of a brigade entering a house and saying to the head: "What? You are still alive? You have not yet died?" He then interrogated the children, and he and his comrades inspected the house, found a little food, and confiscated it.[9] The Party's catawampus reasoning was thus. If you are starving, you are giving all you have to the State, and so, you prove your loyalty to the Party and are good, proud socialists—comrades of the Party. Contrariwise, if you keep food in reserve, even if only for your own subsistence, you have not given all to the State, and so, you are disloyal to the Party and selfish, execrable capitalists—enemies of the Party. Consequently, as a Ukrainian peasant, the surest proof of one's fealty to the state was to die of starvation for the state—a gnarled sort of reasoning but an argument that was entertained by numerous Red Brooms.

Not all collectors were unsympathetic. There was, for instance, mention of the Soviet head of the Ukrainian village Ridnytsya, a certain Burdenko, who discretionarily reduced the output of the peasant-farmers. Burdenko was not punished but merely sent to the village Kozlov.[10]

Fig. 11-1. Children Starving from the Famine in 1922

Source: Wikipedia

---

[8] B.A., "The Warehouses of the 'Grain-Collection Trust' Filled with Grain," in *The Black Deeds of the Kremlin: A White Book*, ed. S.O. Pidhainy, Vol. 2 (Detroit: The Basilian Press, 1955), 558.

[9] Ivan Klymko, "Escape to Donbas," in *The Golgotha of Ukraine*, ed. Stephen Shumeyko (New York: Ukrainian Congress Committee of America, 1953), 20.

[10] *Izvestia*, 1 Jan. 1933.

Why was Burdenko not punished?

The answer is that the Party was becoming aware of the acuteness of the scenario. Things were snowballing. Compulsatory collectivization, dekurkulization, heightened expectations of the yield of grain, and the hyper-aggressive measures of grain collection led to malaise among the Ukrainian peasant-farmers. In effect, farmers stopped working their fields because, at some point, everything produced would be taken from them. The yield of Ukrainian grain was in 1932 some 50 percent of governmental expectation. While the Ukrainian peasant-farmers usually had some 790 million poods of grain for their needs, in that year, they had no more than 215 million poods.[11]

Ukrainian malaise soon became Ukrainian devitalization. Peasant-farmers merely became too enfeebled to work the fields. In the spring of 1932, most districts of Ukraine were suffering from famine. When American reporter Fred Beal wrote to Hryhoriy Petrovsky, president of the Ukrainian Central Committee, about the famine, Petrovsky answered: "We know millions are dying. That is unfortunate, but the glorious future of the Soviet Union will justify it."[12] Late in 1932, numerous thousands of Ukrainians were dying from famine. Ukrainian delegates and Bolsheviks—Mykola Skrypnyk, Hryhoriy Petrovsky, and Vlas Chubar—presented collected documents concerning the famine in Ukraine at the Third All-Ukrainian Party Conference of July 1932. Moscow's high officials, Vyacheslav Molotov and Lazar Kaganovich were present. The Ukrainians enjoined Soviet officials to reduce the demands for the collection of grain lest the famine of 1932 would be greatly exacerbated. Yet Molotov and Kaganovich worried that any concessions to the enjoinments of Ukrainian emissaries would show a weakness in the Party vis-à-vis Ukraine. Demands for requisition were not lessened.

And so, there was no delay in the collection of grain. Amounts to be collected were determined on paper, without allowance for differences in local circumstances. There was, Stalin assumed, the total number of hectares available, and each available hectare was deemed arable regardless of its condition. There then was the maximum yield of a hectare, and that was not determined by inspection of land.[13] As usual with Stalin's regime, there was a wide chasm between theory and reality, and theory ever trumped reality.

---

[11] Ivan Dybynets, "The Organized Preparation of the Famine," in *The Black Deeds of the Kremlin: A White Book*, ed. S.O. Pidhainy, Vol. 2 (Detroit: The Basilian Press, 1955), 435.

[12] Simon Sebag Montefiore, *Stalin: The Court of the Red Tsar* (New York: Alfred A. Knopf, 2004), 84.

[13] Ivan Dybynets, "Excessive Grain-Collection Plans," in *The Black Deeds of the Kremlin: A White Book*, ed. S.O. Pidhainy, Vol. 2 (Detroit: The Basilian Press, 1955), 435.

The Ukrainian economist and engineer M. Hrynko proffers an illustration of Soviet cloud-cuckoo-land—that is, of catering to Stalin at all costs. Transferred to the Kharkiv District Grain-Collecting Committee, Hrynko was bid to list the district's food-products with the aim of seeing what could be sent to the State. Once done, Hrynko was called to the office of Abraham Solomonivich Nus, the director of the committee, and castigated for too few food-products designated for the State. As "proof" of Hrynko's error, Nus showed the former a letter from the Regional Committee of the State that indicated just what grains and just how many grains needed to be sent to the State. Hrynko demonstrated that if the enjoinments were thus conducted, then "in two or three months the population would be left without food and would die of starvation." Nus, agitated, counter-remonstrated: "Are you going to teach me what to do and how to do it? Figures of the amount of food products to be transferred to the State have been given by the Regional Committee—it is an order of the Party and the Government. They know what they are doing. It is not up to us to teach them. These figures have to be met at all costs." Hrynko sums:

> I was convinced that this order of the Regional Committee was consciously calculated to precipitate a state of starvation among the peasant population. I could not participate in this utterly inhuman design. I begged Nus to write to the Regional Committee, and ask them to review their order or to relieve me of my duties.

After, some time there came news from various localities to the effect that the villages were being literally stripped of all grain. The months of February and March showed that the prognosis was correct. The capital of Ukraine was filled with peasant-beggars pleading for bread. The militia could hardly keep up with the removal of corpses.[14]

Fig. 11-2. Cartful of Ukrainian Corpses, 1922

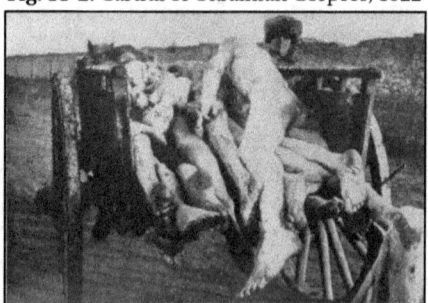

Source: Wikipedia

---

[14] M. Hrynko, "The Party Knows What It Is Doing," in *The Black Deeds of the Kremlin: A White Book,* ed. S.O. Pidhainy, Vol. 2 (Detroit: The Basilian Press, 1955), 438.

There was food in the markets of the largest Ukrainian cities, but it was sparse and inordinately expensive. V. Savur describes the daily scene of the many markets in Kyiv in the years 1932 and 1933.

> The market women sat in the stalls or in rows on the ground selling all sorts of grain by the glassful: wheat, rye, barley, millet corn, groats or some sort of meal, fish cakes, pancakes and little pies with some sort of filling. These were all priced at so many rubles each. Sales of loaves or, more frequently, slices of bread, were carried on "from under the coat." Meat, too, was sold "from under the coat"—it was mostly horse meat of questionable quality. Vegetables, such as potatoes, onions, beets, and carrots, bottled milk, and other dairy products, which were brought to the markets by the farmers from the villages surrounding Kyiv, were very sparse in quantity and extremely expensive.

The markets were ever overflowing with valuable heirlooms—necklaces, ornamental clothing, rugs, tapestries, and jewelry—and such things were bartered for "a few glassfuls of grain."[15]

Those who did not suffer from want of food benefitted greatly at the expense of the starving. Wives of high Soviet officials, Raspreds, combed the markets for bargains. They traded leftovers of food for the starving peasants' heirlooms and other valuable items. A typical exchange might be a large loaf of bread for an exquisitely embroidered shirt or blouse—a ridiculous exchange under normal conditions.[16]

There were also two other groups of people at the markets. First, there were the wives of the workers in factories, who came to the markets with whatever money they had to buy supplementary foodstuffs such as vegetables and milk. Next, there were the moribund, who left their villages, bereft of food, in a desperate attempt to beg for scraps of food in some effort to extend their life for another day. Most of the moribund rummaged through garbage for cores and peelings of vegetables and fruits. Each day, some of them would die and have their corpses packed onto trucks, driven from the city, and buried in mass graves.[17]

---

[15] V. Savur, "Death Claims the Starving at the Markets of Kiev," in *The Black Deeds of the Kremlin: A White Book,* ed. S.O. Pidhainy, Vol. 2 (Detroit: The Basilian Press, 1955), 619.
[16] V. Savur, "Death Claims the Starving at the Markets of Kiev," 619–20.
[17] V. Savur, "Death Claims the Starving at the Markets of Kiev," 620.

"The other children ... drank his blood"
Holodomor

There were efforts to punish Ukrainians for poor yield during the years of famine. A directive was issued that allowed tightened control over the economies of all Ukrainian villages, even those of the poorest peasants. The exchange of commerce between most Ukrainian villagers was forbidden. Workers and peasant-farmers were disallowed to travel within Ukraine without a special passport, the infamous Internal Passport of December 1932, and so they were bound to their village and suffered the fate of other villagers. Ukrainians were also disallowed travel beyond the boundaries of Ukraine—borders were protected by Soviet guards—to prevent the importation of food. Last, there were concerted efforts to prevent any mention of a famine in Ukraine.[18]

With such constraints put into position to ensure the isolation of Ukrainians, many opted for thievery with a large risk of death than to risk certain and slow death through want of food. In the village Chyblyn-Skadiyevsky of Odesa Oblast, the kurkul Malchenko was arrested for having stolen several sheaves of wheat. In Mykhaylivka of Odesa District, Michael Bily and Ivan Sytkevich were sentenced for stealing 35 sheaves of wheat. In Zburivka of Holo-Prystansky District, kurkul Panas Nimych purloined six wagonloads of grain from a collective. In Kopani of the Dniepropetrovsk Oblast, Antin Bondar, the kurkul Bordiuk, and several "semi-kurkuls" were arrested for drilling into and stealing much wheat from a granary. In the village, Yakymivka of Dniepropetrovsk Oblast, a certain Kozlovsky was sentenced for pilfering grain and other counter-revolutionist activities. Vasyl and Elisaveta Kharchenko infiltrated the collective "Stalin" of the village Hnativ of the Rozdilniansky District and stole crops from the collective.[19] All were sentenced to "the higher form of social defense"—execution.

While Ukrainian peasant-farmers were starving and without food, activists were especially guarded about the theft of State-owned grain. More were sent to many Ukrainian collectives to prevent any theft of grain. "Kolhosp [collective] members of Henichevsky District grasped the exceptional importance of the struggle to guard crops this year and, consequently, organized a determined resistance against kurkuls and other hostile elements who coveted the collective farm crops. In 'Stalin' commune, a vigilant detachment was organized, which carefully guarded its crop."[20] At the collective "New Life," guards comprising "better members of the kolhosp" were

---

[18] Ivan Dybynets, "Excessive Grain-Collection Plans," 433–34.
[19] *Izvestia*, 27 Aug. 1932; *Izvestia*, 30 Nov. 1932; and *Izvestia*, 14 Sept. 1932.
[20] *Izvestia*, 28 June 1933.

detached to watch over fields. "They deployed their forces so as to prevent the kurkul remnants from stealing a single kernel of grain."[21] Olena Ivasyn was sentenced to five years imprisonment for "clipping off the unripened heads of the winter crops."[22]

In 1933, numerous watchtowers (Figure 11-3), like those found in concentration camps of northern regions of Odesa and Kharkiv, were built in fields. The rationale for such towers was customary that enemies of the State might at any time "set fire to the collective farm." So, in those watchtowers, there sat armed vigilantes and guards of the GPU to keep the crops from the hungry people of the collectives. When planting, the guards watched so that the hungry members did not dig up planted seeds. When reaping, the guards watched so that the hungry members did not clip heads of the grain.[23] Activists of the Party, too, made rounds through and around the fields of collectives.[24]

Fig. 11-3. Activists on Watchtower

Source: dtkk.ru

---

[21] *Izvestia*, 28 June 1933.
[22] *Izvestia*, 11 June 1933.
[23] P. Onukhrienko, "Watchtowers on the Fields," and P. Chonusky, "Guarding Collective Farms from Own Members," in *The Black Deeds of the Kremlin: A White Book*, ed. S.O. Pidhainy, Vol. 2 (Detroit: The Basilian Press, 1955), 446–48.
[24] V. Maly, "Young Communist Killed a Hungry Woman," in *The Black Deeds of the Kremlin: A White Book*, ed. S.O. Pidhainy, Vol. 2 (Detroit: The Basilian Press, 1955), 447.

By early 1933, any Ukrainians stealing the food of the State were generally shot. On one occasion, members of one Ukrainian collective returned from a day's work, and noticed a group of hungry and disabled men, women, and children being driven by an armed soldier on horseback. "The 'criminals' were all barefoot, ragged and swollen with hunger," and each had a sack of a small amount of grain that they had from left-over grain stalks, which Soviet law had forbidden. They were herded into a barn where they were shot. It was easier for Soviets to execute the incapacitated and emaciated. When not shot, they were merely "left to starve"[25] (Figure 11-4). For the incapacitated and emaciated to remain alive, there was no other option other than to comb the fields for grain and thereby risk execution.

Fig. 11-4. Starving Ukrainian Woman with Son, c. 1932

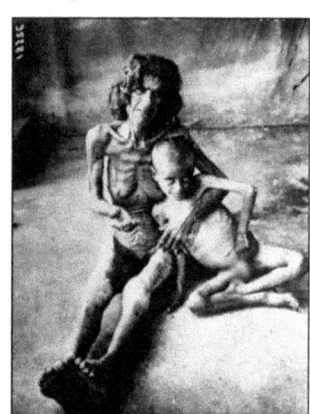

Source: Wikimedia Commons

The Party was playing a sort of game with Ukrainian peasant-farmers. The peasants were starving, yet this was a propitious time to dekurkalize, once and for all, the collectives. The reasoning was thus. Those starving peasants, who were against both the Party and socialization, would, in dire circumstances, steal from the Party and prove themselves to be its enemies. They then could be herded off and shot. Yet, as we have seen, according to that reasoning, the alternative was to prove one's fealty by starving. So, for many peasant-farmers in those parts of Ukraine where food was scarce, death, whether one was "loyal" or "disloyal," was imminent. It was merely a matter of how to die: by execution

---

[25] H.F., "Starving People Sentenced for Gleaning after Reapers," in *The Black Deeds of the Kremlin: A White Book*, ed. S.O. Pidhainy, Vol. 2 (Detroit: The Basilian Press, 1955), 449–50.

or by starvation. Many preferred risking execution. That was at least in defiance of the Party and showed some spark of life.

With want of food, hundreds of thousands died, and the crisis intensified in the spring of 1933. As the snow melted and plants fronded, starving Ukrainian peasants gathered acorns, nettles, sorrel, acacia, insects, snails, worms, marmots, and squirrels to ward off death. Those fortunate enough to live near forests or rivers had more options—e.g., deer, edible plants, or fish—though they risked getting shot for thievery.[26] All land was property of the State.

From 1931 to 1934, as many as eight million persons in the Soviet Union died. Some four million were Ukrainians, and most of the deaths occurred between 1932 and 1933, what is customarily today called by Ukrainians *Holodomor*, or death from hunger (*holod* = hunger) (*mor* = death or plague).[27]

Ukrainians, and all others moribund from hunger, resorted to desperation to ward off starvation. In a village some 30 kilometers south of Kyiv, a family boiled a strange salmagundi comprising bones, pigweed, skin or some sort, and the leather of a boot.[28] In the village Fediivka of Poltava Province, a child was beaten to death for trying to steal onions in a patch.[29] Blacksmith Ilarion Shevchuk, swollen by hunger, went to Viknyna, near Odesa Province, to beg for help. He was led to the fire hall, where men with staves killed him.[30] Victor Kravchenko mentions seeing in a hut, from his days as a young activist in Ukraine, a man fixing a shoe, a boy with a swollen face, and a woman cooking horse dung with weeds.[31]

Some Ukrainians, sensing the inevitability of death, preferred cessation of life to the unremitting pangs of hunger. The most common method of suicide was hanging. In the Ukrainian village, Chrnukhy, of Poltava Oblast, a form activist of the Party begged the district's chief to help his four starving children, who were subsequently placed in a children's home, where two soon died. Some days later, the man hanged himself from a tree near the chief's office.[32]

---

[26] S. Lozovy, "What Happened in Hydach County," in *The Black Deeds of the Kremlin: A White Book*, ed. S.O. Pidhainy, Vol. 1 (Detroit: The Basilian Press, 1955), 248.
[27] The Ukrainian verb *mortyry* means "to poison," "to exhaust," "to torment," and "to drive [one] to death."
[28] Thomas Walker, *New York Evening Journal*, 18 Feb. 1933.
[29] H.F., "Famine in the Village of Fediyivka," in *The Black Deeds of the Kremlin: A White Book*, ed. S.O. Pidhainy, Vol. 2 (Detroit: The Basilian Press, 1955), 531.
[30] Oleksander Hai-Holovko, "The Tragedy of Viknyna," in *The Black Deeds of the Kremlin: A White Book*, ed. S.O. Pidhainy, Vol. 1 (Detroit: The Basilian Press, 1955), 295.
[31] Victor Kravchenko, *I Chose Freedom* (New York: Charles Scribners' Sons, 1946), 119.
[32] Robert Conquest, *The Harvest of Sorrow: Soviet Collectivization and the Terror-Famine* (Oxford: Oxford University Press, 1986), 287.

It was also common for extreme hunger to turn members of a family against each other, and it was very common for villagers to turn against each other. People with food were often murdered for their food. In Bilka Village, Denys Ischenko killed his sister, her husband, and their daughter to get their 30 pounds of flour.[33] Ivan Klymko tells the sordid story of Vasyl Luchko of Lukashiv Grange. Klymko entered Luchko's house and said, "What are you doing Vasyl?" Replied casually Luchko, "I hung my boy." "And where is the other one?" "He is in the storeroom. I hung him." When asked why he hanged both sons, Luchko said: "Because I have nothing to eat. Every time Sanka comes with some bread, she gives it to the children. Now that the two of them are gone, she will have to give me some."[34] Luchko's testimony shows how readily hunger makes a person narrow his focus on reality. One's sole thought at some point becomes self-preservation.

Other persons were killed to serve as food for their murderers—*viz.*, cannibalism. Cannibalism was rife in Ukraine. Writes P. Lykho, "Cases of cannibalism were so numerous that Moscow had to interfere officially, so as to conceal this terrible phenomenon: the Commissariat of Justice of USSR circulated a special letter (Letter 175-K) in which it explained what should be done in cases of cannibalism."[35]

A certain Antin of Tupkalo Grange is mentioned by Ivan Klymko, who, with others, happened to be passing Antin's house on their way to the fields. They smelled rotting flesh and investigated, only to find Anton lying dead near his woodshed. Near him was an axe and chunks of human meat. He had eaten his wife and sister, whose head lay nearby. All that was left of his wife was arms and legs.[36]

J. Chmyr of the village Bridky in Kyiv Oblast writes that he was given the task of gathering the village's corpses.

> Another man and I were ordered to roam over the village and gather up the corpses. Cannibalism raised its ugly head, mothers ate their children and wives their husbands. Nastya Kyzyma ate her husband, Andriyan, and one child, and then she and her remaining five children died.

---

[33] Robert Conquest, *The Harvest of Sorrow*, 257.
[34] Ivan Klymko, "The Horror of the Famine in 1933," in *The Golgotha of Ukraine*, ed. Stephen Shumeyko (New York: Ukrainian Congress Committee of America, 1953), 25.
[35] P. Lykho, "Soviet Documents on the Famine in Ukraine," in *The Black Deeds of the Kremlin: A White Book*, ed. S.O. Pidhainy, Vol. 1 (Detroit: The Basilian Press, 1955), 232.
[36] Ivan Klymko, "The Horror of the Famine in 1933," in *The Golgotha of Ukraine*, ed. Stephen Shumeyko (New York: Ukrainian Congress Committee of America, 1953), 35.

Osadchy's wife ate him when he died, and then told the neighbors that she had buried his bones behind the cottage.[37]

Postman Trokhym Solviychuk of the village Viknyna, near the point of convergence of the oblasts of Vinnytsia, Kyiv, and Odesa, survived by eating the corpse of his wife, who died of starvation and whose corpse was fed to his three children. When the two youngest children were missing, the oldest child ran from home. Authorities dealt with the problem by silence. So gruesome was even the thought of the existence of cannibalism that people were forbidden to speak of it. Any Ukrainian speaking of the horrific crime of cannibalism was "liquidated."[38]

Klymko mentions a meat vendor in Dnipropetrovsk who made his living and kept from starvation by slaughtering villagers and selling the meat to others. Another man and his two sons killed villagers to sustain themselves. At the trial, one son said: "Thank you to Father Stalin for depriving us of food. Our mother died of hunger and we ate her, our own dead mother. And after our mother we did not take pity on anyone."[39]

In all, there are 2,505 documented cases of cannibalism from 1932 to 1933.[40] The actual number of instances, of course, cannot be known.

In Ukraine, death was more prevalent in the fertile areas around the Dnipro River (Figure 11-5 darkest regions)—e.g., oblasts of Kyiv, Cherkasy, Dnipropetrovsk, Zaporizhzhia, and Melitopol—and many regions to the far northeast—e.g., oblasts of Kharkiv, Lysychansk, and Luhansk—than in other areas. In the forested northwest, where beets were commonly grown, the number of deaths was lowest because of the flora and fauna of the forests, rivers, and lakes.[41]

Doctors were forbidden to list starvation as a cause of death, so they referred to some of the effects of starvation—lung disease, kidney failure, heart failure, stomach disease, or poor circulation of blood—as causes of death. One doctor who spoke, with due lack of circumspection, about his sister dying of hunger was given 10 years "without the right of correspondence"[42]—*viz.*, he was taken and shot. Because there was no famine, there could be no cannibalism. By the winter of 1932, so great was the number of deaths that the issuance of

---

[37] J. Chmyr, "Speak Russian or Starve," in *The Black Deeds of the Kremlin: A White Book*, ed. S.O. Pidhainy, Vol. 1 (Detroit: The Basilian Press, 1955), 232.

[38] Oleksander Hai-Holowko, "The Tragedy of Viknyna," in *The Black Deeds of the Kremlin: A White Book*, ed. S.O. Pidhainy, Vol. 1 (Detroit: The Basilian Press, 1955), 295–96.

[39] Ivan Klymko, "The Horror of the Famine in 1933," in *The Golgotha of Ukraine*, ed. Stephen Shumeyko (New York: Ukrainian Congress Committee of America, 1953), 39.

[40] Ivan Klymko, "The Horror of the Famine in 1933," 39.

[41] Robert Conquest, *The Harvest of Sorrow*, 250.

[42] Robert Conquest, *The Harvest of Sorrow*, 259.

certificates of death was deemed bootless.[43] The dead were merely anonymously carted off.

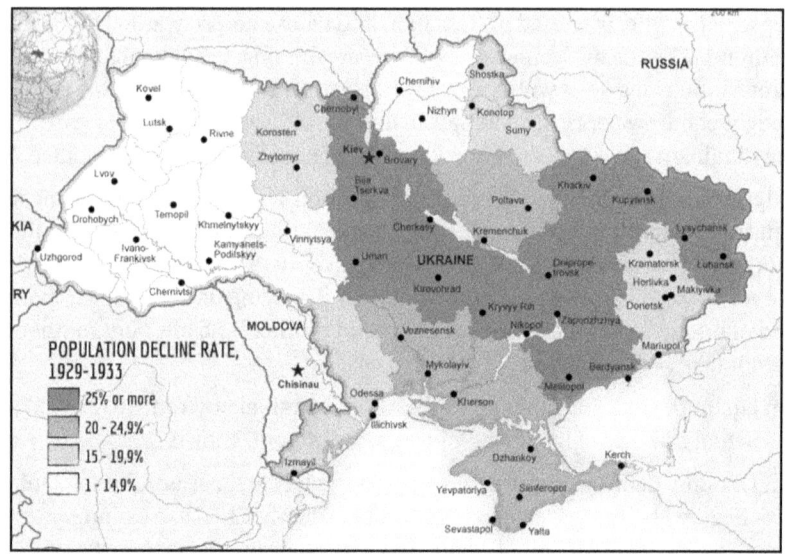

Fig. 11-5. Populational Decline in Ukraine, 1929–1933

Source: Wikimedia Commons

"In the class struggle, philanthropy is evil"

The Fate of Ukrainian Children

The most sadistic aspect of the famine was that when it was disclosed that millions were dying from want of food, nothing was done—at least, not until some critical percentage of Ukrainians had perished to make Stalin concerned about the upcoming spring harvest of 1933. To make matters worse, the crop of grain in 1932, though off, was only 12 percent below the five-year average from 1926 to 1930. Still governmental procurement of grain was up 44 percent. In 1933, of the nearly 70 million tons of grain reaped, not even one-seventieth of that was exported. Moreover, surplus grain was being held in reserve, often within the eyesight of the starving Ukrainians, in the event of a crisis, and in the meantime, millions of peasants from all "classes" were dying. Stalin, as we shall

---

[43] Robert Conquest, *The Harvest of Sorrow*, 250.

see, was aware of that. He did not think that the deaths of millions of Ukrainians constituted a crisis. Perhaps it was merely a statistic.[44]

The most insidious aspect of Stalin's purge of Ukraine concerned the fate of Ukrainian children, from infants to young teens. Children were vulnerable. There was no way to protect them from the iniquities of the famine.

First, children, due to their vulnerability, were often used as food for starving adults. Says Olena Goncharuk: "We were afraid to go out in the village because people were starving and they hunted children. My neighbor had a daughter who disappeared. We went to her house. We found her head separated from her body, and the rest of her was cooking in the oven."[45]

In Kharkiv, a group of women took it upon themselves to protect children from victimization. They turned into an orphanage, an empty shack. The orphanage was customarily noisy. Some of the children in the shack always cried from hunger. On one day, however, the shack was silent, and so some of the women became curious. When entering the orphanage, they found that the children were eating the smallest child, Petrus. "They were tearing strips from him and eating them. And Petrus was doing the same. He was tearing strips from himself and eating them. ... The other children put their lips to his wounds and drank his blood."[46]

Children sometimes were even victimized by members of their families. Marina Strizhachenko killed and ate her child one week after the death of her husband, who died from starvation.[47] In the town of Yahotyn, Sofia Krikhno killed and ate her two children after her husband was imprisoned for not meeting his quota of grain.[48]

Second, children who were deported along with their parents were the most vulnerable humans *en route* to their destination via wagon or train and in the very frigid places of exile. The churches of Vologda, for illustration, were used as waystations for persons exiled to the North. From March to May 1930, up to 25,000 children died *en route* to or in those churches.[49]

Last, there were times when a child had to be sacrificed to save another child. In 1934, one mother, who had three "fine children," explained that the three

---

[44] Stalin is reputed to have said, "If only one man dies of hunger, that is a tragedy. If millions die, that's only statistics." *Washington Post*, 20 Jan. 1947.
[45] Ivan Klymko, "The Horror of the Famine in 1933," in *The Golgotha of Ukraine*, ed. Stephen Shumeyko (New York: Ukrainian Congress Committee of America, 1953), 39.
[46] Ivan Klymko, "The Horror of the Famine in 1933," 39.
[47] K.S., "A Mother Eats Her Child," in *The Black Deeds of the Kremlin: A White Book*, ed. S.O. Pidhainy, Vol. 2 (Detroit: The Basilian Press, 1955), 655–56.
[48] V. Platavka, "In a Mad Fit She Ate Her Children," in *The Black Deeds of the Kremlin: A White Book*, ed. S.O. Pidhainy, Vol. 2 (Detroit: The Basilian Press, 1955), 656–58.
[49] Robert Conquest, *The Harvest of Sorrow*, 285.

thrived only because she allowed the three others, the least robust and intelligent, to die in the famine.[50]

Activists and officials of the Party were taught not to worry too much about the deaths of children of kulaks—the enemies of the State. One district secretary was chided for his sympathy toward a kulak's children. "Do not think of the kulak's children. In the class struggle, philanthropy is evil."[51] The message in all such instances was the same. The child of an enemy of the state would grow up to be an enemy of the state. Thus, when a parent was adjudged to be a kulak, so too were all members of the family, even infants, and so too were friends, even associates. The notion of regarding philanthropy as an evil in the struggle of classes was queer, as the promise of communism was essentially philanthropic—a better world for all.

Children who were not labeled kulaks were targeted by the Party with propaganda concerning the greatness of Stalin and the Party and the myriad benefits of collectivization and loyalty to the Party. Spoon-fed the notion that enemies of the State were everywhere—that even the most unsuspicious characters could be kulaks—peasants were conditioned, mostly through fear of repercussions, to report any suspicious activities to the Soviet of their village. They were even encouraged to search for suspicious activities in their household. That had become one of Stalin's decrees: A true "comrade" was one who searched everywhere for anti-Leninists. Those who never saw suspicious activity were unquestionably kulaks.

A child could prove his worth to the State by turning on a parent. That sometimes happened. In the Soviet village Gerasimovka, there is the story of Pavlik Morozov (1918–1932), then 14, who "unmasked his father who sheltered the kulaks," to the Soviet of the village—at least, that is the Stalinized account. The boy was presumably cornered and killed by peasants of the village, including members of his family, but the Soviets, moved by his heroism in defense of the Party's principles, established a museum in his name and a statue. In 1948, there was even a stamp (Figure 11-6) commemorating his proud deed.[52] There are also the stories of Pronya Kolibin, 13, who reported to authorities that her mother stole grain, and of Pioneer Sorokin of North

---

[50] Robert Conquest, *The Harvest of Sorrow*, 285–86.
[51] Merle Fansoid, *Smolensk under Soviet Rule* (Cambridge: Harvard University Press, 1958), 231.
[52] Yuri Druzhnikov has reasonably challenged the official story in *Informer 001, or The Myth of Pavlik Morozov*. He maintains that Pavlik turned in his father to the NKVD at the behest of his mother, who wanted revenge on a cheating husband.

Caucasus, who had his father arrested after he saw his father illegally filling his pockets with grain.[53]

Fig. 11-6. Stamp Commemorating Pavlik Morozov, 1948

Source: Wikipedia

And so, Stalin aimed to install full socialization through the collectivization of peasants' farms in all parts of the USSR by destroying all bonds of cultural identity inimical to the spread of socialism: identity through religion, language, and even through consanguinity.

Children of kulaks, themselves branded as kulaks, were especially vulnerable. They had few options if they wished to survive. When a family of kulaks was dispossessed from their home or when a father was exiled, such children sometimes wandered the streets of their village in search of food and a place to stay. Few villagers were disposed to provide succor, for any sort of succor would be sympathy to an enemy of the State—proof that one, too, was a kulak. At times, it was best for members of a family to break up the family—to let each member forage for food on his own. Older children would sometimes be sent by parents to a nearby city with the hope of scrounging out a living.

---

[53] Robert Conquest, *The Harvest of Sorrow*, 295.

In Ukrainian cities, there were orphanages and predatory gangs of children.

Orphanages were often hopelessly overcrowded and impossible to manage. In Kirovograd in the oblast of the same name, the orphanage became so overcrowded that children were moved to a newly constructed Children's Town—a walled outdoor "haven" outside the town where children were left to fend for themselves without the superintendency of adults—hence, the name. Some foraged for food and survived; most died. At night, dead children were thrown onto trucks and taken to burial pits and hastily heaped into them, always overfilled and only scantily covered with earth. So hastily were those "funereal" activities undertaken that it was common for bodies to fall off a truck in transit. Dogs and wolves would "exhume" the corpses, hurriedly covered with a few shovelfuls of dirt.[54]

With orphanages usually overfull, orphaned children often became úrkas—hooligans or street thugs. By joining together with other parentless and homeless boys who were hungry, a boy could survive, but he would have to lose whatever ruth he had. Survival depended on ruthlessness. Úrkas would steal, maim, and even murder to survive.

UPSHOT

I begin this chapter with some discussion of the famine in the Russian republics of 1921–1922. Like the famine of 1932–1933, that famine was the result of a lack of grain for peasant-farmers due to the theft of grain and other foodstuffs from farmers to sustain the Bolsheviks in the Russian Revolution. Ukraine, the breadbasket of the RFSFR, was especially targeted. Some one million Ukrainians died in that famine. There was an appeal to global philanthropy, but that assistance came to Ukraine only after there was relief for Russia.

The Great Famine of 1932–1933 was more devastating and brutal. Some four million Ukrainians died, and, as I show in the next chapter, there are few reasons to believe that the famine was not intentional. It is very likely that Stalin's aim was to punish Ukrainians for their resistance over the years to collectivize. That is the subject of chapter 12.

---

[54] David E. Bonior, "Remembrance of Ukraine Famine," in *Extension of Remarks*, 8 Sept. 1993: 20, 494, https://www.govinfo.gov/content/pkg/GPO-CRECB-1993-pt14/pdf/GPO-CRECB-1993-pt14-3-3.pdf, accessed 23 Nov. 2022.

Chapter 12

Holodomor, Causes & Consequences

"Under the direct leadership and directions of the Central Committee of the Communist Party and personally of comrade Stalin, we smashed the Ukrainian nationalist counterrevolution."

~Pavel Postyshev

In this chapter, I aim to complete my expiscation of the series of events as they unfolded that led to the deaths of some four million Ukrainians through want of food, with a focus on the years 1932 and 1933. In doing so, I say little of the numerous thousands of deaths of Ukrainians in Soviet prisons and gulags, some of which were covered in prior chapters.

"Impoverishment and pauperism in the countryside…"
Mission Accomplished!

While millions of Ukrainians were starving to death, Stalin's speeches in the early 1930s mention merely the vast Soviet victory of full collectivization.

On January 7, 1933, Stalin delivered his report, titled "The Results of the First Five-Year Plan," thought mistakenly by the Soviets to be a "private, national affair," but proven to be "the concern of the whole international proletariat." In that report, Stalin limns many "fundamental tasks" of the First Five-Year Plan—each of which might, with some clemency for Stalin's lack of logical acumen, be considered mutually entailing. In the USSR, says Stalin, there is zero unemployment and "impoverishment and pauperism in the countryside have been done away with."[1]

The express goal of the plan, says Stalin, has been to convert the Soviet Union into an "industrial country," without capitalist elements. Such widespread industrialism involves "transfer [of] small and scattered agriculture onto the lines of large-scale collective farming, so as to ensure the economic basis of

---

[1] J.V. Stalin, "The Results of the First Five-Year Plan," in *Marxists Internet Archive*, https://www.marxists.org/reference/archive/stalin/works/1933/01/07.htm, accessed 12 Jan. 2023.

socialism in the countryside and thus to eliminate the possibility of the restoration of capitalism in the USSR." In the industry of Soviet cities, "the capitalist elements have been completely and irrevocably ousted from industry, and socialist industry has become the sole form of industry in the USSR." The steel, tractor, automobile, machine-tool, chemical, aircraft, agricultural, electrical, oil, coal, metallurgy, and textile industries all thrive now. Along with such successes, the Party has carried to completion, at least "in the main," collectivization of peasants' farms, as it has "already completed the collectivization of the principal regions of the USSR."[2] There is, however, a failure to mention that such completion has occurred not willfully, but coercively.

In the collectives, the abuses of the kulaks are gone, as there is no longer a class of kulaks. In liquidating the kulaks as a class, the penurious bednyaks have forgotten their low-class status, for they are no longer exploited. "They were people who usually lacked either seed, or horses, or implements, or all of these, for carrying on their husbandry. The poor peasants were people who lived in a state of semi-starvation and, as a rule, were in bondage to the kulaks." The scenario today has changed. By joining collectives, the poor peasant-farmers have found liberation and "security."[3] The language, it is worth noting, only factors in circumstances. There is no accommodation for differences in constitution or differences determined by habit. Give the poor peasants seed, horses, and implements, the argument goes, and they will produce farmed goods as well as did the kulaks. The argument is again paralogistic.

The Soviet economy is flourishing, too; so are individual laborers. There has been a noticeable increase in the national income—an increase of 85 percent in 1932 from 1928—and so, an increase in the incomes of the workers and peasants"—a 67 percent increase in wages in 1932 from 1928. Everyone is working, and everyone is happy.[4]

There are sprinkled into the speech, as is Stalin's wont, numerous key quotes from Lenin to give the speech its proper authorial grounding.[5]

There are two noteworthy omissions in the speech. First, there is conveniently, as we saw in prior chapters, no mention of the gross, suffocating inflation that has much reduced the purchasing power of that increase of wages such that 90 percent of a worker's wages are spent on food. Second, Stalin cold-shoulders the great famine that was occurring while he speaks about his colossal victories

---

[2] J.V. Stalin, "The Results of the First Five-Year Plan."
[3] J.V. Stalin, "The Results of the First Five-Year Plan."
[4] J.V. Stalin, "The Results of the First Five-Year Plan."
[5] J.V. Stalin, "The Results of the First Five-Year Plan."

and Stalin's Red Brooms continuing to rob the peasant-farmers of whatever grain and foodstuffs they can find (Figure 12-1).

In 1932, with the famine having taken root in Ukraine, Kazakhstan, and Northern Caucasus, the yield of grain was 32 percent below average, while there was a considerable increase in procurement of grain—44 percent.[6] Moreover, during the critical years of famine, Stalin continued to export considerable amounts of grain to glean money for Soviet industry. Export of grain from the years 1930 to 1933 are as follows:

1930 → 48 million poods (867,000 tons),

1931 → 51 million poods (920,887 tons),

1932 → 18 million poods (325,019 tons), and

1933 → 10 million poods (180,566 tons).[7]

Fig. 12-1. Red Brooms (Buksyors) "Appropriating" Foodstuffs from Oleksiyivka, Kharkiv, 1932

Source: Wikipedia

Those figures indicate a considerable drop-off in the exportation of grain in the years 1932 and 1933—the most acute years of the Ukrainian famine. Still, as we saw earlier, there was plenty of Ukrainian grain in Russia, and the grain

---

[6] Robert Conquest, *The Conquest of Sorrow: Soviet Collectivization and the Terror-Famine* (Oxford: Oxford University Press, 1986), 194–95.
[7] Edvard Radzinsky, *Stalin* (New York: Anchor, 1997), 259.

exported in 1932 and 1933 could have been used to mitigate the famine in Ukraine. It was not. Grain was earmarked for the workers in the Soviet cities, not for the Ukrainian peasant-farmers, the people responsible for that grain. The farmers were left to starve.

Numerous Ukrainian peasant-farmers, of course, began to die, and by famine's end, the Ukrainian peasantry would be more than decimated. Some four million people, approximately 18 percent of the Ukrainian population, would perish.

The numbers in this chapter and the last indicate that high-level Soviet officials, including Stalin, had to know that famine in Ukraine was inevitable. Having some percentage of the Ukrainian population would die, thought Stalin, would have beneficial consequences. It would teach the intransigent Ukrainians a valuable lesson: not to resist collectivization and not to push for independence.

Fig. 12-2. Mass of Graves near Kharkiv, 1933

Source: Wikimedia Commons

When it was time to ready for the upcoming spring harvest in 1933, there was a severe shortage of farmers in Ukraine. A critical mass of the population had perished in the famine—Figure 12-2 shows a mass burial in 1933 near Kharkiv—and, of those peasants who remained alive, many were too enfeebled to farm. Requisitions for grain were officially surceased on March 15, 1933. There was also a subsidy of seed parceled to Ukraine for the upcoming harvest several weeks earlier.[8] The number of deaths diminished markedly by May's end.

Those reversals of the Party's policies vis-à-vis *prodrazvyorstka* are evidence of Stalin's recognition of a famine, destroying much of Ukraine and State-

---

[8] *Pravda*, 18 Feb. 1933, and 15 Mar. 1933.

caused, insofar as Stalin recognized that the spring's harvest was in jeopardy. There needed to be seed for sowing and there needed to be farmers to do the sowing and reaping. This is an excellent example of Stalinist brinkmanship. Yet, with many millions of Ukrainians exiled and left to starve and with the early harvest at risk, it is clear that Stalin had gone beyond the brink.

The lack of Ukrainian peasant-farmers was perhaps a way, in Stalin's eyes, of solving the nationalist problem. The exiled and dead Ukrainians could be replaced by Russian peasants. Russian peasants could be brought into the peasant-decimated Ukrainian villages and those of other decimated areas, like the North Caucasus, with a substantial Ukrainian population.

"A jealous god"
Red Brooms as Stalinist Sadists

The question must now be asked: Given the indescribably large number of testimonies of cruelty to peasants—tortured, worked to death in exile, pushed to death from starvation, and sentenced to exile "without the right to correspond"—how is it that activists could be so cruelly indifferent to the sufferings of others, children especially, reduced to beggary, scrounging, or under the heavy burden of exile?

Many activists merely bought into the frenzied atmosphere of Stalinist Marxism: everyone giving to the state which would return generously all things equally to all persons—thereby, the horrors of capitalism could be forfended. During the rule of the tsars, generations of Russians lived as serfs. With the uprisings (e.g., Bloody Sunday, 1905), the entrance of Russia into World War I, the subsequent abdication of Tsar Nicholas II in March 1917, and the years of civil war till the Bolsheviks claimed control of Russia, Russians were exhausted, and the slogans of the Bolsheviks held out the promise of true democracy through socialism, the end of suffering for the *hoi polloi*, industrial and agricultural yield to equal and perhaps surpass capitalistic countries, and the promise of a parochial and soon a global utopia. The young Russians, whose parents and grandparents iterated and reiterated stories of the stormy revolutionary years, were especially excited and wished to follow up on and justify the sanguinary efforts of parents and grandparents. Those young Russians were eager activists of the Party's Komsomol. Stalin was fighting for a better world, and so he could be forgiven for sometimes taking radical actions to bring about that better world. If genuine enemies of the people, anti-revolutionaries, were thwarting those efforts, it was necessary to nullify those actions by quashing the anti-revolutionaries. It was thus right to take anything or all things from those who would hoard for themselves. Enemies of the Party were enemies of the people.

I illustrate such enthusiasm for Bolshevism by reference to three strong young advocates of Bolshevism, who were also three Ukrainians—Victor Kravchenko, Petro Grigorenko, and Lev Kopelev—each of whom has left behind an autobiography.

Ukrainian Victor Kravchenko (1905-1966) was a proud member of the Komsomol of the USSR. His grandfather lived through the feudalism of tsarist times, and his father lived through the revolution and the civil war. Given what his father and his father's father suffered, Bolshevism seemed to promise golden days. Moreover, as an activist in the Komsomol, there was a sense of belonging—of working with other youths toward something meaningful and substantive. Belonging to the Komsomol became his life. He pledged to "work harder, to disdain money and foreswear personal ambition." As an activist, Kravchenko "served on all kinds of committees, did missionary work among the non-Party infidels, played a role in frequent celebrations," such as the opening of a new factory or a new mine, installation of new machinery in a plant, or success in meeting a scheduled production goal.[9]

For Kravchenko, "the Party Line ... became more important than any personal interests," which was an axiom of Bolshevism. The godlessness of Marxism was replaced by the worship of mechanization. "The modern machine, as symbol and substance of industrialization, loomed large in our lives, intensifying every day of existence. The machine became a jealous god to be appeased. It acquired an almost mystic power in the everyday life of the country. The distress of 'humanitarians' seemed merely a leftover from a strange past."[10] For years, it was easy, says Kravchenko as his autobiography unfolds, to rationalize abuses of the Party as mere glitches on the path to the joy of a world without classes and the numberless problems they gave humanity.

Kravchenko was enjoined on a few occasions to travel as a Red Broom to Ukrainian villages, report his observations, and act effectively to find grain wherever it might be hidden during the years of famine. At Petrovo, noticing gross enfeeblement, starvation, and corpses strewn throughout the village square, he used humanitarian methods that won over the peasants, at odds with Bolshevik directives, to bring in the harvest ahead of schedule, though the confiscated grain left little for the town's peasants.[11] His enthusiasm for the express aims of the Party slowly waned. Though he had many years of successful work as an engineer in the system, he was accused by the NKVD of

---

[9] Victor Kravchenko, *I Chose Freedom* (New York: Charles Scribner's Sons, 1946), 38.
[10] Victor Kravchenko, *I Chose Freedom*, 50.
[11] Victor Kravchenko, *I Chose Freedom*, 110–31.

being an enemy of the State and spent many years trying to clear his name. On several occasions, he even considered release from his hellish existence by a bullet to his brain.[12] He eventually defected to the United States.

Ukrainian Petro Grigorenko (1907–1987), who would become a high-ranking general in the Red Army, was also an active member of Komsomol. Grigorenko felt passionately and enthusiastically that he and fellow activists in the Komsomol were participating in something enormous, something world-changing. "Everywhere, the press and radio reported, there were successes." Stalin's published speeches were mesmerizing. "Stalin was adroit at advancing ever new and ever larger tasks. The people were tantalized by the goals he set before us." Grigorenko mentions "A Year of Great Change" (1929) and "Dizzy with Success" (1930) as especially moving speeches.[13] When schooled for two years at the Kharkiv Construction Engineering Institute, he and his classmates were spoon-fed the principles of Marx, Lenin, and Stalin to be "active warriors for the victory of worldwide socialism."[14]

When Grigorenko had become somewhat drawn to the writings of Trotsky concerning the eternal revolution—Grigorenko says, "Could Trotsky be right?"—he read Stalin's 1924 essay, "Trotskyism or Leninism," and became thoroughly convinced of the success of "building socialism in our country"— *viz.*, one-country socialism. Says Grigorenko: "I agreed with Stalin's every word. He liberated me from all doubts." Grigorenko would thereafter always have with him the essay to be used as "my best weapon during arguments with Trotskyites."[15] He, too, would soon sour on the villainous activities of the NKVD, as his friends and associates began to disappear and when it was evident that the Chekists aimed to arrest, and perhaps execute him.

---

[12] Victor Kravchenko, *I Chose Freedom*, 230.
[13] Petro Grigorenko, *Memoirs* (New York: W.W. Norton, 1984), 28 and 35.
[14] Petro Grigorenko, *Memoirs*, 35.
[15] Petro Grigorenko, *Memoirs* (New York: W.W. Norton, 1984), 25

Fig. 12-3. Dr. Lev Kopelov, 1980s

Source: Wikipedia

Finally, there is the testimony of Kyiv-born and former Soviet Bolshevist Dr. Lev Kopelev (1912–1997, Figure 12-3) in his memoirs after his early years of Stalinist activism. I include a large chunk of his recollections of being young and bewitched by the empty promises of Stalinism and willingly doing the Party's dirty work as Komsomol.

> I firmly believed that the ends justified the means. Our great goal was the universal triumph of Communism, and for the sake of that goal everything was permissible—to lie, to steal, to destroy hundreds of thousands and even millions of people, all those who were hindering our work or could hinder it, everyone who stood in the way. And to hesitate or doubt about all this was to give in to "intellectual squeamishness" and "stupid liberalism," the attribute of people who "could not see the forest for the trees."

> I believed what Trotsky and Bukharin were saying, when I saw that "total collectivization" meant—how they "kulakized" and "dekulakized," how mercilessly they stripped the peasants in the winter of 1932–33. I took part in this myself, scouring the countryside, searching for hidden grain, testing the earth with an iron rod for loose spots that might lead to grain. With the others, I emptied out the old folks' storage chests, stopping my ears to the children's crying and the women's wails. For I was convinced that I was accomplishing the great and necessary transformation of the

countryside; that in the days to come the people who lived there would be better off for it; that their distress and suffering were a result of their own ignorance or the machinations of the class enemy; that those who sent me—and I myself—know better than the peasants how they should live, what they should sow and when they should plough.

In the "terrible spring of 1933," adds Kopelev, he witnessed much starvation. There were women and children with "distended bellies, turning blue, still breathing but with vacant, lifeless eyes." There were "corpses in ragged sheepskin coats and cheap felt boots; corpses in peasant huts, in the melting snow of the old Vologda, under the bridges of Kharkiv." Such dreadful things he witnessed without insanity or any thought of suicide. Kopelev still dutifully went about his task of taking "peasants' grain the winter" and persuading "barely walking, skeleton-thin or sickly-swollen people" to enter and to work the fields.

Kopelev, overall, kept the faith. "I believed because I wanted to believe. Thus, from time immemorial men have believed when possessed by a desire to serve powers and values above and beyond humanity: gods, emperors, states; ideals of virtue, freedom, nation, race, class, party."[16]

Kopelev's "confession" here is clean and candid, and so I have chosen not to paraphrase. He mentions a "great goal": the "universal triumph of Communism." Such a goal is so worthwhile that even the loss of millions of lives would be worth it. The short-term sufferings of the peasants who resisted that goal were deserved. They were victims of their own ignorance and of the propaganda of the enemies of Stalinism. In the words of the former activist, "Those who sent me, and I myself, know better than the peasants how they should live, what they should sow and when they should plow." That was the anti-liberalism of Stalin. It was better for kulaks, as enemies of the utopianism of socialism, to perish than to impede the implementation of socialism. With the promise of Xanadu not only for Soviets, but also for all humans, it would be no large thing to eliminate those who preferred their own happiness and blocked the path that led to the prosperity and happiness of all. There, too, would be an added benefit. It will be a lesson to the others.[17]

Yet there was also the issue—and this applies to other young activists in the Komsomol—that the lure of Bolshevism was so great that it was like a religion for Kopelev. Kopelev admits readily to forgiving the misdeeds of the Party even when he was their object. Bolshevism gave meaning to his life. "That vision was essential to me as a source of spiritual strength, of my conception of myself as

---

[16] Lev Kopelev, *The Education of a True Believer* (New York: HarperCollins, 1980), 11–12.
[17] Lev Kopelev, *The Education of a True Believer*, 12.

part of a great whole. Without that conviction, my life would lose its meaning—my past life and whatever lay ahead."[18]

As we saw at the end of the prior chapter, Stalin ever shied away from exorbitant promises. He ever shied away from vivid, explicit discussion of the Bolshevik utopia. Alexander Barmine, a former official of the Party who was not exterminated in Stalin's Great Purge of 1937–1938 (discussed further in the epilog), said that when he campaigned for Bolshevism, his message in gist was this: "Join a party which offers you neither privileges nor advantages. If we win, we build a new world. ... Who is not with us is against us!"[19]

Given Barmine's expression of the message preached to him, it is difficult to grasp the lure of Stalinist socialism. Its chief attraction, one might argue, was that it was not capitalism. Yet there was some pledge of adventure. As a committed Bolshevik, one would be part of a team of revolutionaries aiming to build a new and better world. For people who had survived the turmoil of the lengthy Russian Revolution and who were told stories by parents or grandparents of life in feudalist Russia prior to the revolution, the promise of a new world, a stable world, must have sounded wholly alluring. There is also the pledge of inclusion. One could be a proud, card-carrying Bolshevik who would take part in the march toward that new, stable world. With this pledge of inclusion, there concomitantly came the threat of exclusion. Refusal to become a Bolshevik, given the logic of "Who is not with us is against us," meant that one was an enemy of the people. For Stalin, there was nothing in between the two. They were mutually exclusive and mutually exhaustive.

There is a second reason for explaining acts of unspeakable cruelty: a visceral, psychological element to Kopelev's apology. As Sigmund Freud rightly notes, strong prohibitions, such as the prohibitions of killing and incest, are put into place because humans have strong impulses to act in such ways. Freud writes, "Men are not gentle creatures who want to be loved, and who at the most can defend themselves if they are attacked; they are, on the contrary, creatures among whose instinctual endowments is to be reckoned a powerful share of aggressiveness."[20] In other words, it would be fatuous to have axial laws against vile human actions such as killing other humans and against incest unless we had strong impulses to act in such ways. Thus, part of the appeal of Stalinism was its Party-sanctioned brutality. For Stalin, lying, spying, turning against one's

---

[18] Lev Kopelev, *The Education of a True Believer*, 93.
[19] Alexander Barmine, *One Who Survived: The Life Story of a Russian under the Soviets* (New York: G.P. Putnam's Sons, 1945), 67.
[20] Sigmund Freud, *Civilization and Its Discontents* (1930, S.E., XXI: 111).

family, stealing, and even murder are permissible, even laudatory, if they are done in the interest of the Party.

A third reason why many activists were transported to large acts of cruelty was coercion. Many felt forced to behave cruelly so as not to be victims of cruelty at the hands of the Party. For Stalin, it was always either-or; skepticism was never an option. It was a matter of working to destroy the kulaks or being dubbed kulak. We have seen illustrations of this in prior chapters. Moreover, the *modus operandi* of the GPU/NKVD was always this: guilty until proven innocent. As the *soi-disant* "good Chekist" Aleksei Gershgorn said to Victor Kravchenko during his ceaseless sessions of interrogation of Kravchenko, "Everyone is guilty unless he can prove his innocence." The system literally ran on mutual distrust. "Mutual distrust was not merely a fact in the Soviet *apparat*. It was the recognized, obligatory way of life, the only chance of survival."[21]

Fourth, members of the Party feared both losing the benefits of membership and suffering the miseries of non-membership. A card showing membership in the Party meant escaping the fate of the penurious by having a job with pay usually sufficient for subsistence. In the village Lypkivka, near Kharkiv, a Bolshevik named Hurenko was given *carte blanche* to organize the farms into a collective. Yet if he failed, he would be deprived of his Party membership, which at least assured him and his family of survival. The kurkuls of the village had been removed, and he had only to "convince" the lowly bednyaks to collectivize. Yet he could not do so through arguments. Therefore, he removed the poor peasant-farmers to a large house, where he lit a fire and closed the dampers so that the thick smoke choked the peasants, whose lives were at stake. With guards at the doors, no one could leave. When all were nearly asphyxiated by dense smoke, Hurenko allowed the farmers to leave the house and to consider once more the aidful benefits of joining the collective. Those who refused would be forced, at the point of a rifle, to return to the house. It comes as no surprise that all peasants, now seeing the "numerous benefits" of collectivizing, voluntarily signed the document.[22] Hurenko kept his card.

Again, the Party employed "criminals, sadists and other degenerate elements" to employ dekurkulization. That made cruelty easy. Stepan Kavun mentions a certain Anton Oleksiyovich Orlenko, who visited the village Viytivka in Central Ukraine. Says Kavun: "He carried out all the orders of the government without question, even if it meant taking the life of a human being. He swept out the last kernels of grain from pots and cans, thus sentencing young children to certain death. The word Orlenko was sufficient to frighten playful children into absolute

---

[21] Victor Kravchenko, *I Chose Freedom*, 257 and 398.
[22] W. Slobidsky, "Forced to Join Collective Farm by Poisoning" and H. Senko, "History of the Destruction of the Ukrainian Orthodox Church," in *The Black Deeds of the Kremlin: A White Book*, ed. S.O. Pidhainy, Vol. 2 (Detroit: The Basilian Press, 1955), 284.

silence and the grown-ups went out of their way to avoid him. He carried a pistol with him wherever he went, always looked filthy and cursed everyone within hearing." Orlenko's unusual cruelty, however, was noticed. He was reprimanded and sent to prison for a year, but he was there as a guard, not a prisoner. After his year, he was sent to other villages as a grain-collecting specialist.[23]

Sixth, last, and following the lead of the boy who, along with his brother and father were on trial for killing others and eating and selling the meat, desperation, driven by fear of starvation, led some persons to commit vile acts—e.g., to turn on family or fellow villagers for promise of gain or to kill others for food. As the boy said, once the first act was committed, other such acts were a matter of course. Having eaten his mother once she starved to death, it was no large atrocity to seek out the meat of other humans as food to eat and to sell. Likewise, some became Red Brooms and committed foul, sometimes violent, deeds against peasant-farmers simply because they believed that there was no alternative course of action.

---

[23] Stepan Kavun, "Sadists, Government Representatives," in *The Black Deeds of the Kremlin: A White Book*, ed. S.O. Pidhainy, Vol. 2 (Detroit: The Basilian Press, 1955), 145.

Chapter 13

Stony Soviet Silence

"My father had to give everything to the collective farm—our cow, horse, even our bucket. My mother was very angry."

~Petro Mohalat

Ukrainian P. Lykho mentions top-secret Soviet documents that were disclosed in September 1941, when German soldiers assaulted the town of Chronykhy and sealed off possible routes of escape. Caught unawares, Soviet officials did not have the time to bury the documents, which consisted of papers from Chornukhy County Party Committee, Chornukhy County Branch of the NKVD (formerly GPU) and Militia, Special Branches of Chornukhy County Executive Committee, Chronukhy County Military Committee, Chornukhy County Prosecuting Office, Chornukhy Branch of the State Bank, and Chornukhy County Inspecting Office of Peoples' Domestic Economy Inventory. The documents concerned the collection of grain from kolhosps (Rus., kolkhozes), where it was ordered that "severe measures" be taken about what to do about cannibalism, about "tens of thousands of hundred-weights of valuable grain" that was left to rot when it should have been delivered to the State, and about the maximum amount of reaped grain (10 percent) that should be left in kolkhozes "for the subsistence of the kolkhoz-workers," *inter alia*. Those documents, says Lykho, "signed by Stalin himself, show that the famine of 1932–1933 in Ukraine was created by Moscow—by the Communist Party and the Government."[1]

Is Lykno correct? Did Stalin not only know of the famine but also plan the famine?

There is too much evidence, limned in this chapter, to make believable that high officials of the Party, Stalin especially, did not know of the famine. That said, the official response of the Party to any assertions of a famine in Ukraine was incredulity, ridicule, or silence. The question to be answered is whether the famine was planned.

---

[1] P. Lykho, "Soviet Documents on the Famine in Ukraine," in *The Black Deeds of the Kremlin: A White Book*, ed. S.O. Pidhainy, Vol. 1 (Detroit: The Basilian Press, 1955), 232.

"No sooner had we crossed over into Russian territory..."
Bolshevik Knowledge of the Famine

Officials of the Bolshevik Party were aware of the famine and how it debilitated Ukraine through the deaths of hundreds of thousands of Ukrainians. "A little time spent at just one [Ukrainian] market-place," says Ukrainian A. Savur, "was enough for anyone to realize in all its enormity the horror of the famine which had Ukraine and all its villages in its grip." Their response, dictated by Soviet propagandists, was scripted and bromidic. "Those are all 'enemies of the people' and kurkuls who will not work." There are economic problems, but "there is no famine. Anyone who says there is a famine is an enemy of the people and the Soviet Government."[2]

Gen. Petro Grigorenko tells of a conversation with Stanislav Kossior, secretary of the Central Committee of the Ukrainian Communist Party, in the summer of 1930. Kossier related to Grigorenko of the Ukrainian peasant-farmers' "new tactic"—refusing to bring in their harvest while they live on hidden grain to "choke the Soviet government with the bony hand of famine." He sums, "We will show him what famine is." The argument was that if Ukrainians want to start a famine in Russia, then Russia will start a famine in Ukraine.

Kossier told Grigorenko that he and other buksyors were to go to the farms and search for and confiscate all the "harvested grain they have in their pits." Grigorenko, filled with disgust after hearing Kossier's plan, met with Yasha Zlochevsky, head of the Komsomol Committee, and related what Kossier had said. Zlochevsky replied that all the Bolsheviks, even Stalin, knew of that plan, so it was bootless to complain about Kossier to a higher official. He bid Grigorenko to do honestly his work and try to convince the Ukrainian peasant-farmers to bring in their harvest in keeping with the government's requisition, while stealing away some grain for themselves.[3]

There are also the testimonies of travelers who, for some reason, were allowed to travel during the famine from Russia to Ukraine or from Ukraine to Russia.

Ukrainian engineer M. Rusetsky in 1932 was serving in the Soviet army just outside Moscow during the first year of rampant famine. While famine raged in Ukraine—Rusetsky knew of it from relatives whom he had been assisting with packages of food—no one in Moscow could believe that there was famine in Ukraine. Yet the engineer in that year helped many peasants from the villages

---

[2] V. Savur, "Death Claims the Starving at the Markets of Kiev," in *The Black Deeds of the Kremlin: A White Book*, ed. S.O. Pidhainy, Vol. 2 (Detroit: The Basilian Press, 1955), 621.
[3] Petro G. Grigorenko, *Memoirs* (New York: W.W. Norton, 1982), 36–37.

of Northern Ukraine escape its borders and form "a complete small town of navvies"[4] near Moscow.[5]

S. Zapolenko, a laborer in a chemical factory in the Donbas region, was given a 30-day vacation. He returned to Pushcha Vodytsya near Kyiv and witnessed *en route* numerous corpses of bloated bodies from starvation. Trucks would come to collect the bodies of the dead or moribund—it was customary to treat the nearly dead as dead—to dump them into a large pit. Wandering through Kyiv, he noted that the streets were teeming with villagers in search of food. Each day, thousands of people would line up at each shop with the hope of purchasing or bartering for bread. Lines were frequently broken by mounted soldiers who struck the hungry peasants with knouts, only to reveal several dead bodies hidden behind the lines. On his return to his job, he said, "You could not get food at any price at any of the stations along the way, but at every station there were corpses, and more corpses."[6]

With 10 days left on his vacation, Zapolenko agreed to travel with Russian coworkers to their village. Of his return to Russia, he writes:

> Once again, I was passing through Ukrainian territory and observing the familiar scenes of famine. But no sooner had we crossed over to Russian territory than everything changed. Life was proceeding in a normal fashion. There was not the faintest trace of any famine on the way to my friend's village, which was about 25 kilometres from Tula. I could have bought all kinds of food at the stations. At the collective farm in their village, likewise, there was not a single sign of famine. The young people enjoyed themselves after their day's work was done. They held parties in the evenings.[7]

From an artel in Yahotyn from Poltava Oblast, Ukraine, Panas Skirda was sent to Russia for grain. On a train from Kyiv to Mikhaylivsk on the eastern border of Russia, there was no food. "Once we crossed the border into Russian territory more and more food became available. In Moscow there was an abundance of everything and it was cheap." In Kashino, some 180 miles from Moscow, 16 kilograms of rye could be bought for 3.5 rubles. At that same time, the same amount of rye cost 350 rubles in Yahotyn, in the heart of the grain-growing area

---

[4] Construction workers for canals, roads, and damns, etc.
[5] M. Rusetsky, "Flight into Moscow," in *The Black Deeds of the Kremlin: A White Book*, ed. S.O. Pidhainy, Vol. 2 (Detroit: The Basilian Press, 1955), 627–28.
[6] S. Zapolenko, "No Famine in Russia," in *The Black Deeds of the Kremlin: A White Book*, ed. S.O. Pidhainy, Vol. 2 (Detroit: The Basilian Press, 1955), 628–29.
[7] S. Zapolenko, "No Famine in Russia," 629.

of Poltava. Skirda adds that there was an abundance of Ukrainian grain during the famine in Russia, but little to be had in Ukraine.[8]

Last, I return to Grigorenko, who traveled back to Ukraine upon hearing of his seriously ill father. At Belgorod, he saw hordes of people begging for bread. "The farther our train traveled into Ukraine the more starving people I saw." At his village, Borissovka, the streets were eerily empty, there was no barking of dogs, and no one, whom he greeted, returned his greeting—a most non-Ukrainian behavior. On retrieval of a horse-drawn cart for his sickly father, Grigorenko passed two corpses in the street. He protested to the Central Committee, the local perpetrators were punished and food was sent to the village. For many years, Grigorenko was convinced that his experiences were due to parochial abuses. Only later did he become aware that "the Central Committee was preparing a mass famine for the collective farms of Ukraine, of the Don, of the Kuban, of Orenburg and of a number of other areas for the winter of 1932–33."[9]

Nonetheless, the testimonies of such travelers told to Russians were habitually met with disbelief, scorn, or laughter. Zapolenko writes of sharing a smoke with an old man at the latter's house and telling the old man of what he had seen when he traveled through Ukraine. The old man merely laughed in disbelief.[10] The old man's response was graspable. If there had been a large famine in Ukraine, would Russians not be suffering from a lack of food? Were they not part of the USSR? Food was not scarce in Russia, so there could be no scarcity of food in Ukraine. Moreover, if there had been a large famine in Ukraine, would the Soviet newspapers not have mentioned it?

There were concessions by Stalinists, writes Ivan Dubynets, that the Party struggled mightily with Ukrainian peasant-farmers over collectivization, but never was there any mention of famine

> In summing up achievements in agriculture and collectivization at the end of the first Five-Year Plan, the Communist press did not gloss over, but openly admitted a host of incredibly harsh and cruel forms of struggle between Communist authority and peasant population. It admitted forced collectivization; the slaughter of livestock by the peasants; the destruction of agricultural stock and machinery; direct, occasionally armed, anti-Soviet insurrections; the killing of activists and burning of their settlements; mass sabotage; even the collaboration of

---

[8] Panas Skirda, "There Was an Abundance of Ukrainian Bread in Russia, in *The Black Deeds of the Kremlin: A White Book*, ed. S.O. Pidhainy, Vol. 2 (Detroit: The Basilian Press, 1955), 630.
[9] Petro G. Grigorenko, *Memoirs*, 42–43.
[10] S. Zapolenko, "No Famine in Russia," 629–30.

Communists with anti-Soviet elements; but nowhere does it mention the famine or its demographic results.[11]

"You are a good storyteller"
Just What Did Stalin Know

We have seen in the prior section that numerous officials of the Party knew of the famine. Yet, is it possible that Stalin did not know of it?

There are no documents to indicate that Stalin directly and unmistakably recognized famine in Ukraine in the early 1930s. Yet he and other high officials of the Party knew about it. All information of any significance made its way to Stalin. The significant question is this: Was it planned? Did Stalin implement the aggressive grain-collection policy late in 1932 in full knowledge that it would result in famine?

Nonetheless, all instances of mention to Stalin of famine in Ukraine and in other severely hit regions were sloughed off by Stalin as daft. For illustration, Roman Terekhov, who was the First Secretary of the Kharkiv Provincial Committee, is said to have brought up the notion of bringing in grain to help the victims of the Ukrainian famine. Stalin is reported to have replied: "You are a good storyteller. You have made up such a fable about famine, thinking to frighten us, but it will not work. Would it not be better for you to leave the post of provincial committee secretary and the Ukrainian Committee and join the Writers' Union? Then you can write your fables and fools will read them."[12]

Yet we must not be misled by Stalin's tergiversations. Words for Stalin were not significant insofar as they could be put together to express truthful assertions. He was no analytic philosopher, agonizing over the precise meaning of each word, strung together in a sentence, and of each sentence, strung together in a paragraph. Words, for Stalin, were to be used to get others to do what he wanted them to do. Stalin chose guardedly his words in transmissions to others, his lackeys, so that he could never be trapped by them—for example, he seldom said literally just what he wanted others to do—but there was for those directly beneath and loyal to him a way of cleanly deciphering or decoding his missives so that his instructions were fully grasped. One must consider merely the

---

[11] Ivan Dubynets, "The Suppression of the Effects of Famine and the Strengthening of the Collective Slave System," in *The Black Deeds of the Kremlin: A White Book*, ed. S.O. Pidhainy, Vol. 2 (Detroit: The Basilian Press, 1955), 681.
[12] Robert Conquest, *The Harvest of Sorrow*, 324–25.

euphemism attached to a sentence of exile "without the right to correspond." That meant "Kill the bastardly kulak!"

Stalin did know of the famine. The evidence, which I sum below, is incontrovertible.

Stalin, as we have seen, was informed by Ukrainian leaders that the Ukrainian quotas of 1932 were unjustly excessive and impossible to meet. He ignored that information.

Moreover, Stalin enjoined that grains of seed for the upcoming harvest in 1932 throughout Ukraine were not to be stored in kolhopses, but in the granaries nearby or those of the nearby cities.[13] That maneuver is inexplicable unless one presumes that his fear was that the Ukrainian peasants would eat the grains of seed and not use them for the spring harvest. Figure 13-1 shows an armed guard in front of one of the doors of a building converted to a granary.

Also, the border of Russia and Ukraine was blockaded heavily by Soviet guards.[14] Those who traveled through Russia and Ukraine at the time of the famine noted the scarcity of food throughout Ukraine and the plentifulness of food throughout Russia. That was not accidental. It was planned, and no such plan could have taken place without the approbation of the Party's Boss.

Fig. 13-1. Soviet Guard by Granary, c. 1932

Source: Wikimedia Commons

---

[13] B.A., "The Warehouses of the 'Grain-Collection Trust' Filled with Grain," in *The Black Deeds of the Kremlin: A White Book*, ed. S.O. Pidhainy, Vol. 2 (Detroit: The Basilian Press, 1955), 558.
[14] Mykola Prychodko, "The Year 1933 in Soviet Ukraine," in *The Black Deeds of the Kremlin: A White Book*, ed. S.O. Pidhainy, Vol. 1 (Detroit: The Basilian Press, 1955), Vol. 1, 236.

Furthermore, Stalin received reports from the NKVD of a famine and millions of deaths in Ukraine. Iona Yakir, Commander of the Ukrainian Military District, had asked Stalin for grain to give to the Ukrainian peasant-farmers. He was told to confine his advice to military matters. Vlas Chubar, Chairman of the Ukrainian Council of People's Commissars, asked Stalin for food "at least for the starving children" in Ukraine. Stalin's curt reply was this, "No remarks on that question."[15]

Again, there is also the Party's official reversal of policy vis-à-vis the thorough collection of grain in the spring of 1933. That makes sense only if he is addressing a nodus: lack of grain to be collected or lack of peasant-farmers for the upcoming spring sowing, or both.[16]

In addition, and as we saw in Chapter 10, there is the concomitant Soviet aim of destroying Ukrainian culture and aiming to Russify and secularize Ukrainians that was occurring throughout the years of famine. Famine would only have helped to facilitate de-Ukrainization and would have allowed for the possibility of an influx of Russians to replace the discordant, dead Ukrainians.

Finally, it is almost certain that Stalin's second wife, Nadezhda Alliluyava (1901–1932, Figure 13-2), a plain woman of a serious though mercurial bent, often told him stories of famine in Ukraine. On advice from Nikolai Bukharin, Nadya matriculated at the Industrial Academy, where she was privy to all the gossip and news that could not be found in the State-run newspapers: the aggressive collection of grain, widespread famine in Ukraine, orphaned children begging for bread, and even cannibalism.[17]

Stalin's wife likely killed herself with a bullet to her heart[18] from a small revolver on November 5, 1932, though it is possible that Stalin had her killed. The setting was a dinner party at Marshal Klementy Voroshilov's villa near Stalin's, where there was tension between Nadya and Stalin throughout the evening. Nadya, who had the volatile mood swings of her husband, is said by Nadya's brother to have brought up the famine. Stalin rudely dismissed the comment as "Trotskyite gossip."[19]

---

[15] Robert Conquest, *The Harvest of Sorrow*, 325–26.

[16] There was here the additional nodus of large opposition to Stalin's leadership at the time. Failure of collectivization, Soviet runaway inflation, and the famine led to the popularity of more moderate Bolsheviks, like Sergei Kirov, about whom I shall write in the afterword.

[17] Anne Applebaum, *Red Famine: Stalin's War on Ukraine* (New York: Anchor: 2017), 221–25, and Edvard Radzinsky, *Stalin* (New York: Anchor, 1997), 272–304.

[18] Of her death, Stalin merely posted a one-sentence editorial in *Pravda*. "My sincere thanks to the organizations, institutions, comrades and friends who have expressed their condolences on the occasion of the passing away of my beloved friend and comrade, Nadezhda Sergeyevna Alliluyeva-Stalina." *Pravda*, 18 Nov. 1932.

[19] Alexander Barmine, *One Who Survived: The Life Story of a Russian under Stalin* (New York: G.P. Putnam's Sons, 1945), 264.

Fig. 13-2. Nadezhda Alliluyava, Stalin's Second Wife

Source: Wikipedia

"Their foul clothing reeked revoltingly"

The Party's Response

There was no need for the Party's propaganda at the time to cover up the famine. Silence was the most effective tool. When questions pressed officials concerning the possibility of a large-scale famine in Ukraine, Stalin and his officials acknowledged numerous Ukrainians dying from starvation, but likely no more than in any other trying years. Moreover, high officials were wont to add that those peasants could have prevented their deaths by being good kolkhozniks, instead of sworn enemies of the people. Says Dubynets of the official Soviet response, "There was no famine but … the kurkuls … [who] refused to work on the collective farms were starving as a result of their lack of co-operation." And so, eyewitnesses' accounts were casually and conveniently dismissed because such persons were kurkuls.[20]

Admission of a famine, Stalin certainly thought, would only have done him harm. Though production of essential goods in factories throughout the USSR had improved remarkably since the implementation of the Five-Year Plan, the pie-in-the-sky goals of the plan had not been met. Moreover, success in

---

[20] Ivan Dubynets, "The Suppression of the Effects of Famine and the Strengthening of the Collective Slave System," in *The Black Deeds of the Kremlin: A White Book*, ed. S.O. Pidhainy, Vol. 2 (Detroit: The Basilian Press, 1955), 682.

collectivizing Soviet farms had come at the loss of some eight million Soviets—half of whom were Ukrainian. Export of grain in 1933 was one-fifth of what it was in 1931, and so the policy of *prodrazvyorstka* had proved to be disastrous. Finally, the USSR at the end of the Five-Year Plan was suffering from suffocating inflation. All leading members of the Party were fully aware of such things. Stalin knew that his leadership was at stake, and open admission of a large-scale famine would have only made the scenario worse.

When reports surfaced in countries like England or the United States about the atrocity, the response of such countries was negligible. Russia, after all, was a valued ally in World War I, as Russia suffered the brunt of the casualties, and there was general acknowledgment that the crisis, if real, was an internal matter.[21] If Russia was not asking for international assistance, as it did in 1921, the crisis was manageable, not as large as several individual reports have claimed. Moreover, the United States was not in the position to agitate the USSR, as it had in 1933 recognized the legitimacy of the USSR, which would soon become a member of the League of Nations.

Moreover, there were testimonies of foreigners who visited the USSR during the height of famine and were introduced to what appeared to be nothing but an economic machine, well-oiled and running smoothly.

George Bernard Shaw, a Marxist sympathizer, visited the USSR in 1931 and had a two-hour audience with Stalin. To the editor of *Manchester Guardian*, Shaw wrote:

> Particularly offensive and ridiculous is the revival of the old attempts to represent the condition of Russian workers as one of slavery and starvation, the Five-Year Plan as a failure, the new enterprises as bankrupt and the Communist regime as tottering to its fall. Although such inflammatory irresponsibility is easily laughed at, we must not forget that there are many people not sufficiently well informed politically to be proof against it, and that there are diehards among our diplomats who still dream of starting a counter-revolutionary war anywhere and anyhow, if only they can stampede public opinion into the necessary panic through the press.[22]

Again, there was *The New York Times*' correspondent Walter Duranty, who lived in Moscow from 1922 to 1936. Duranty fashioned himself to be an

---

[21] Many English-speaking people are today still in the dark concerning the gloomy years from 1928 to 1933.
[22] George Bernard Shaw, "Social Conditions in Russia," in *The Manchester Guardian*, 2 Mar. 1933.

objective reporter of life in the USSR. Stalin fitted Duranty with an automobile, a large flat, and even a mistress. He privileged the reporter twice with interviews, and Duranty won the Pulitzer Prize in 1932 for his cheery articles on collectivization and Stalin's Five-Year Plan. Yet Duranty, perhaps fearing damage to his credibility for his prior published reports,[23] slowly came to recognize the reality of famine in Ukraine and the Soviet cover-up, but published nothing on that.

British Journalist Gareth Jones, however, was the first foreigner to notice the devastation in Ukraine. On a train from Moscow to Kharkiv in 1933, Jones alighted some 40 miles north of Kharkiv and set out, with a stuffed backpack, on foot. He passed through over 20 villages and collectives, and he documented what he had witnessed.

> I crossed the border from Great Russia into Ukraine. Everywhere I talked to peasants who walked past. They all had the same story. "There is no bread. We haven't had bread for over two months. A lot are dying." The first village had no more potatoes left and the store of *burak* ("beetroot") was running out. They all said: "The cattle are dying, *nechevo kormit* [there's nothing with which to feed them]. We used to feed the world & now we are hungry. How can we sow when we have few horses left? How will we be able to work in the fields when we are weak from want of food?"

When Jones, on foot, was asked by a Soviet militiaman about what he was doing, he was forced to take a train to Kharkiv, his intended destiny. Still, in Kharkiv, he documented the effects of famine on urbanites.[24]

Jones' articles were anonymously published but with heavy edits to anti-USSR comments, and they had little effect. Duranty himself attacked Jones. He accused Jones of hyperbolizing. From a 40-mile walk through the Ukrainian countryside, summed Duranty, Jones concluded that all Ukraine suffered from famine. Yet Jones was an upstart journalist of 27 years; Duranty was a Pulitzer winner. That alone settled the debate in the minds of most. It is perhaps best to say that many just did not care if Ukrainians were dying if the USSR did not care.

Bolsheviks, however, could not forever remain silent. Russia's official response was that reports of mass famine were being spread by counter-revolutionists. A typical response, here to a pamphlet citing much evidence of

---

[23] Anne Applebaum, "How Stalin Hid Ukraine's Famine from the World, in *The Atlantic*, https://www.theatlantic.com/international/archive/2017/10/red-famine-anneapplebaum-Ukraine-soviet-union/542610/, accessed 13 Jan. 2023.

[24] Anne Applebaum, "How Stalin Hid Ukraine's Famine from the World."

Soviet violence apropos of Ukrainians, is given on January 3, 1934, by Maksim Litvinov, People's Commissar for Foreign Affairs by Stalin at the time:

> I am in receipt of your letter of the 14th inst., and thank you for drawing my attention to the Ukrainian pamphlet. There is any amount of such pamphlets full of lies circulated by counter-revolutionary organizations abroad, which specialize in the work of this kind. There is nothing left for them to do but to spread false information or to forge documents.[25]

In sum, the official Bolshevik response was that there was no famine, and rumors of one were merely promulgated by the ever-present enemies of the State.

There was a sound reason for high officials of the Party never to discuss the possibility of a famine in Ukraine. Beginning in 1929, Stalin began to press hard for the collectivization of all farms in the USSR. Formal admission of a large-scale famine in Ukraine through assisting the dying with food, seemingly plentiful in Russia, was, by implication, formal admission that Stalinist collectivization was failing. No one near or under Stalin was willing to state that Stalin's collectivization was failing lest they be sent away "without the right to correspond."

A stark illustration is the testimony of M. Rusetsky, an engineer of the Albert Kahn Company based in Detroit, who came to Russia to work. He and others passed through several Ukrainian villages, and in all, "not a living thing was to be seen, not even a cat or a dog." When the engineers arrived at their destination, each was given "a loaf of delicious, well-baked bread, some sausage, and hot broth with meat in it," as the men sat on a grassy hilltop near a ravine.

> We no sooner began to eat then out of the ravine came crawling famished old people and children who no longer had the strength to walk, and began to beg us for food. Their foul clothing reeked revoltingly, since they were so enfeebled that they could no longer cope normally with the eliminative processes. We were so horrified by the sight that we gave them our entire lunch, even though we ourselves were hungry. We unwittingly did these poor people more harm than good, for the majority of them, having neither seen nor tasted bread for a long time had lost the ability to digest it, and died within two days as a result of overeating.[26]

---

[25] Dmytro Solviy and Stephen Shumeyko, *The Golgotha of Ukraine*, 5.
[26] M. Rusetsky, "The Harvest Campaign of 1933," in *The Black Deeds of the Kremlin: A White Book*, ed. S.O. Pidhainy, Vol. 2 (Detroit: The Basilian Press, 1955), 684–85.

Fig. 13-3. Cartoon Drawing of Starving Peasant Asking a Russian Soldier for Bread, 1933

Source: Wikimedia Commons

After the lunch that the engineers missed, they were summoned to a meeting by local members of the Party. They were told that they had merely witnessed "the enemies of the collective system." An official added in reply to questions concerning no aid given to the starving peasants: "We Communists have a different conception of the decrees of Party and Government. We should help those 'reapers' as you have entitled them to die and not raise them up again. They are enemies of the Soviet Government, madly opposed to collectivization. They want to force the Party and the Government to their knees, but they will never succeed in this."[27]

Izvestia, in a rare concession of a famine of some sort, at one point reported saboteurs at work against the State. Those arrested were charged with deliberate destruction of machinery in collectives, burning Machine-Tractor Stations and linen mills, stealing food from the stock of collectives, sabotaging the operations of seeding and harvesting, and slaughtering of livestock. "The evidence resulting from the investigations and from the confessions of the arrested saboteurs proves that the prisoners' intention had been to disorganize agriculture and produce famine in the land." There followed a list of 35 persons,

---

[27] M. Rusetsky, "The Harvest Campaign of 1933," 685.

awaiting execution; 22 persons awaiting 10-year exiles; and 18 persons, awaiting eight years of imprisonment.[28] The implication here was that the peasant-farmers, qua saboteurs, were attempting to cause a famine in the USSR, and the result, at least implicitly, was that they themselves were starving because of their misdeeds.

Given the enormous amount of evidence of the famine—much of which has surfaced long after the fact—and given the nearly complete, stony silence from Soviet sources concerning it—it was not mentioned in newspapers, in speeches, on the radio, by officials of the Party—it is impossible, I maintain, to assert that officials of the Party from Stalin downward, were not aware of a famine and it is very likely that it was planned by Stalin. It was merely covered by silence. It was understood by all that mere mention of the possibility of a famine was sufficient for imprisonment, even execution.

Fig. 13-4. Ukrainian Peasants Fleeing from their Village in Search of Food, 1933

Source: Wikimedia Commons

Emaciated peasants left their villages (Figure 13-4) to roam the Ukrainian cities' streets, but Soviets on those same streets said nothing of famine. One urban worker sent to the country to help with the harvest, notes: "At work one spoke of the famine or of the bodies in the streets, as if we were all part of a conspiracy of silence. … The rumors were confirmed when the townspeople were ordered to the countryside to help with the harvest and saw for themselves whence had come the living skeletons that haunted our city streets." Health-care workers were enjoined to come up with causes of death, like cardiac arrest or

---

[28] *Izvestia*, 4 and 12 Mar. 1933.

infectious disease, that were effects of starvation on certificates. In some provinces, books with registers of deaths were merely confiscated under the pretense that kulaks had infiltrated the registries. There were problems and shortages of food in places, but there never was any famine.[29]

"The deviation towards nationalism..."

Genocide

Moscow's cover-up worked for decades. It was only in the 1980s that Ukrainians across the globe, through persistence over decades, were able to inform the general global public of the Stalin-sanctioned atrocity. Says scholar Frank Sysyn (my numbers):

> Success in bringing the famine to the public's attention in the 1980s was primarily due to four projects: (1) production of the film *Harvest of Despair* (1984); (2) the organization of scholarly conferences and publications, above all, Robert Conquest's *Harvest of Sorrow* (1986); (3) the establishment of a US Congressional Commission on the Ukrainian famine (1985); and (4) the convening of an international commission of inquiry into the famine (1988). The diverse Ukrainian communities in the diaspora did not have a unified plan, but each of the projects influenced the others and served to bring the famine to the attention of the wider public.[30]

Were Stalin and other high-level officials of the party responsible for genocide?

According to Article 2 of the United Nation's Convention of the Prevention and Punishment of the Crime of Genocide, published in 1948, "genocide" is defined thus (again, my numbers):

> Genocide means any of the following acts committed with intent to destroy, in whole or in part, a national, ethnical, racial or religious group, as such: (1) Killing members of the group; (2) Causing serious bodily or mental harm to members of the group; (3) Deliberately inflicting on the group conditions of life calculated to bring about its physical destruction in whole or in part; (4) Imposing measures intended to

---

[29] Anne Applebaum, *Red Famine: Stalin's War on Ukraine* (New York: Anchor: 2017), 355–56.
[30] Frank Sysyn, "The Ukrainian Famine of 1932–3: The Role of the Ukrainian Diaspora in Research and Public Discussion," in *Studies in Comparative Genocide*, ed. Levon Chorbajian and George Shirinian (New York: St. Martin's Press, Inc., 1999), 189.

prevent births within the group; or (5) Forcibly transferring children of the group to another group.³¹

If we allow that Ukrainians are a distinct national or ethnic group—and that seems likely from our discussion in chapter 10—then it is impossible not to conclude that not only the Famine of 1932–1933, but also the numberless actions of violence against Ukrainians, both peasants and the education (consider the execution of the kobzars in chapter 10), in the early twentieth century were aimed at the destruction of Ukrainians as a national or ethnic group, at least through mass murder of millions of Ukrainians, from simple peasants to members of the intelligentsia, in an effort to thwart the nationalist movement and to impose willful acceptance of collectivization. As Orest Subtelny writes, "At best, Stalin viewed the deaths of millions as a necessary cost of industrialization. At worst, he consciously allowed the famine to wipe out resistance in a particularly troublesome region of his empire."³² Serhii Plokhy adds, "The regime singled Ukraine out for especially harsh treatment, as it was crucial to the fulfillment of Moscow's economic plans."³³ In Stalin's words: "If we do not start fixing the situation in Ukraine right away, we may lose Ukraine. ... In the Communist Party of Ukraine (500,000 members, ha-ha), there is no lack (yes, no lack!) of corrupt elements, committed and latent Petliurites, and, finally, outright agents of Piłsudski. As soon as things get worse, those elements will not hesitate to open a front within (and outside) the party, against the party."³⁴

The question now to be asked is whether Stalin and his minions—and I do not use "minions" pejorative but descriptively—knew that compulsatory collectivization and other anti-Ukrainization policies would lead to a large-scale famine in Ukraine prior to their implementation. If not, was it merely the case that his aggressive policies of implementing socialism with his Five-Year Plan had for him the welcome, but unanticipated, effect of the deaths through starvation of some four million Ukrainians?

Much has been and continues to be written and there seems not to be consensus. Robert Conquest and Anne Applebaum each argue that Stalin did not plan for famine from the start. Conquest maintains that Stalin was fully informed about the famine while it occurred. "That Stalin was fully informed does not quite prove that he had planned the famine from the first. His

---

31 "Genocide," *United Nations, Definitions*, https://www.un.org/en/genocideprevention genocide.shtml, accessed 13 Jan. 2023.
32 Orest Subtelny, *Ukraine: A History* (Toronto: University of Toronto Press, 1992), 416.
33 Sergii Plohky, *The Gates of Europe: A History of Ukraine* (New York: Basic Books, 2021), 250.
34 Sergii Plohky, *The Gates of Europe*, 251.

continuing to employ the policies which had produced the famine after the famine had clearly declared itself, and indeed to demand their more rigorous application, does, however, show that he regarded the weapon of famine as acceptable."[35] Anne Applebaum strongly suggests that Stalin was innocent of intentionally bringing about famine. He merely wished to meet quotas, and in doing that, he decreed that anyone keeping reserves of grain was guilty of "theft of state property." What happened to Ukrainian peasant-farmers was of little concern. "Stalin knew that the methods being used were damaging, and he knew they would fail. But he allowed them to continue for several fatal months, during which time millions died."[36]

Neither argument is cogent.

First, there is Conquest's *ad ignorantiam* argument: Being fully informed during the famine and his continued employment of strong-arm tactics does nowise "prove" that he had planned from the beginning on a famine. That one might concede, yet they certainly do not "prove" that Stalin did *not* have famine all along in mind. I will also add misuse by Conquest of "prove," which is a term best left to mathematicians and logicians, who concern themselves with deductions. Here we are in the realm of inductive arguing.

Second, there is Applebaum's argument—that Stalin implemented highly aggressive policies of *prodrazvyorstka* without knowing in advance that they would lead to famine. Stalin certainly registered mentally that the aggressive requisitions of grain during the Russian Civil War led to rife famine in 1921, and it is too much to believe that Stalin had forgotten that lesson. *Pace* Applebaum, I counter with an alteration of her text, "Stalin knew that the methods being used were damaging, and he knew they would lead to famine"—a suitable punishment for obdurate Ukrainians.

From the perspective of inculpation, which thesis is true might not matter much. Most of the dying through starvation, up to 80 percent, was in Ukrainian or large Ukrainian regions like North Caucasus, not in Russia. Of many millions who died from the famine—starvation occurred in the North Caucasus, the lower Volga area, and Kazakhstan—some four million were Ukrainians. Almost 20 percent of Ukraine's population was lost in the famine. Kyiv and Kharkiv Oblasts were hardest hit, as each lost over one million people. There is considerable evidence that Ukrainians—on account of intransigence, that is, unwillingness to collectivize in conjunction with their desire for autonomy and, consequently, their linkage with the capitalist West—were singled out for punishment, hence the concentration of deaths in that republic of the USSR.

---

[35] Robert Conquest, *The Harvest of Sorrow* (Oxford: Oxford University Press, 1986), 326.
[36] Anne Applebaum, *The Red Sorrow*, 228–29.

The aggressive policy of collection of Ukrainian grain was happening concomitantly with the move to quash Ukrainian nationalism.[37]

UPSHOT

Stalin's violent treatment of Ukrainians begs this question: Did Stalin hate Ukrainians?

Stalin, a Georgian, had no especial ethnic execration of Ukrainians and no especial love of Russian culture. It is likely that he, like other Russian rulers before him, never fully recognized their ethnicity to be distinct from that of Russia. Ukrainians were merely enemies because of circumstances. Stalin aimed to socialize the USSR and Ukraine—"a republic whose economic and human resource potential equaled that of all the other national republics put together"[38]—was the key republic to the success of that goal. Failure to win over the grain-rich republic to socialism would, in Stalin's eyes, mean failure of the experiment of one-country socialism. Yet Ukrainians, peasant-farmers particular, were obstinate and disobliging, and thus, they needed to be forced to remain with the union of republics. Stalin did not hate Ukrainians. He merely hated any person or group of persons that were albatrosses to his ideals.

The Ukraine, which emerged after the Great Famine, comprised broken people. The peasant-farmers who survived had lost their pluck. They "willfully" joined the collectives. There was not much choice. Collective farms were taxed at a rate much lower than independent farms, and only collective farms were given governmental assistance in the spring of 1933. By decade's end and with the influx of numerous thousands of Russians into Ukraine to work the overgrown fields, nearly 100 percent of all arable Ukrainian land was collectivized, though the yield was unimpressive. Furthermore, to "incentivize" the Russification of Ukraine, Stalin expunged more than one-half of the high-ranking Ukrainian officials from key positions by the summer of 1933 and replaced them with Soviet officials whose allegiance to the Party was less dubious[39]—a strange thing to do for someone who consistently preached respect for the cultural differences in the USSR.

Yet Ukrainian nationalism, as a deviation from socialism, was nowise to be tolerated. He says in an address in January 1934 to the Seventeenth Congress, "The deviation towards nationalism is the adaptation of the internationalist policy of the working class to the nationalist policy of the bourgeoisie. The deviation towards nationalism reflects the attempts of 'one's own,' 'national' bourgeoisie to undermine the Soviet system and to restore capitalism."

---

[37] Serhii Plohky, *The Gates of Europe*, 252–53.
[38] Stanislav Kul'chyts'yi, "The Holodomor of 1932–33: How and Why?" in *East/West: Journal of Ukrainian Studies*, Vol. 2, No. 1, 2015: 114.
[39] Serhii Plohky, *The Gates of Europe*, 254–55.

Nationalism is a deviation because "it is a departure from Leninist internationalism"[40] and a regression to capitalism. I return to this address in the afterword.

---

[40] J.V. Stalin, "Report to the Seventeenth Party Congress of the Work of the Central Committee of the CPSU(B)" (26 Jan. 1934), in *Marxists Internet Archive,* https://www.marxists.org/reference/archive/stalin/works/1934/01/26.htm, accessed 14 Jan. 2023.

Chapter 14

Stalin's Marxist Utopia

"The people who cast the votes decide nothing. The people who count the votes decide everything."

~Joseph Stalin

We have seen in previous chapters, from the testimonies of Lev Kopelev and others, that many young activists of the Party were swept to enthusiastic pro-Bolshevik action by the speeches of Stalin concerning the successes of one-country socialism and the promise of a better life: Stalin's Marxist utopia. Yet Stalin, as we have come to see, was well-schooled in the art of tergiversation. Precision of expression, too, was anathema, for then he, and not others, would be responsible for failures of policy, cleanly articulated.

Stalin's speeches, overall, tended to focus on what needed to be done in the short term—e.g., his series of Five-Year Plans[1]—and he seldom said anything about what Soviets might enjoy once one-country socialism was fully, or mostly, implemented. This chapter is an attempt to tease out Stalin's utopia.

"A good life cannot be obtained without effort"
What Is to Be Done?

On October 22, 1924, and some eight years prior to the large-scale famine in Ukraine, Stalin gives a speech to the secretaries of rural party units of the USSR. He begins aggressively—by castigation. All reports mention successes of the work in the countryside, but not defects. Second, all reports focus on the mood of members of the Party, not of non-Party peasant-farmers. The work in the countryside has been weak, and that is astonishing. "Is not agriculture developing? Have the conditions of the peasants not improved during the past two years since the surplus-appropriation system was abolished? Are the growth of industry and the supply of urban manufactures not easing the conditions of the peasants? Has not the stable currency eased the conditions of

---

[1] From 1928 to 1953, there would be four Five-Year Plans.

the peasants?" To understand the weakness of the Party's work in the countryside, one must first, adds Stalin, understand its strength in cities[2]—again, the notion that rural areas must be urbanized.

In towns and cities, there is an enormous mass of many hundreds of thousands of non-Party workers. From those, the Party recruits members, non-Party actives, through its successes in the industries of the cities. "Hence, the non-Party active is not only a connecting bridge, but also the very ample reservoir from which our Party draws new forces. Without such an active our Party could not develop. The Party grows and gains strength *if* a wide non-Party active grows and gains strength around the Party. The Party grows sick and feeble *if* there is no such active."[3]

In the countryside, there are tens of millions of peasant-farmers, but only a "thin network of Party units" and an "equally thin network of non-Party peasants who sympathize with the Party." How can a thin network of non-Party peasants link the numerous peasant-farmers to the Party? It cannot. "Hence, our Party's chief task in the countryside is to create a numerous, non-Party peasant active, numbering several hundred thousand, capable of linking the Party with the tens of millions of toiling peasants."[4]

How is that to be done?

Stalin's solution, in 1924, is sensible, democratic, and humane. Communists must treat the non-Party man as an equal. There must be, in Lenin's words, mutual confidence. Communists must teach and learn from peasant-farmers, otherwise, they will not gain the farmers' trust needed for feeding urban laborers pursuant to Stalin's plan of accelerating output in Soviet industry.[5] Yet, freed from the servitude of feudalism in the time of the tsars, the class of peasant-farmers now "has forgotten the landlords and is now concerned about ... selling its grain at the highest possible price,"[6] which nowise benefits the Party. That, at least, was the rhetoric of that day, not long after the death of Lenin.

On January 11, 1933, while the famine in Ukraine rages, Stalin again delivers a speech on defects of the Party's work in the countryside. There is no longer concern about mutual confidence, about treating peasant-farmers as equals. The concern is that procurements of grain were more difficult in 1932 than in

---

[2] J.V. Stalin, "The Party's Immediate Tasks in the Countryside," (26 Oct. 1924), in *Marxists Internet Archive*, https://www.marxists.org/reference/archive/stalinworks/1924/10/26.htm, accessed 12 Apr. 2023.
[3] J.V. Stalin, "The Party's Immediate Tasks in the Countryside."
[4] J.V. Stalin, "The Party's Immediate Tasks in the Countryside."
[5] J.V. Stalin, "The Party's Immediate Tasks in the Countryside."
[6] J.V. Stalin, "The Party's Immediate Tasks in the Countryside."

1931, while harvest, Stalin's figures show, was improved in 1932.[7] There is no mention of millions of Soviets, and half of them being Ukrainians, having died or on their way to dying in a Party-imposed famine. The focus is on how to make the collectives prosperous.

Fig. 14-1. Joseph Stalin at the Tehran Conference, 1943

Source: Wikimedia Commons

One month later, Stalin states that the collective-farm path is difficult but adds, with philosophical triteness, that "a good life cannot be obtained without effort." Moreover, the current difficulties "seem mere child's play" when compared to those that workers' faced 10 to 15 years ago. He sums: "Socialism is a good thing. A happy, socialist life is unquestionably a good thing. But all that is a matter of the future. The main question now is not what we shall achieve in the future. The main question is: What have we already achieved at present?" He adds at the end of this lengthy speech: "The destinies of nations and of states are now determined, not only by leaders, but primarily and mainly by the vast masses of the working people. The workers and the peasants, who without fuss and noise are building factories and mills, constructing mines and railways, building collective farms and state farms, creating all the values of life,

---

[7] J.V. Stalin, "Work in the Countryside" (11 Jan. 1933), in *Marxists Internet Archive*, https://www.marxists.org/reference/archive/stalin/works/1933/01/11.htm, accessed 6 Jan. 2023.

feeding and clothing the whole world—they are the real heroes and the creators of the new life."[8]

What is noteworthy here and something that typifies Stalin's somewhat colorless, pedestrian speeches is the depiction of unfussy, selfless laborers giving their all for the State and even for the prospect of the socialization of the world. Yet Stalin ever eschews discussion of how Stalinist Marxism will improve life for the average "proletariat"—that is, why it will be better to escape classes for the liberating uniformity of classlessness promised by Marx. There continue to be difficulties, Stalin notes, but they are not so bad when compared to those problems fronted by laborers nearly a generation ago. We are told not to question the value of socialism: Its value is obvious. "Socialist life is unquestionably a good thing." Nevertheless, why would anyone be moved by that uninformative, flavorless claim? Peasant-farmers clearly were not. Soviets are again asked to trust that there will be a future in which the present and past problems will have evanesced.

Millions of Soviets, Ukrainians among them, would be sacrificial lambs for Stalin's socialist propaganda—it is reasonably estimated that throughout his sanguinary tenure as dictator of the USSR, up to 20 million people were killed[9]—as the means of instantiation of Stalin's utopia, which might profitably be likened in his mind to a well-working machine, given his frequent references to industrializing the countryside. For Stalin, it is the machine that matters, not its parts. In a large, efficient machine, all the parts work together, while each has a critical function, though many parts will have the same function. When all parts perform their function well, the machine efficiently produces what it is designed to produce. Moreover, because numerous parts have the same function, the parts are replaceable.

For Stalin, for socialism to work, the whole of the USSR must be socialized. Cities must be industrialized, and there must be laborers for the raw materials needed for factories. The countryside, too, must be industrialized. The perceived inefficiency of numerous small farms scattered in a large area of land can be mitigated by collectivizing farming: having one large farm absorb the small farms and placing the large farm under the ownership and direction of activists of the state. Within a socialized republic, there will be unity, and not merely a sense of unity, engendered by all persons having a strong sense of working

---

[8] J.V. Stalin, "Speech Delivered at the First All-Union Congress of Collective Farm Shock Brigadiers" (19 Feb. 1933), in *Marxists Internet Archive*, https://www.marxists.org/reference/archive/stalin/works/1933/02/19.htm, accessed 6 Jan. 2023.

[9] Simon Sebag Montefiore, *Stalin: The Court of the Red Tsar* (New York: Alfred A. Knopf, 2003), 643, and Timothy Snyder, *Bloodlands: Europe between Hitler and Stalin* (New York: Basic Books, 2010), 384.

toward something common and "unquestionably" good, at least inasmuch as Stalinism steers clear of the inequalities of industrialized capitalism.[10] If, in the process of bringing about this Marxist utopia, millions of lives have to be lost and the system will benefit by the free slave-labor of prisoners (most wrongly sentenced) in prisons and gulags, then that is a price worth the effort.[11]

"A good life cannot be obtained without effort"
Stalin & the Good Life

I have just sketched, briefly, a picture of what must be done to implement Stalin's one-country socialism, and it does not sound, unless the sketch is too sketchy, all that inviting.

What does Stalin himself say about his socialist utopia?

When one combs Stalin's writings, one finds little about Stalin on the good life. Much of what he writes concerns the eschewal of the bad life lived by the millions exploited by rich capitalists. Philosopher Geroid Tanquary Robinson notes that there are 179 references to "dictatorship of the proletariat" and only three to "communist society" where, according to Marx, dictatorships and states have wholly disappeared. "By and large his comments on the Communist Utopia are brief, scattered, incomplete, sometimes obscure, and sometimes at least outwardly self-contradictory."[12]

Yet, the expiscation of his works allows some discussion of Stalin's sense of utopia. Stalin, as we have seen, was committed to one-country socialism as the first and decisive step toward global socialism. That entails, *inter alia*, the integration of Ukraine, Caucasia, Belarus, and Russia into the USSR. Though Stalin pays lip service to voluntarism and federalism as needed for integration, his coercive and sanguinary actions betray commitment to the Russification of Soviet republics through dictatorship from Moscow, and Russification implies the eventual disappearance of all cultural differences. Stalin was also

---

[10] Geroid Tanquary Robinson, "Stalin's Vision of Utopia: The Future Communist Society," in *Proceedings of the American Philosophical Society*, Vol. 99, No. 1, 1955: 11–21.

[11] One of the guiding principles of Leninism, gleaned from revolutionist Peter Tkachev, was that there could be a major revolution without popular consent—a strange concept, if the revolution is on behalf of the people. If successful, the revolutionists would lead the ignorant peasants toward a brighter future. To guard against opposition to the paradisiacal ideology of the revolutionists, Tkachev advocated extermination of oppositional elements, even if that meant extermination of most of the population. Edvard Radzinsky, *Stalin* (New York: Anchor, 1997), 34.

[12] Geroid Tanquary Robinson, "Stalin's Vision of Utopia," 12.

committed to an industrial model of agriculture and consolidation of urban industry and rural agriculture into an "organic" whole, hence my metaphor of a well-working machine. With the industrialization of both cities and the countryside, there would be no class of people for capitalists to exploit, for there would be no capitalists and no longer any poor. Moreover, there would be a centrally directed system of barter to supplant money. Last, mechanization would become the religion of the State. In the poster below (Figure 14-2), prelates of the Orthodox Church cower as a mighty Soviet tractor approaches.

Fig. 14-2. Soviet Anti-Religion Poster of Unknown Date

Source: 123RF

Yet things were abysmal, not favorable, in Russia during and at the end of the First Five-Year Plan. The promise of Leninist socialism was more and better goods produced more cheaply than in capitalist countries, and thus, a better quality of life than in capitalist countries.

That promise never materialized. In 1930, says Alexander Barmine, "manufactured goods and food were much scarcer than money, and money was scarcer than jobs."[13] All were proclaimed boastfully by the Party to be working, yet quality food was scarce and inordinately priced. Wages were improved, but the extra money had no purchasing power because by 1933, inflation was suffocating. "The ruble, little by little, had fallen until its purchasing power was ten, twenty, thirty, or forty times lower than that of 1926, according to the articles purchased." A laborer, who earned 100 to 200 rubles a month, paid one ruble for a kilo of black bread, two rubles for a kilo of white bread, nine rubles for a kilo of rice, 10 rubles for a kilo of sugar or meat, over 10 rubles for 10 eggs, some 25 rubles for a kilo of butter, and up to 150 rubles for one pair of shoes. Most laborers sustained themselves and their families on black bread, buckwheat, potatoes, and cabbage. An average industrial laborer would spend 90 percent of his earnings on food.[14] High officials of the Party, however, suffered no such inconveniences. They worked hard but lived lavishly and sybaritically, had many servants and guards in the estates of the removed wealthy bourgeois, and took many vacations. They were not overly concerned about the plight of the "proletariats."

Soviet industry, too, was in shambles. The top-heavy bureaucracy made the efficiency of production impossible. It was a thick system that customarily promoted the inept, the unintelligent, and the inefficient—those who chummed up to the *Vozhd* or his underlings—and spies were everywhere. Managers were given impossible production demands that sometimes could be met in the short term, though they were unsustainable in the long term. Barmine, who spent much time in Soviet industrial production, illustrates a state-of-the-art ball-bearing factory, Sharikopodchipnik, built and supervised by a certain Bodrov. By enjoinment of the Politburo, Bodrov was forced to up production to two million bearings per month. He met those demands at the expense of his machines, which ran non-stop. Following Stalin's principle that producers can produce more if pushed to do more, Grigory Ordjonikidze, People's Commissar for Heavy Industry, demanded three million bearings per month. Bodrov insisted that that goal could not be met. Bodrov "disappeared" and was replaced by another engineer, Melamed, who boasted that he could produce the extra bearings and did so for three months. It was soon disclosed that many of the bearings were faulty due to defective, "overwrought" machines. As an "enemy of the people" for allowing the machines to deteriorate, Melamed too "disappeared."[15]

---

[13] Alexander Barmine, *One Who Survived: The Life Story of a Russian under Stalin* (New York: G.P. Putnam's Sons, 1945), 197.
[14] Alexander Barmine, *One Who Survived*, 208–9.
[15] Alexander Barmine, *One Who Survived*, 210–11.

What happened in Sharikopodchipnik typified what was happening in Soviet factories throughout the USSR. That is confirmed by Victor Kravchenko who was chief engineer at a pipe plant in Nikopol. When the story came out of the miraculous output of a certain Stakhanov in a coal mine in Donetz Basin—this man is said to have mined 102 tons of coal in one shift—the achievement was celebrated throughout the USSR. That scrap of propaganda was created to boost morale and inspire workers to increase productivity. Yet it had the "capitalist" result of splitting laborers into "Stakhanovites" and mere laborers: the former were given a better wage and added perks; the latter and the overwhelming majority of laborers were given a reduced wage. On one media-covered shift of Stakhanovites in Kravchenko's plant, production was increased by eight percent, and there were plaudits for the laborers and overseers. What was not reported was that what was gained by the Stakhanovite shift was more than lost on the other two shifts, where laborers underperformed, because they felt themselves insignificant. The overall result of the propaganda was that there was a higher bar set for production goals but no overall improvement in the total money given to laborers.[16] Moreover, there was again no consideration for the maintenance of the machines in the factory.

The real cost of production, despite inordinately low wages for laborers, was very much greater in the USSR than in capitalistic countries. First, lack of competition from other businesses simpatico made overseers and workers lethargic and uncreative. Next, workers lacked incentive to work enthusiastically and efficiently—fear was the sole motivator—and they seldom worked enthusiastically and efficiently. They were just too exhausted from overwork, lack of incentives, indescribably poor housing, and lack of healthy food, priced out of the reach of laborers. Again, when production was poor, lack of profit was compensated for by a cut in the wages of laborers, who were seldom incentivized by the promise of greater pay, but mostly by loss of current pay. Last, with heavy industries, no decisions could be rendered without Stalin's approval, and that massively delayed or annulled many significant projects. Sums Alexander Barmine: "Since thousands of relatively unimportant, as well as all-important, problems must pass through Stalin's hands for the final decision, the top is always jammed. Weeks are spent in waiting: commissars wait in Stalin's office; presidents of companies wait in the offices of the commissars; and so on."[17] Yet prior to a proposal or problem reaching Stalin, Victor Kravchenko mentions the slowing of its movement due to the ponderous bureaucracy: "hundreds of useless officials on futile jobs" who involved themselves in the process, if only to save their own skins. Moreover, proposals

---

[16] Victor Kravchenko, *I Chose Freedom* (New York: Charles Scribners' Sons, 1946), 187–89.
[17] Alexander Barmine, *One Who Survived*, 213.

and problems were often brought to a halt by the "feverish spying, denunciations and investigations" of Chekists, always looking for omnipresent saboteurs.[18] All persons had always to prove their essentiality in the process.

And so, by the end of the Five-Year Plan in 1933, the promised utopia was a dystopia. One-country socialism was a failure, as famine raged throughout many of the republics of the USSR, Ukraine especially. Stalin covered himself by blaming every catastrophe on the vaunted enemies of the Party, now within the Party.

What, however, is Stalin's vision of global socialism?

Stalin never said much about that topic. "All that," he was wont to say, "is a matter of the future." Yet global socialization, not merely Marxizing Russia or the USSR, was the aim of committed Marxists like Lenin and Trotsky. Marxists, Stalin included, were not nationalists. Neither Lenin nor Trotsky thought that there was much chance of global socialization happening from Russia, an enormous boondocks. The revolution needed to start from an inveterate capitalist Western country like Germany, the country of the great Marx, which had fully experienced the "defects" of free markets. Neither Lenin nor Trotsky thought that there was any chance of Russia, as a union of republics, becoming a self-sustaining socialist "democracy." Stalin did, or at least he aimed to find out, even though the USSR had never entered the capitalistic phase of the dialectical process.

Yet, if we do extrapolate from Stalin's vision for the USSR, then we can say that Stalinism aimed to free people from the yoke of ownership, in which few people owned much and expropriated the labor and lives of others, owning scant or nothing. This freedom, through the promise of mass equalitarianism of some sort, would be ushered in and overseen by a centralized governing power—and that for Stalin was Stalin—which would militate for all farmers and laborers who would lose themselves in their love of labor and love of the Party, the secular religion of the Stalinist proletariat. Infusion through workers losing themselves in their labor because of their love of the Party, was essential to Stalin's scheme. Bolsheviks were expected to place their Party above all other concerns—even their lives. Communists were given duties, *nagruzki*, in keeping with their time and talents. Involvement in many *nagruzki* entailed that a Bolshevik was involved in many parts of the labyrinth of everyday Bolshevik activities.[19] That showed his loyalty to Stalin, but with greater visibility, it also greatly increased the possibility of proving oneself an enemy of the Party.

---

[18] Victor Kravchenko, *I Chose Freedom*, 329.
[19] Alexander Barmine, *One Who Survived*, 157–59.

What about the notion of "mass equalitarianism"? Stalin does address that issue early in 1934 with reference to conceivable objections to life in an artel where there are differences in personnel because of differences in duties.

> By equality Marxism means, not equalization of personal requirements and everyday life, but the abolition of classes, i.e., (A) the equal emancipation of all working people from exploitation after the capitalists have been overthrown and expropriated; (B) the equal abolition for all of private property in the means of production after they have been converted into the property of the whole of society; (C) the equal duty of all to work according to their ability, and the equal right of all working people to receive in return for this according to the work performed (*socialist* society); (D) the equal duty of all to work according to their ability, and the equal right of all working people to receive in return for this according to their needs (*communist* society). Moreover, Marxism proceeds from the assumption that people's tastes and requirements are not, and cannot be, identical and equal in quality or quantity, whether in the period of socialism or in the period of communism.[20]

It is manifest that conditions C and D are problematic. Pursuant to Stalinist Marxism, it is the Party (Stalin) that measures the quality and quantity of the work performed by laborers. It is the Party (Stalin) that determines the needs of the workers and hence, what return laborers are to get for their work. Conditions C and D also show that equality entails selfless work for the sake of the Party. Conditions C and D are so vaguely articulated that they, in effect, are discretionary, and the discretion here is that of Stalin.

Despite the "abolition of classes," the Stalinist Soviet Union was neatly echeloned. "The system was set up so that a man worked only among people of his particular social group, lived only among them, shopped only among them, and socialized with no one else."[21] Even in the large factories, there was strict separation of the common laborers, the engineers, and higher foremen, and the officials of the Party—each with its own cafeteria in the factory and each with its own living conditions thereafter. Laborers often lived in crude and filthy barracks, while higher foremen and engineers had sanitary and spacious houses, and high officials of the Party had large residences with servants. The

---

[20] J.V. Stalin, "Report to the Seventeenth Party Congress" (26 Jan. 1934), in *Marxists Internet Archive*, https://www.marxists.org/reference/archive/stalin/works1934/1/6.htm, accessed 23 Jan. 2023.
[21] Petro G. Grigorenko, *Memoirs* (New York: W.W. Norton, 1982), 207–8.

latter two groups had assistants in the factory and it was commonplace for assistants to be informants to the GPU.[22] Moreover, there were also levels of membership in the GPU or NKVD, whose numerous tens of thousands of members were scattered throughout the USSR and across the globe. So, there is not much here to say about the riddance of classes in the promise of utopia.

I turn to the measured words of biographer Edvard Radzinsky to sum up the promise of Stalin's utopia:

> There would be a single bank, a single economic plan, a peasantry organized in collective farms, and a pyramid of lesser leaders, all-powerful at their own level. At the top of the pyramid would be the Supreme Leader, his word instantly made flesh in the lesser leaders. There would be ruthless discipline, ruthless punishments. Gigantic resources would be concentrated in the hands of the state and the leader. He would be able to create a huge industrial economy. And hence a huge army. And then, … The Great Leninist Dream of World Revolution.[23]

I merely add to Radzinsky's colorful, but accurate assessment that to get to that utopia—"all that is a matter for the future"—millions of lives would have to be sacrificed and at Stalin's discretion.

UPSHOT

I have shown in this chapter the execrable consequences of the aggressive implementation of Stalin's Five-Year Plan. In the effort to industrialize the countryside, Stalin forced independent farmers to collectivize, and his coercive policies were especially severe in Ukraine. Consequently, millions of Ukrainians were dispossessed, sent to gulags as free labor for the State, or left to starve through highly aggressive, often violent, means of *prodrazvyorstka*—i.e., grain-collecting campaigns.

Despite the atrocities in Ukraine and in other republics of the Soviet Union, at the end of the Five-Year Plan in 1932, when the deaths from starvation began to mount, Stalin claimed enormous successes for Soviet Russia. The plan showed that the working class could shatter the old and build the new, that socialism could be grounded and thrive in one country, and that capitalism was not the best system of economy. In a speech delivered on January 7, 1933, Stalin vaunts:

---

[22] Victor Kravchenko, *I Chose Freedom* (New York: Charles Scribners' Sons, 1946), 174–76.
[23] Edvard Radzinksy, *Stalin* (New York: Anchor Books: 1997), 232.

> We did not have an iron and steel industry, the basis for the industrialization of the country. Now we have one. We did not have a tractor industry. Now we have one. We did not have an automobile industry. Now we have one. We did not have a machine-tool industry. Now we have one. We did not have a big and modern chemical industry. Now we have one. We did not have a real and big industry for the production of modern agricultural machinery. Now we have one. We did not have an aircraft industry. Now we have one. In output of electric power we were last on the list. Now we rank among the first. In output of oil products and coal we were last on the list. Now we rank among the first.[24]

Stalin sums with habitual hypocrisy and hyperbole, "The results of the Five-Year Plan have shown that the capitalist system of economy is bankrupt and unstable; that it has outlived its day and must give way to another, a higher Soviet, socialist system of economy; that the only system of economy that has no fear of crises and is able to overcome the difficulties which capitalism cannot solve, is the Soviet system of economy."[25]

The hyperbole and hypocrisy, given the state of the Soviet economy at the end of Stalin's Five-Year Plan, is evident and shameful. Yet that is the nodus of the philosophy of consequentialism. One can always justify large current flagitiousness by the promise of a not-too-distant future in which flagitiousness will be absent. That has been the promise of numerous tyrants over the centuries. The result is always that the tyrant and his minions live extravagantly and hedonistically at the expense of the people that they "love and protect."

Nonetheless, Stalin was wedded to a theory that had never been tested, to a theory to which he was wholly emotionally attached, and he was not about to let reality get in the way of his commitment to it. In his mind, problems existed, but they were due to the ever-present enemies of the people, which had to be liquidated—the so-called "wet work" of the Party—if that "happy socialist life," which was "unquestionably a good thing," could ever take root.

In the latter years of the 1930s, Stalin likely gave up the dream of socialism's promise of a local or global utopia. His focus would become sustaining and, if possible, growing his dictatorial powers and rewarding profligately his "friends."

---

[24] Joseph Stalin, "The Results of the First Five-Year Plan," in *Marxists Internet Archive*, https://www.marxists.org/reference/archive/stalin/works/1933/01/07.htm, accessed 22 Nov. 2022.
[25] Joseph Stalin, "The Results of the First Five-Year Plan."

Afterword

On January 26, 1934, Stalin addresses the Seventeenth Party Congress. He limns numerous victories of the Party. The anti-Leninist Trotskyites have been quashed and scattered. Nationalist deviators, Ukrainians especially, have also been quashed and scattered.[1]

How have those victories happened?

At the Fifteenth Party Congress, Stalin says, there were concessions by the Party that there were anti-Leninists, and so there was a need for a war against them. At the Sixteenth Party Congress, that war was waged and won. Yet now, the country has been industrialized, the kulaks have been liquidated, and "complete collectivization has triumphed." He sums, "There is nothing to prove and, it seems, no one to fight. Everyone sees that the line of the Party has triumphed." There then, of course, are also the requisite numerous quotes from Lenin's speeches and writings [2] to support his claims.

Stalin, of course, glossed over the many hundreds of thousands who were victims of starvation, the many hundreds of thousands who were in the prisons and gulags.[3]

With nothing to prove and no one to fight, one might ask, "What [else] is to be done?"

That is an idle question. Stalin would find someone else to fight. He ever needed to have someone to fight—kulaks, enemies of the Party, counter-revolutionists, or anti-Leninists—and always they were everywhere. Enemies, as we shall also see, were forever needed to secure his leadership.

The 1930s would be a decade of large changes in Stalin's Party, which were a natural extension of his sanguinary actions to enforce collectivization. He sought to strengthen and consolidate his role of *Vozhd* of the Party—he began

---

[1] J.V. Stalin, "Report to the Seventeenth Party Congress of the Work of the Central Committee of the CPSU(B)" (26 Jan. 1934), in *Marxists Internet Archive,* https://www.marxists.org/reference/archive/stalin/works/1934/01/26.htm, accessed 14 Jan. 2023.

[2] E.g., V.I. Lenin, "On Deceiving the People with Slogans about Liberty and Equality," in *Works,* Vol. 24, 293–94.

3 For more, see Oleg Khlevniuk and Marta D. Olynyk "Comments on the Sort-Term Consequences of the Holodomor," in *Harvard Ukrainian Studies,* Vol. 30, No. 1.4: 149–61.

to liken himself to a godlike tsar[4]—by making sure that those nearest to him were completely devoted to and had unconditional faith in him, with devotion and faith in him being the criteria by which he judged others. To consolidate his role as the Party's "tsar," he took to eliminating anyone who might pose any danger to his leadership, which was essentially dictatorial.

The most imminent danger to Stalin was Sergey Kirov (1886–1934, Figure A-1)—the rising star of the Party. Kirov was young, handsome, winsome, eloquently persuasive in speech, and at least as popular as Stalin, as the ovation of his speech at the Party's Sixteenth Congress early in 1934 showed. Unlike Stalin, Kirov was a moderate. He maintained that some amount of discordance in the Party was good, and thus, his advocacy for leniency toward dissidents within the Party. And so, many "Oppositionists," among them Kamenev and Zinoviev—there was large, mostly quiet, for fear of recrimination, opposition to Stalin's leadership due to the bunglesome manner in which Stalin pushed for socialism in his Five-Year Plan—were brought back, and integrated, into the Party. Oppositionist Martemyan Ryutin, whom Stalin had ousted from the Party and whom Stalin wished to see executed, was granted a stay by the Politburo on account of Kirov.

Fig. A-1. Sergey Kirov

Source: kratkoebio.ru

---

[4] Diary of Maria Svanidze, 29 Apr. 1935, "He once said of the ovations he received, 'The people need a tsar,' i.e., someone to reverence, someone to live and work for." Edvard Radzinsky, *Stalin* (New York: Anchor, 1997), 333. For more, see Sheila Fitzpatrick, "The Boss and His Team: Stalin and the Inner Circle, 1925–33," in *Russian Politics from Lenin to Putin*, ed. Stephen Fortescue (New York: Palgrave-Macmillan, 2010), 51–75.

Afterword

Stalin's popularity, notwithstanding the resounding ovations he typically received during and after a speech, was at its nadir. Many in the Party wished to see him replaced. He could, and would, profit much from the liquidation of Kirov, who posed a serious threat to his leadership of the Soviet Union and failed to speak to Stalin with the customary deference that others showed him,[5] and that wet task is just what occurred. Kirov was assassinated on December 1, 1934. That event, which might have occurred at the behest, certainly subtly, of the Boss, led to a radical shift in Stalin's policies.[6]

Stalin grieved openly and bitterly over the expiration of Kirov, whom Stalin in some measure much loved. It is extraordinary that Stalin could so easily put to death so many whom he loved, admired, and respected, and show above-board grief on their passing.[7] He doubtless consoled himself by entertaining the notion that those whom he condemned to death were condemned for the future good of the Party—*viz.*, that putting to death such persons was evidence of the Boss' devotion to the cause.

With Kirov's death, Stalin, who contemned the moderate turn of the Party, turned it in an intolerably Leftist direction. He would now nowise tolerate dissent. To eliminate the possibility of ascent of another Kirov, if Stalin was behind the killing, or to identify those behind Kirov's murder and those plotting to overthrow the government, if Stalin was not behind the killing, he would liquidate anyone who might pose the least threat to his leadership. Thus, there began what has come to be dubbed the "Great Purge" or the "Bolshevik Terror" of 1936–1938, and that marked a sea change in Stalin's political commitment to Marxism.

The Bolshevik Terror was a top-to-bottom, thorough expurgation of anyone who knew anything about Stalin's rise to leadership and his means of maintaining power or anyone who was intimately involved in the Russian Revolution and Civil War. That would entail, ironically, riddance of almost all the Old Guard—all who participated in the Russian Civil War, all who helped to bring the Bolsheviks to power, all the loyalists of Lenin. It began, logically enough, with leaders of the Party who had too much popularity or power, and then there followed generals of the army, chiefs of industry, key diplomats in

---

[5] Artyom recalls a mocking toast to Stalin by Kirov. "A toast to Stalin, the great leader of all peoples and all times. I am a busy man but I have probably forgotten some of the other great things you have done too." Simon Sebag Montefiore, *Stalin: Court of the Red Tsar* (New York: Alfred A. Knopf, 2004), 131.

[6] For more on Kirov, see Alexander Barmine, *One Who Survived: The Life Story of a Russian under the Soviets* (New York: G.P. Putnam's Sons, 1945), 247–53, especially 253n1.

[7] That is perhaps something he learned from his alcoholic father. It is not uncommon for alcoholics to act with dreadful cruelty, when drunk, and wake the next day as if nothing untoward has happened, or say, "I was drunk."

and outside of Russia, and even eventually those police who were doing the dirty work of following, arresting, and exterminating "Oppositionists" or "enemies." Most of Stalin's political "comrades" from the days of Lenin—e.g., Lev Kamenev and Grigory Zinoviev of the Left; Nikolai Bukharin and Alexei Rykov of the Right;[8] and Leon Trotsky (removed as commissar of war in 1925, expelled from the Party in 1929, and killed, while in exile, in Mexico City in 1940) were liquidated.

While the proximate cause of the purge was the death of Kirov, the rationalization was given in a singular speech on March 3, 1937, to the Plenum of the Central Committee of the Bolsheviks. There are anti-Leninists, says Stalin, who "mask themselves as Bolsheviks." Zinovievites and Trotskyites have gathered around them "every hostile bourgeois element" and have entered the confidence of the Party. As members of the Party, they seek to destroy the Party. "Their strength lies … in their possession of a Party card [that] … gains for them political confidence and opens to them all our institutions and organizations. … By possessing Party cards and pretending to be friends of Soviet power, they have deceived our people politically, abused confidence, wrecked on the sly, and revealed our state secrets to the enemies of the Soviet Union," across the globe.[9]

Comrades of the Party, adds Stalin, seem to have forgotten one singular fact: capitalist encirclement. "They have forgotten that Soviet power was victorious in only one-sixth of the world, that five-sixths of the world is in the possession of the capitalist states.[10] They have forgotten that the Soviet Union finds itself encircled by capitalist states."[11]

What is capitalist encirclement?

"It means that there is one country, the Soviet Union, which has established at home a Socialist order, and that there are, besides, many countries, bourgeois countries, which continue to carry on the capitalist form of life and which encircle the Soviet Union, waiting for the opportunity to attack it, to crush it, or, in any case-to undermine its might and to weaken it."[12]

By implication, Stalin asserts the success of one-country socialism, but concedes its tenuousness because of capitalist encirclement. The obvious

---

[8] Mikhail Tomsky committed suicide in August 1936.
[9] J.V. Stalin, "Defects in Party Work and Measures for Liquidating Troskyite and other Double-Dealers" (3 Mar. 1937), in *Marxists Internet Archives*, https://www.marxists.org/reference/archive/stalin/works/1937/03/03.htm, accessed 16 Jan. 2023.
[10] A singular and false claim.
[11] J.V. Stalin, "Defects in Party Work and Measures for Liquidating Troskyite and other Double-Dealers."
[12] J.V. Stalin, "Defects in Party Work and Measures for Liquidating Troskyite and other Double-Dealers."

result of capitalist encirclement is that many anti-Leninists have infiltrated the USSR. Thus, Stalin in 1936 undertakes an enormous expurgation of the Soviet Party to rid of all bourgeois elements, hence the Bolshevik Terror.

In anticipation of the effects of Stalin's barmy turn of mind, many members of the Party, fearing the worst, left the Party and left Moscow and other prominent Soviet cities and fled to villages, towns, and cities remote from direct Bolshevik influence. That mass evacuation, in some measure, worked to Stalin's advantage in the eyes of the ignorant masses. This mass evacuation of Bolsheviks was to the Soviet *hoi polloi* proof not only of capitalist encirclement but also of capitalist penetration.

The theatricality of the Great Purge was evident in its tripartite wave of show trials in which those indicted, often guilty of doing nothing or of nothing but what they were "asked" to do, were forced to admit through "confession" their anti-Leninist intentions. The first show trial (19–24 August 1936) featured the trials of Lev Kamenev and Grigory Zinoviev, but included 14 others (all shot); the second (23–30 January 1937), Yuri Pyatakov and Karl Radek and 15 others (13 shot); the third (March 1938), Nikolai Bukharin, Genrikh Yagoda (former head of NKVD), and Alexei Rykov and 19 others (18 executed).[13] Confessions were almost always forthcoming, for the means of torture and blackmail were sophisticated, visceral, and effectual. Innocent members of one's family would, if needed, be brought into play. Stalin would often feign astonishment that an important member of the Party was guilty of sabotage. He would often remark, as part of the pageantry, something like, "I cannot believe that ******* is an enemy of the people, but, you see, he signed his confession."

Those brought to trial, once humiliated by confession, were sometimes (provisionally) acquitted such that they were assured of having won, again, their Boss' approbation. Stalin would then reward such repenters with promise of a promotion within the Party, only to have them again arrested and later executed.[14] The sadism of that process, which was, in effect, a game that was reserved for his greatest enemies—e.g., anyone who might have at one time betrayed or slandered him, who was popular, or who knew too much about his rise to power as a slyboots—betrays a warped mind and greatly unstable, volatile person.

To complement the circus-nature of the in-camera trials, libraries were purged of many materials in Stalin's later effort to reinvent and rewrite Soviet

---

[13] Leon Sedov, *The Red Book: On the Moscow Trials* (New York: New Park, 1980), https://www.marxists.org/history/etol/writers/sedov/works/red/index.htm, accessed 12 Apr. 2023.
[14] Justin Ramos-Flynn, "Stalin's Victims from the Great Purge," https://scalar.usc.edu/works/stalins-victims-from-the-great-purge/moscow-trials, accessed 16 Jan. 2023.

history. Back-issues of the State-sanctioned newspapers, *Pravda* and *Izvestia*, were unavailable to patrons.

Fig. A-2. Nikolai Bukharin, 1926

Source: Wikipedia

Stalin's treatment of the brilliant and highly popular young theoretician of the Party, Nikolai Bukharin (1888–1938, Figure A-2), key confessor of the third kangaroo court, offers a fit illustration of Stalin's sadism. Bukharin began his work as a revolutionist on the Bolshevik Left, those opposed to Lenin's moderate New Economic Policy, but was led to the conservative Right, which he came in time to lead. Bukharin, on account of his moderatism and popularity, fell into disfavor with Stalin when the latter pushed for strong-arm means of collectivizing farms as part of his Five-Year Plan. Bukharin was expelled from the Party in 1929.[15]

Bukharin was arrested on February 27, 1938, as part of the Bolshevik Terror and imprisoned. In prison, he was exposed to harsh conditions much too severe for the frail intellectual. While imprisoned, Bukharin sent Stalin 43 letters, most groveling and ingratiatory. The broken man readily "admitted" to many wrongdoings against Stalin and the Party, and he begged for clemency. In one letter to the *Vozhd*, Bukharin writes: "All my dreams recently have come down to one thing—to stick closely to the leadership and to you ... to work with all my strength, subordinating myself completely to your advice, instructions,

---

[15] Paul R. Gregory, Politics, *Murder, and Love in Stalin's Kremlin: The Story of Nikolai Bukharin and Anna Larina* (Stanford: Hoover Institution Press, 2010), chap. 17.

and requirements."[16] Stalin, perhaps frustrated that there was nothing left of Bukharin to break, replied to none of the letters. A man, broken, is no longer any fun.[17] Bukharin was shot on March 15, 1938.

There were also purges within the swollen People's Commissariat of Internal Affairs (NKVD), which was itself a huge bureaucracy with hundreds of thousands of members scattered across the globe, all of whom were doing the filthy deeds of the Party under the psychotic guidance of Stalin. I mention merely some of the most noteworthy arrests. Genrikh Yagoda, on September 26, 1936, after a letter from Stalin, was removed as head of the NKVD and replaced by Nikolai Yezhov, a diminutive man with a profound work ethic and little sexual discretion, who undertook the affairs of the show trials during the Great Purge.[18] Yagoda would be later arrested in March 1937 and tried on March 21. Found guilty, he was shot. Yezhov would soon arrest his deputy, Yuri Pyatakov, who would be shot on January 30, 1937. Stalin also had Karl Pauker, who headed Stalin's personal security, arrested and shot.

The purges also included the most prominent members of the People's Commissariat of Foreign Affairs (NKID), and the effects on Soviet diplomacy were disastrous. Writes Teddy Uldricks:

> The list of Stalin's victims read like a who's who of Soviet diplomats. The victims included Deputy Foreign Commissars N.I. Krestinskii and G. Ia. Sokol'nikov, as well as former Deputy Commissar and then Ambassador to Turkey L.M. Karakhan, Ambassador to Finland E.A. Asmus, Ambassador to Hungary A.A. Bekzadian, Ambassador to Latvia S.I. Brodovskii, Ambassador to Poland Ia. Kh. Davtian, Ambassador to Norway I.S. Iakubovich, Ambassador to Germany K.K. Iurenev, Ambassador to Turkey M.A. Karskii, Ambassador to Rumania M.S. Ostrovskii, Ambassador to Spain M.I. Rosenberg, Ambassador to Afghanistan B.E. Skvirskii, Ambassador to Mongolia V.K. Tairov, and Ambassador to Denmark N.S. Tikhmenev; and Narkomindel department heads V.N. Barkov (chief of protocol), E.A. Gnedin (press chief), D.G. Shtern (of the Second Western Division), and V.M. Tsukerman (of the

---

[16] Bukharin to Stalin 15 Apr. 1937. Edvard Radzinsky, *Stalin* (New York: Anchor, 1997), 375.
[17] Barmine relates that Kamenev once heard from Stalin that his greatest pleasure was the plot of revenge, and its successful execution, against an enemy. Alexander Barmine, *One Who Survived: The Life Story of a Russian under the Soviets* (New York: G.P. Putnam's Sons, 1945), 266.
[18] Nikita Petrov and Marc Jansen, *Stalin's Loyal Executioner: People's Commissar Nikolai Ezhov, 1895–1940* (Stanford: Hoover Institution Press, 2002), 187–88.

Central Asian Division), to name only a few of the more prominent officials.[19]

Those activists most faithful to him—those activists who were carrying out his vile schemes in such a manner that Stalin could not be inculpated—were usually executed merely because in doing what they were enjoined to do, they knew too much and what they knew might be leaked. Sufficient grounds for execution, or exile if lucky, were the things someone might do, not what they have done. As Stalin once told Lavrenti Beria, who would head the NKVD after the arrest and execution of Nikolai Yezhov in the third show trial: "An Enemy of the People is not only one who does sabotage but one who doubts the rightness of the Party line. And there are a lot of them, and we must liquidate them." It mattered little to Stalin and his sadistic liquidators whether many innocents were put to death in the purge. The key was to get an "enemy" among the innocents. There was even a Russian term, *frantsuskaya borba* or "French wrestling," used for the killing of an innocent.[20]

In addition to expurgations within the NKVD and NKID, Stalin unsurprisingly commissioned purges in the Red Army. Some 47,000 officers were dismissed, and many of them were exterminated. Stalin feared a military uprising and coup. Most of the highest-ranking officials of the army had been shot, e.g., Marshals Tukhachevsky, Yegorov, and Blukher. Generals Khalepsky, Yakir, Alksnis, Eydeman, and Uborevich, as well as Admirals Muklevich and Orlov, were also there. Commissar Ordjonikidze, a close friend of Stalin, was poisoned, while Commissar Gamarnik, foreseeing his execution, committed suicide.[21] The effect of the expurgation of his top military officials was colossal. Stalin's vindictiveness and idiocy, resulted in millions of dead Red soldiers in World War II, as young Russian soldiers were led into battle by green young officers, untested in the craft of warfare.[22] Yet Stalin thought that it was better to remove them and replace them with younger and untried officers, who owed their post to him than to run the risk of a military uprising.

---

[19] Teddy J. Uldricks, "The Impact of the Great Purges on the People's Commissariat of Foreign Affairs," in *Slavic Review*, Vol. 36, No. 2: 188.
[20] Simon Sebag Montefiore, *Stalin*, 243 and 245.
[21] Edvard Radzinsky, *Stalin*, 8–9 and 370–73.
[22] Peter Whitewood, "Rethinking Stalin's Purge of the Red Army, 1937–38," in *University of Kansas Blog*, https://www.google.com/url?sa=t&rct=j&q=&esrc=s&source=eb&cd=&cad=rja&uact=8&ved=2ahUKEwiJs_Ltxr8AhVUFlkFHbSCCOYQFnoECBAQAQ&url=https%3A%2F%2Funiversitypressblog.ku.edu%2Funcategorized%2Frethinking-stalins-purge-of-the-red-army-1937-38%2F&usg=AOvVaw1b5ROyfJFqBJ1GTaQPOUXj, accessed 28 Jan. 2023.

Along with the expurgation of members of the Old Guard, numerous thousands of non-Russians—e.g., Ukrainians, Poles, and Germans—were arrested.[23] From 1937 to 1938, some 270,000 Ukrainians were arrested, and many of them were shot[24]—so much to illustrate Stalin's snowballing sadism and insanity.

To please Stalin, Yezhov and his deputy, Mikhail Frinovsky, pushed and propelled Order Number 00447 to the Politburo: Regions of the USSR were to be assigned quotas of persons to be exiled and persons to be executed. The initial proposal mandated that 72,950 were to be shot; the actual number of murders was 386,798, over five times the proposal. Overall, from 1937 to 1938 alone, up to 1.5 million people were arrested and 700,000 were shot.[25] Michael Ellman states that the total number of deaths from 1937 to 1938 was from 950 thousand to 1.2 million.[26]

The randomness of the many arrests and lack of discretion in the executions are manifest in a comment by Yezhov, speaking to Chekists at the Officers' Club: "There will be some innocent victims in this fight against Fascist agents. We are launching a major attack on the Enemy; let there be no resentment if we bump someone with an elbow. Better that ten innocent people should suffer than one spy get away. When you chop wood, chips fly."[27] Thus, the harm of letting one spy escape prosecution is greater than the elimination of 10 innocents.

It was a general rule that when someone was declared to be an enemy of the people, those others near him were to be punished through exile or execution, for they likely knew what he knew and likely too were of the same anti-Bolshevist disposition. Those empowered with deciding whether someone was a threat to the socialist experiment were Stalin, Molotov, Kaganovich, and Voroshilov, from the Politburo, and Yezhov as head of the NKVD, though Yezhov too would be arrested for anti-Lennist activities, executed (4 Feb. 1940), and replaced by Lavrenty Beria.[28]

The expurgation of the Old Guard allowed Stalin to replace them with his own people, young men who had no experience of the revolution and civil war and who were his lackeys because they owed their careers to Stalin. They would

---

[23] Edvard Radzinsky, *Stalin*, 331–32.
[24] Serhii Plohky, *The Gates of Europe: A History of Ukraine* (New York: Basic Books, 2021), 254.
[25] Simon Sebag Montefiore, *Stalin*, 228–29.
[26] Michael Ellman, "Soviet Repression Statistics: Some Comments," in *Europe-Asia Studies*, Vol. 54, No. 7, 1151–72.
[27] Simon Sebag Montefiore, *Stalin*, 218.
[28] Report of Court Proceedings in the Case of the Anti-Soviet 'Bloc of Rights and Trotskyites,'" 2–13 Mar. 1938, Verbatim Report (Moscow: Peoples Commissariat of Justice of the USSR, 1938), https://archive.org/details/in.ernet.dli.2015.150911/page/n4/mode/1up, accessed 14 Jan. 2023.

readily believe that those eliminated really were enemies of the Party. They knew no better. Expurgation would also, as I have already noted, allow Stalin to rewrite Soviet history by eliminating the extraordinary achievements of men like Trotsky, Kamenev, Zinoviev, Rykov, and Marshal Tukhashevky. Figures A-3 and A-4 offer one illustration of Stalin's efforts to rewrite history. The first is a picture of him walking with the diminutive Yezhov, at Stalin's left. In the second, Yezhov has been removed.

Fig. A-3. Stalin with Yezhin   **Fig. A-4.** Stalin without Yezhin

Source: Wikipedia

One here might come to Stalin's rescue by noting that Trotsky and even Lenin were advocates of violence to advance the interests of Bolshevism, so Stalinism was merely an offshoot of Leninism. While that must be conceded, there is nothing in the Bolshevik Terror or in Stalin's handling of Ukrainian collectivization and nationalism that smacks of actions in the interest of advancing Bolshevism—the global dictatorship of the proletariat, which at least promised, on average, a better life for all persons. Stalin's sanguinary actions were in the interest only of the parochial dictatorship of the Boss. In addition, it was, we have seen, Stalin who initiated intolerance of and violence toward members within the Party, even those of high rank, and that led to violent measures against any member of any rank within the Party.

That leads to this question: Was Stalinism really an offshoot of Leninism?

Because of Stalin's autarchy, it is difficult to assess the extent to which Stalin was an unswerving disciple of Lenin. His devotion to Lenin, and Marx, occurred in some measure because he was weaned on their milk, and as a Bolshevik, Stalin found purpose. Yet he knew nothing other than Leninism and was incapable of creating a theoretical path of his own. Leninism was his religion, and life without it was unendurable.

Nonetheless, in the end, Stalin was committed only to Stalin, and he sought absolute power through others, showing complete sycophantic deference to him. Groveling sycophancy was, to him, an intoxicant. Nothing pleased Stalin more than seeing powerful men with powerful ideas, like Bukharin, kneel and cringe before him, admit to crimes in which they were uninvolved, beg for forgiveness, entreat his leniency, promise unconditional fealty, and then ... suffer extermination. Stalin, says biographer Simon Montefiore, was fond of revealing that his "greatest pleasure [was] to choose one's victim, prepare one's plans minutely, slake an implacable vengeance, and then go to bed. There is nothing sweeter in the world."[29] One must assume that such a "pleasantry" led to a deep, peaceful sleep. The Bolshevik Terror of 1936–1938 was, thus, to him, not only a needed liquidation of enemies of the people—and all enemies of the people were by then equivalent to enemies of Stalin—it was also a perversely delightful experience of revenge that ultimately led to inner calm, for the nonce.

There is more to say about the Bolshevik Terror. It is stark evidence of Stalin giving up on the Marxist experiment and contenting himself not with one-country socialism—he was by then aware that it could not work as a better alternative to capitalism—but one-person socialism: his dictatorship and his personal well-being, which included taking good care of those who cared for him.

Leninist Marxism was built on two presuppositions: first, that State control over production of all sorts would lead to economic development that exceeded that of capitalist countries, and second, that that economic development would lead to a standard of living for laborers that exceeded that of capitalist countries. Yet after the general failure of his First Five-Year Plan, Stalin's commitment to Marxism was, at best, lukewarm. By the time of the Bolshevik Terror, it was merely nominal. Anyone sincerely committed to the spread of Marxism would not exterminate, by the thousands, those Bolshevik patriots who have done the most for the cause of socialism. It might be that Stalin came to see that socialism was no improvement over capitalism—that elimination of private property, fixing wages for work, and industrializing all sectors of production would not lead to utopia.

What can we say of Stalinism at this point?

Adjudged from the perspective of its aim of successful implementation of Marxist-Leninism in the USSR, Stalinism can only be seen to be a colossal failure. Failure was at the root of the theory, which could never in his lifetime be put into praxis. Stalin ever expressed purchase of two axioms—willful acceptance of Stalinist socialism and respect for diversity of cultures in socializing them—but he consistently contravened those axiomata in practice,

---

[29] Simon Sebag Montefiore, *Young Stalin* (New York: Vintage, 2008), 295.

chiefly in Ukraine; hence he merely paid mouth honor to those axiomata. Ukrainian peasant-farmers repudiated collectivization and demanded respect, along with members of the intelligentsia, for their Ukrainian culture.

It was only through policies that encouraged violence and mendacity, through fear and ignorance, that Stalin would avowedly achieve any degree of success in Stalinizing Ukraine. Yet through fear and ignorance, he collectivized the intransigent Ukrainians, inasmuch as, after the Great Famine, Ukrainians complied with his directives, though the republic was in shambles. That compliance was willful insofar as a people, completely beaten to a state of obedience—and Stalin's sadistic treatment of Bukharin here again comes to mind—could be said to possess a will. As with Bukharin, Stalin doubtless experienced large pleasure in hearing about the enormous sufferings of millions of the execrable kurkuls in the Ukrainian countryside.

Stalin ever kept Soviets in the dark concerning the truth about the Party's successes with socialization. He controlled the Soviet media—the Party-run newspapers were replete each day with stories of the great successes of Soviets, true to Stalinist ideals, who prospered despite the weighty obstacles of enemies of the State—and he also kept visits by foreign correspondents at a minimum so that the other five-sixths of the world could be readily deceived about the successes of socialism in the USSR. Stalin also liquidated all persons who might be of the slightest danger to his dictatorship and replaced them with loyalists until such time that those loyalists, too, needed to be supplanted because, knowing too much, they could no longer be loyalists.

***

In this book, I have focused on Stalinism from 1928, the provenance of the Five-Year Plan, to 1933, the year that the Great Ukrainian Famine had mostly ended. My focus has been the effects of his policies on Ukrainians, though it has been shown that his autocratic, self-serving policies hurt almost all Soviets. With the death of Lenin, Stalin, through callidity, taciturnity or dissimulation, and through the acquisition of intimate knowledge of the workings of the Party by doing much of Lenin's dirty work, a true factotum, slowly and surprisingly became the key figure of the Party. By 1930, he was unquestionably its "Boss."

The Boss succeeded through smoke and mirrors. His Five-Year Plan had noteworthy industrial successes, but the overall effect was to bankrupt the economy and destroy Ukraine. He ever concerned himself with the possibility of losing Ukraine—the most important of all Soviet republics. To Stanislav Kosior, Ukrainian Secretary-General of the Communist Party and member of the Politburo, he writes on April 26, 1932: "It seems that in some regions of Ukraine, Soviet power has ceased to exist. Is this true? Is the situation so bad in Ukrainian villages? What is the GPU doing? Maybe you will check this problem and take measures."[30] Kosior, with Vlas Chubar, was doing much of the dirty work for Stalin in Ukraine, yet he became an enemy of Stalin when he asked for food to be sent to starving peasant-farmers during the famine. He was arrested by Stalin on May 3, 1938, and confessed to being a Polish spy when his 16-year-old daughter was raped in front of him. He was shot on February 26, 1939.[31]

Prior to that six-year span of time from 1928 to 1933, with the existence of Lenin's New Economic Policy and its reversal of stringent State controls over other Soviet republics, there were large hopes and dreams by many Ukrainians of an independent Ukrainian republic or perhaps even of a separate Ukraine, as even Stalin always tended to recognize explicitly any republic's right to secede from Moscow. Those hopes of independence were dashed with Stalin's ascendency to the head of the Party and his implementation of his Five-Year Plan, which used propaganda, dissimulation, lying, and violent coercion to implement socialism throughout the USSR.[32] The consequences of that plan burked Ukrainians' hopes of nationalism and more than decimated the Ukrainian population, as it crushed into quiet submission those Ukrainians who did not perish through labor, exile, or famine, and I say nothing of the all-too-numerous non-Ukrainians who suffered likewise.

By 1933, we might note that Ukrainians who warmed to Stalinism had learned many valuable lessons concerning the good life in a Stalinist State—in the satirical words of former Soviet ambassador Alexander Barmine, the "new society with abundance and happiness for all."[33] They learned how to endure torturously long bread-lines, how to live in flats that were said to be homes, how to work for a less-than-subsistence wage at factories and yet to subsist, how to rat on fellow Ukrainians who voiced any discontent about Stalinism, how to take orders in collectives from managers who knew nothing about farming, and how, to ensure their own survival, to ignore the cries of fellow Ukrainians suffering from want of food, displacement, or torture. Those who learned the most, most importantly, learned that there was a genuine secular alternative to the God they had once blindly worshipped: "Tsar" Joseph Stalin.

---

[30] Simon Sebag Montefiore, *Stalin: The Court of the Red Tsar* (New York: Alfred A. Knopf, 2004), 88.
[31] Roy Medvedev, *Let History Judge: The Origins and Consequences of Stalinism* (New York: Columbia University Press, 1976), 296.
[32] Following Lenin, Stalinists that the dictatorship of the proletariat demands use of force—"there is no dictatorship without the use of force"—unimpeded by laws. J.V. Stalin, "Questions Concerning Leninism" 25 Jan. 1926), in *Marxists Internet Archive*, https://www.marxists.org/reference/archive/stalin/works/1926/01/25.htm, accessed 15 Mar. 2023.
[33] Alexander Barmine, *One Who Survived: The Life Story of a Russian under Stalin* (New York: G.P. Putnam's Sons, 1945), 96.

Figure Credits

Map 1: Ukraine's Ecological Zones, 1937, courtesy Ukrainian Research Institute, Harvard University, https://gis.huri.harvard.edu/galleries?page=1

Map 2: Wheat-Growing Areas in Ukraine, 1937, courtesy Ukrainian Research Institute, Harvard University, https://gis.huri.harvard.edu/galleries?page=1

Map 3: Collective Farms by in Ukraine 1932, courtesy Ukrainian Research Institute, Harvard University, https://gis.huri.harvard.edu/collectivization

Map 4: Total Direct Famine Losses of Population in Ukraine, 1933, courtesy Ukrainian Research Institute, Harvard University, https://gis.huri.harvard.edu/galleries?page=1

Figure 1-1: Joseph Stalin, 1920, public domain (PD), https://en.wikipedia.org/wiki/Joseph_Stalin#/media/File:Stalin_1920-1.jpg

Figure 1-2: Vladimir Lenin at Sverdlov Square with Leon Trotsky and Lev Kamenev, Moscow, May 1920, PD, https://en.wikipedia.org/wiki/Vladmir_Lenin#/media/File:Lenin_Speech_in_May_1920.png

Figure 2-1: Vladimir Lenin, Confined to Wheelchair, March 1923, PDF https://en.wikipedia.org/wiki/Vladmir_Lenin#/mdia/File:%D0%9B%D0%B5%D0%BD%D0%B8%D0%BD_%D0%B2_%D0%93%D0%BE%D1%80%D0%BA%D0%B0%D1%85_(1923).jpg

Figure 3-1: Leon Trosky, PD, https://en.wikipedia.org/wiki/Leon_Trotsky#/media/File:Trotsky_reading_The_Militant,_circa_1936.jpg

Figure 3-2: Stalin with Rykov, Kamenev, and Zinoviev in 1925, PD, https://en.wikipedia.org/wiki/Joseph_Stalin#/media/File:Stalin_Rykov_Kamenev_Zinoviev_1925.jp

Figure 4-1: Woman Goading Emaciated Horses on a Collective-Farm, PD, Author Unknown, *The Black Deeds of the Kremlin: A White Book Vol 1*. SO Pidhaini ed. Toronto: Canada, 1953

Figure 4-2: Vladimir Krikhatsky (1877–1942), *The First Tractor*, date unknown, https://commons.wikimedia.org/wiki/File:Wladimir_Gawriilowitsch_Krikhatzkij__The_First_Tractor.jpg#/media/File:Wladimir_Gawriilowitsch_Krikhatzkij_-_The_First_Tractor.jpg

Figure 4-3: Serednyaks, Bednyaks, and Kulaks, 1926, PD, https://en.wikipedia.org/wiki/Collectivization_in_the_Soviet_Union#/media/File:Three_broad_categories_of_the_peasants.jpg

Figure 5-1: Ivan Vladimirov, *Prodrazvyorstka*, 1922, PD, https://en.wikipedia.org/wiki/Ivan_Vladimirov#/media/File:Ivan_Vladimirov_requisitioning.jpg!HD.jpg

Figure 5-2: Peasant-Farmers Headed for Work, PD, https://www.ukrainianworldcongress.org/russias-long-history-of-deporting-ukrainians/

Figure 6-2: Buksyors Showing their Spoils, PD, https://ukrainegenocide.com/history/

Figure 7-1: "Liquidate the Kulaks" Parade, PD, https://en.wikipedia.org/wiki/Dekulakization#/media/File:Dekulakisation_in_the_USSR_V_3.jpg

Figure 7-2: Solovky Special Camp, PD, https://en.wikipedia.org/wiki/Solovki_prison_camp

Figure 8-1: Exiled Female Kulaks Deforesting, PD, https://en.wikipedia.org/wiki/Dekulakization#/media/File:Kulak_women1930.jpeg

Figure 9-1: Haymakers, Volodymyr Orlovskyi, 1787, https://euromaidanpress.com/2020/01/03/ukraine-at-the-break-of-20th-century-as-seen-by-landscape-painters/

Figure 10-1: Bourgeoisie, Priest, and Kulak Pulling Alexander Kolchak, Viktor Deni, 1919, PD, https://library.brown.edu/cds/Views_and_Reviews/date_lists/1918-25.html

Figure 10-2: Mykola Skrypnyk, PD, https://www.encyclopediaofukraine.com/picturedisplay.asp?linkpath=pic%5CS%5CK%5CSkrypnyk%20Mykola%20(photo).jpg&page=pages%5CS%5CK%5CSkrypnykMykola.htm&id=14457&pid=3976&tyt=Skrypnyk,%20Mykola&key=Skrypnyk%2C+Mykola

Figure 10-3: Ukrainian Kobzars Mykhailo Kravchenko and Petro Dravchenko, 1902, PD, https://www.encyclopediaofukraine.com/picturedisplay.asp?linkpath=pic%5CK%5CO%5CKobzars%20Mykhailo%20Kravchenko%20Petro%20Drevchenko.jpg&page=pages%5CK%5CO%5CKobzars.htm&id=5953&pid=3221&tyt=Kobzars&key=Kobzars%2C+%D0%BA%D0%BE%D0%B1%D0%B7%D0%B0%D1%80%D1%96%3B+kobzari

Figure 10-4: Ivan Vladimirov, *Confiscation of Church Property in Petrograd*, 1922, https://en.wikipedia.org/wiki/1922_seizure_of_church_valuables_in_Russia#/media/File:Ivan_Vladimirov_confiscation-of-church-property-in-petrograd-1922.jpg

Figure 11-1: Children Starving from the Famine in 1922, PD, https://en.wikipedia.org/wiki/Droughts_and_famines_in_Russia_and_the_Soviet_Union

Figure 11-2: Cartful of Ukrainian Corpses, 1921, PD, https://commons.wikimedia.org/wiki/Category:Starving_people_in_Ukraine#/media/File:Victims_of_Soviet_Famine_1922.jpg

Figure 11-3: Activists on Watchtower, PD, https://dtkk.ru/kraj-kraevedov/attachment/f-13-p-post/

Figure 11-4: Starving Ukrainian Woman with Son, PD, https://picryl.com/media/golodomor-v-kazahstane-2-57b02d

Figure 11-5: Populational Decline in Ukraine, 1929–1933, Wikimedia Commons, https://commons.wikimedia.org/wiki/File:Ukraine_famine_map.png

Figure 11-6: Stamp Commemorating Pavlik Morozov, 1948, PD, https://en.wikipedia.org/wiki/Pavlik_Morozov#/media/File:Rus_Stamp_PMorozov-1950-40.jpg

Figure 12-1: Red Brooms (Buksyors) "Appropriating" Foodstuffs from Oleksiyivka, Kharkiv, 1932, PD, https://en.wikipedia.org/wiki/Economic_repression_in_the_Soviet_Union#/media/File:HolodomorVyizdValky.jpg

Figure 12-2: Mass of Graves near Kharkiv, 1933, PD, https://commons.wikimedia.org/wiki/File:Sowjetunion_1935,_Leichen_der_Verhungerten_werden_in_Massengr%C3%A4bern_verscharrt.jpg

Figure Credits

Figure 12-3: Dr. Lev Kopelev, Wikipedia, courtesy Elke Wetzig (Elya), https://en.wikipedia.org/wiki/Lev_Kopelev#/media/File:Lew_Kopelew.jpg

Figure 13-1: Soviet Guard by Granary, c. 1932, PD, https://commons.wikimedia.org/wiki/Category:Holodomor#/media/File:Holodomor17.jpg

Figure 13-2: Nadezhda Alliluyava, Stalin's Second Wife, pd, https://en.wikipedia.org/wiki/File:Nadezhda_Alliluyeva_1.jpg

Figure 13-3: Cartoon Drawing of Starving Peasant Asking a Russian Soldier for Bread, 1933, PD, https://commons.wikimedia.org/wiki/Category:Holodomor#/media/File:%D0%9C%D0%B8%D1%85%D0%B0%D0%B9%D0%BB%D0%BE_%D0%9C%D0%B8%D1%85%D0%B0%D0%BB%D0%B5%D0%B2%D0%B8%D1%87_%D0%A5%D0%BB%D1%96%D0%B1_1933.jpg

Figure 13-4: Ukrainian Peasants Fleeing their Village in Search of Food, 1933, PD, https://commons.wikimedia.org/wiki/Category:Holodomor#/media/File:Abb._10._Der_Hunger_treibt_die_Bauern_auf_der_Wanderung.jpg

Figure 14-1: Joseph Stalin at the Tehran Conference, 1943, PD, https://en.wikipedia.org/wiki/Joseph_Stalin#/media/File:StalinCropped1943(b).jpg

Figure 14-2: Soviet Anti-Religion Poster of Unknown Date, PD, https://ttps://www.123rf.com/photo_18079656_communist-propaganda-poster-period-before-1930.htm

Figure A-1: Sergey Kirov, PD, https://kratkoebio.ru/kirov-sergej-mironovich-kratkaya-biografiya/

Figure A-2: Nikolai Bukharin, 1926, PD, https://en.wikipedia.org/wiki/Nikolai_Bukharin#/media/File:Bucharin.bra.jpg

Figures A-3 and A-4: Stalin with and without Yezhin, PD, https://en.m.wikipedia.org/wiki/File:Stalin_and_Molotov_along_the_Volga_Don_Canal,_Nikolai_Yezhov_removed.jpg

Index

A

Alliluyava, Nadezhda: 187, 188
Applebaum, Anne: 195
Artemenko, Danylo: 104–5
Austro-Hungarian: 3

B

Barmine, Andrew: 10, 27, 28, 67, 178, 204, 205–8, 217n17, 223
Beria, Lavrenti: 218, 219
black market: 56, 57
Bloody Sunday: 2
Bolshevik Leftism and Rightism: 30n6, 216
brigadiers: xiv, 62–68, 75, 82–83, 90–92, 103, 113, 153
Bukharin Nikolai: xix, 187, 214–17
buksyors: see brigadiers

C

cannibalism: 85, 162–63, 181, 187
Capitalism: 50, 51, 77, 136, 210
Central Rada: 3n3
Cheka: xiii n1, 101
Chernyshevsky, Nikolai: 16, 50
Chicherin, Georgy: 43
Chorny, Stepan: 75–76
Conquest, Robert: 67, 195–96
Czar Alexander II: 2
Czar Nicholas II: 2

D

Davrichewy, Damian: 15

Deuscher, Issac: 106
Djugashvili, Vissarion: 14, 16
Du Bois, W.E.B. 34
Duranty, Walter: 189–90

F

Famine of 1921: 5–6, 145, 152
Famine of 1932–1933: xviii, 47, 151–68, 195, 200
Far Eastern Republic: 43
Fedorchenko, F.: 104
Five Ears of Grain Law: 129
Five Year Plan: xviii, 8. 31n11, 32, 38, 49, 50, 53, 54, 68, 81, 88, 106, 108, 121, 169, 184, 188–190. 196, 199, 204, 207, 209, 210, 212, 216, 221, 222, 223

G

GPU: xii n1, 33, 75, 86, 90, 99, 103, 112, 118, 119, 124, 129, 148, 159, 179, 181, 209, 222
Geladze, Ekaterina Georgievna: 14
Georgia: 1, 9, 11–12, 14, 16, 22, 33, 41–42, 44, 81, 97, 98, 100, 197
Goncharuk, Olena: 165
Gosplan: 57
grain collection: xvi, xvii–xviii, 4, 59, 63, 65, 66, 70, 70n23, 73, 76, 81–85, 91, 108–14, 117, 123, 128–29, 136, 151–52, 153, 155–56, 165, 172, 177, 180, 181, 185, 187, 209
Grigorenko, Petro: 104, 116, 118, 149, 174, 175, 182, 184
gulags: see labor camps

H

Holodomor: see Great Ukrainian Famine

I

Individual Farmer Plan: 94, 99, 103
Internal Passport: 129, 158
Ivanovich, Kyzma: 56

J

Jones, Gareth: 190

K

Kaganovich, Lazar: 11
Kaledin, Alexey: 40
Kamenev, Lev: xix, 14, 19, 20, 30–32, 212, 214, 214, 220
Kazakhstan: 133
Kazbegi, Alexander: 16
Kershaw, Ian: 33
Kirov, Sergey: 212–13
kolkhoz: see state-owned farms
komnezamy: see Poor-Peasant Committees
Komsomol: see Young Activists
Kopelev, Lev: 174, 176, 177, 178, 199
Kravchenko, Victor: 28, 56, 64, 92, 101, 109, 152n5m, 161, 174, 179, 206–7
Kronstadt Rebellion: 5
Kyiv-Rus': xxi, xxiv–xxv

L

labor camps: 69, 73, 75, 97–103
League of Nations: 189
Lenin, Vladimir: xix, xxii, 2, 4, 6, 11, 20–26, 27, 28–29, 30, 30n8, 31–32, 34, 35, 36–37, 39m 39n28, 41, 42–43, 45, 48, 49, 50, 53, 62, 65, 76, 77, 78, 107, 109, 134, 140, 141, 142, 144, 152, 170, 175, 198, 200, 203n11, 204, 207, 209, 211, 213–15, 216, 220, 221, 222, 223, 223n32
Litvinov, Maksim: 191
Luchko, Vasyl: 162
Lypkivsky, Vasyl: 145

M

Magocsi, Paul Robert: xxiii, xxiv
Marx/Marxism: xvi, xv, xvi, xviii–xx, 1, 6, 8,12, 13, 24, 29, 33–36, 38,39, 41, 42, 48, 49–50, 51, 52, 54, 61, 67, 68, 69, 73, 74, 76–77, 80, 89, 91, 92, 94, 109, 124, 125, 133, 136, 137, 141, 142, 143, 144, 149, 150, 173, 174, 175, 189, 199–210, 213, 220, 221
Maslivets, Y.: 94, 98
Mdivani, Polykarp: 42
Mensheviks/Menshevism: 29
Molotov, V.M.: 26, 106, 128, 155, 219
Morozov, Pavlik: 166–67
Myshuha, Luke: 107

N

NATO: xxvi
NKVD: xiii-n1, 64, 106, 166n52, 175, 179, 181. 187, 209, 215, 217, 218, 219
New Economic Policy: xviii, 6, 48, 49, 144, 223
Nus, Abraham Solomonivich: 156

O

October Revolution: 32, 40
Odzhonidkidze, Sergo: 41

P

Pereprygin, Lidia: 12
Petliura, Symon: 40
Petrovs'kyi, Hryhoryi: 128
Pidhainy, S.O.: 47, 100–1
Plokhy, Serhii: xxiii, 195
Politburo: 20, 33
Poor-Peasant Committees: 4, 69, 79, 108, 114, 118, 125, 126, 127, 128, 133, 135, 136, 137, 181
prodrazvyorstka: see Stalin and grain collection
Putin, Vladimir: xxi–xxii, xxiii, xxv, xxvi, 93
Pyatakov, Yuri: 67, 217

R

Radzynsky, Edvard: 209
Revolution of Dignity: xxvi
Robinson, Geroid: 203
Rodzyanko, Mikhail: 40
Rusetsky, M.: 182–83, 191
Russian Civil War: 3, 67
Russian Soviet Federative Socialist Republic: 4–6, 8, 48, 151–52
Rykov, Alexei: 30
Ryutin, Martemyan: 212

S

Samsonov, T.: 144
Savur, S.: 157
Sepity, Andriy:103
Shaw, George Bernard: 189
Shlikhter, Alexander: 4–5
Sholokhov, Mikhail: 86
Shvets, K.: 104
Skirda, Panas: 183
Soloviy, Dmytro: 154
Solviychuk, Trokhyum: 163
Special Military Operation: xiii, xvi, 93
Stalin, Joseph
   ambition of: 21, 29
   biography of: 8–17
   brutality/sadism of: 92, 108, 202, 211–22
   on classes of peasants: xv–xvi, 57–58
   and collectivization: xv, 8, 47–59, 61–74 70n23, 88, 109–14, 124
   and compulsory collectivization: 61–74, 88, 109–14
   and dekulakization/dekurkalization: xviii, 63, 75–88, 89–105, 107–114, 126, 133
   Dizzy with Success: 121–23
   on equality: 205
   and eulogy of Lenin: 23–24
   and gigantism: xiv, 49, 209
   and grain collection: 62, 72, 85, 109, 111, 112, 114, 123, 151, 172, 189, 209
   and Great Purge: 214–20
   and industry: 49, 54, 77, 202, 205–7
   knowing of famine: 172, 182–88
   kulaks/kurkuls: xvi, xvii, xix, 53, 56–59, 60–69, 70, 73, 76–88, 89–106, 112, 117, 121, 123–25, 127, 135–37, 154, 166, 167, 170, 178, 179, 194, 211
   and branding: 92–94
   and dispossession of property: 94–97
   exile of: 76, 97–103

on Lenin (first impression): 13
and methods of coercion: xix
and perception of Ukraine: xiv, 134
and religion: 80, 87, 144–150
and roles in Party, 19–20
and Russification: 1
and Show Trials: 215–17
socialism/Marxism/Leninism of: xv, xxiii, 33–38, 50–52, 77, 214, 221–22
and utopia: 199–210
versus independence of peasants: xv, 39n27, 135, 137–44
versus cultural differences: xv, 1, 41, 42–43, 132–33, 135
view of Ukrainians: xix
as Vozhd (Boss): 134, 205, 211, 216, 222
on willful integration of republics: xxii
Work in the Countryside: 135–37
Strumilin, Stanislav: 68
Subtelny, Orest: 3, 195
Svanidze, Mari: 212n4
Sverdlov University: 24
Sybirny, Pavel: 87

T

Terekhov, Roman 185
Tkachev, Peter: 203m11
Transcaucasian Socialist Federative Soviet Republic: 42, 44
Treaty of Brest-Litovsk: 2–3
Treaty of Versailles: 3
Trotsenko, Ivan: 97
Trotsky, Leon: 10–11, 14, 19, 20, 22, 26, 28–32, 35, 36, 38, 48, 76, 107, 109, 121, 175, 176, 207, 214, 220

Trotsky's Permanent Revolution 36

U

Ukraine/Ukrainians
children during Famine: 164–68
economy of: xxv–xxvi
ethnicities within: xxiv, xxiv n7
genocide of: 194–97
and independence: xxiii, 3, 39
intelligentsia of: xiv, xvii, 7, 81, 131, 195, 222
kobzars: 143–44
as Little Russia: 1
and meat: 115n19
nationalism of: 131–150, 197, 211
natural resources of: xxv
resistance to collectivization: 114–19, 125, 128
rivers of: xxv
Russification of: 41, 133
starved by Stalin: 128
Ukrainization of 7–8
Union of Soviet Socialist Republics, formation of: 6, 33, 44, 48, 49, 50, 52, 78
United States: xxv, 189

V

Vasylenko, Vasyl: 147
Voroshilov, Klementy: 187

W

War Communism: 4, 5, 48, 62, 151
World War I: 2–3

Y

Yakir, Iona: 187

Yanukovych, Viktor: xxvi, xxvi n13
Yagoda, Genrikh: 217
Yavdas, M.: 148
Yemchenko, E.: 96
Yezhov, Nikolai: 217, 219, 220
Young Activists, Group of: 56, 64, 80, 98, 104, 118, 145, 146, 173m 174m 175m, 176, 177, 182

Z

Zapolenko, S.: 183, 184
Zinoviev, Grigori: xix, 17, 20, 30–32, 212, 214, 215, 220